T0304916

UNDERCLASS

UNDERCLASS
A Memoir

Dr Jessica Taylor

CONSTABLE

CONSTABLE

First published in Great Britain in 2024 by Constable

1 3 5 7 9 10 8 6 4 2

Copyright © Dr Jessica Taylor, 2024

The moral right of the author has been asserted.

A CIP catalogue record for this book
is available from the British Library.

ISBN: 978-1-40871-695-3 (hardback)
ISBN: 978-1-40871-992-3 (trade paperback)

Typeset in Sabon LT Std by SX Composing DTp, Rayleigh, Essex
Printed and bound in Great Britain by Clays Ltd, Elcograf S.p.A.

Papers used by Constable are from well-managed forests
and other responsible sources.

MIX
Paper | Supporting
responsible forestry
FSC® C104740

Constable
An imprint of
Little, Brown Book Group
Carmelite House
50 Victoria Embankment
London EC4Y 0DZ

An Hachette UK Company
www.hachette.co.uk

www.littlebrown.co.uk

For us both
For neither of us exist without the other
And neither of us succeed without the other
We are whole only when we honour every part
of ourselves

Contents

UNDERCLASS

1

What kind of alleyway is this?

Autumn 2016

'I said, if you touch me again mate, you're going through that fucking window over there.'

My body shook. My heart raced. I hated people touching me.

'Jessica!' My mum clapped her hand over her mouth, blushed red, and apologised repeatedly to the dentist.

I batted his hands away from my mouth.

'I told him twice, Mum. I'm not numb yet, that stupid shit hasn't worked again!'

The dentist took two steps back from me, peeled off his gloves one by one, and slapped them down on the edge of the sink. He snatched his blue face mask off, and glared at me through little rectangular glasses.

Suddenly, he exploded.

'Get out of my practice right now. And don't you ever come back! You are banned!'

Ironically, just as he banned me from my third dental practice in a year, my mouth finally went numb.

I slobbered and slurred another insult at the dentist as my mum pulled me off the chair and shoved me out of the room. For good measure, he followed us down the stairs and past reception, as he yelled in front of his anxiously waiting patients that I was to be banned for life.

At fourteen years old.

'What on earth did you do in there?' The receptionist shook her head in disbelief that the ordinarily kind and quiet old man had such an outburst at a patient.

I shrugged at her, and joked, 'He wouldn't give me a sticker.'

That earned me a sharp slap up the back of the head and Mum gritted her teeth.

'Shut the fuck up,' she growled under her breath, and then returned to being her polite, bubbly self, apologising profusely for her unruly chav of a daughter.

'She's just . . . she's . . . very frightened of the dentist . . . I am so sorry, it won't happen again.' My mum did her best to convince the receptionist to keep me on their books.

'It won't happen again because she is never to be seen in this practice again!' the dentist raged to his receptionist. She looked up at me, over the top of her computer.

Half of my mouth grinned at the receptionist, and the other limp half let out another mouthful of slobber onto my navy-blue Carlotti hoodie.

I could have sworn she stifled a giggle. She put her head down and tucked her hair behind her ear.

On reflection, it can't be easy being a dentist. In what other job do you get up, get ready, go to work, and meet people all day who tell you that they hate you right before they ask you to fix their teeth? Dentists must be told, 'I hate the dentist', like thirty times a day. You don't go to your hairdresser and tell her, 'I hate hairdressers', moments before you ask her to bleach your whole head, do you?

'Jessica.'

'Jessica.'

'Jessica, are you listening?'

I shook myself out of the memory of threatening to throw the dentist out of the third-floor window, and stared back at the two professors in the tiny, stuffy office we were crammed into.

No one tells you that when you 'make it' to the top in academia, they give you a draughty closet to live in, like Harry Potter's under-the-stairs bedroom. The one next door was just used to pile expensive bicycles in. There was a sign on the door where they had scratched out a retired professor's name, and written 'BIKES'. Every evening, the lecturers had to untangle them like an oily old necklace, the pedals and chains all mashing into each other.

White middle-class passive-aggressive academics, all being awfully polite whilst blaming each other for the mess of their fold-up bikes.

I didn't even know what a university was until I rocked up at mine at twenty-five.

I grew up on a diet of raunchy coming-of-age American comedies like *American Pie* and *Road Trip*. All of my knowledge of college and university came from those films. No one in my family had ever mentioned university to me, let alone been to one.

I thought universities were all in the US, and I had to earn a basketball scholarship to go there. I figured that once I got there, I would have to pick a sorority and live in a huge wooden house with the girls from *Legally Blonde*.

As you can imagine, having gotten all of my academic knowledge from films, it was rather the anti-climax to finally go to university. I didn't get a sorority. I didn't get a road trip. But on the plus side, I also didn't have to worry about earning a basketball scholarship either, which would have been extremely difficult at 5ft 5in.

I went to university to become a psychologist, and my family kept asking me how night school was going. Like they thought I was doing a still life drawing course. I wished I was. My drawing was shocking, come to think of it.

'Yeah, sorry, I was just thinking . . .'

It wasn't a lie.

We are all technically 'just thinking', aren't we?

I didn't need to tell them that I was thinking about how aggressive I used to be as a teenager, and how lucky they were that I wasn't fourteen any more.

'We just don't think this is realistic, Jessica. The scenario you have written up for this study . . . it's just . . . far-fetched.'

'How is it far-fetched?'

I looked at them both, wondering if they had ever been anywhere near a council estate, or if it was something they had just seen on TV.

Malcolm tried to smooth over the comment, but his lip curled up into laughter as he tried.

'Your scenario for this study. A woman walks through a dangerous alleyway in broad daylight, and she's mugged and assaulted? It's just . . . what kind of alleyway is this? Where does this poor woman live?'

He sniggered, and Laura stifled a chuckle.

I feigned confusion, told them I didn't follow, but I knew exactly where this was going. It was going the way it always went.

'Well, I just think it would be more realistic if we said the alleyway was dangerous at night-time, you know, in the dark.'

Malcolm surprised me. I always had him down as quite street-smart for a posh white dude. He seemed to have travelled, but then, people with money don't tend to travel to dilapidated old mining towns, and he had recently got back from visiting his friends in Thailand for a month. Maybe he didn't have as much about him as I had assumed.

'Why?'

'Because . . . well, it's just not realistic to have an alleyway that's dangerous in broad daylight, is it?' He was still smiling at me, but smiling at me like I was being a bit silly. Like he was trying to get a small child to realise they were being daft about wanting to get on the bouncy castle after four ice creams, and needed to sit down and stay still for a while.

'Why?' I tested, raising one eyebrow.

Laura piped back up again to save her colleague, whom I was slowly backing into a corner of his own construction.

'I know I certainly haven't lived anywhere with an alleyway I couldn't walk down in the middle of the day, Jessica. It just seems so unrealistic that no one would believe it.'

Malcolm nodded enthusiastically and tapped his biro on the side of his slim face. They looked at each other and nodded again.

'I agree. I've lived in many places and there has never been an alleyway I couldn't walk down. I think we should just remove this scenario. Either that, or you need to rewrite it, and make it clear that it's dangerous, but because it's dark.'

I raised my eyebrows at them both.

Well, good for them. Bloody good for them. They'd never lived anywhere with a dangerous alleyway. Wasn't that wonderful?

It wasn't even called an 'alleyway' where I grew up. It was a gully. But these two didn't know what a gully was, so I had to say alleyway.

There were plenty of them dotted around Stoke, but there were two I used frequently. One was fairly safe in the

5

daytime, but a risk at night-time. It ran from my street to the high school. It was covered in permanent marker graffiti: who was shagging who, rumours about STDs, doodles of dicks and ganja leaves, and threats to knock out your dad. It was where a few of the smaller deals would go down, and I had only had serious trouble in there once.

But the other one, the other one made my blood run cold. I would rather walk the extra ten minutes around it than go through that death trap no matter what time of day it was.

In fact, I would rather walk barefoot on broken glass than walk through that gully. It was shaped in a zigzag, and covered by overgrown trees and barbed wire fences which meant there were two corners with no natural light.

Everything was dumped down there. The paperboys hid their hundreds of undelivered copies of *The Advertiser* there, until the ground was grey, sloppy papier mache. So many thousands of newspapers were discarded down there that it looked like it was covered in a permanent layer of snow no matter the season. Well, the kind of snow that is left after the cars had been driving through it for two days and it looked like grey sludge. The stuff you get told off for making snowballs out of because it's not fun any more, and you are just throwing dirt and ice at kids by that point.

The addicts used it to shoot up, and then discard their dirty needles on the floor. The gangs used it to do everything from deal drugs, to holding up drunk old veterans for their wallets. People hung around in that gully when they didn't want to be seen. Only the hardest kids played truant in there.

Jase went down there on his new bike once, and came out with no bike, and a nice new thick lip. Hannah got chased in there by Chris's mum who was wielding a carving knife like she was in a slasher movie (again), and instantly wondered whether it would have been safer out there with his mum, than in there with those shady bastards.

'On my estate, there were gullys ... alleyways you couldn't walk down in the day or the night.'

Laura looked down, but Malcolm choked back laughter.

I realised that once again, I was sat in a room of fellow psychologists who had absolutely no idea what the real world was like. Both of Laura's parents were successful law professors, and Malcolm's father was one of the most successful psychologists in Australia. They lived lives I didn't even know existed until I had met them and heard them tell their stories. I didn't tell them that one of my parents was an alcoholic and the other was unemployed. Doesn't have the same ring to it.

'Is that so?' he teased, chuckling.

'Yeah. It is. Loads of people live in areas like that.' I wasn't laughing. I held eye contact with Malcolm until he became uncomfortable and fell silent. As he put his head down, Laura had seemingly composed herself, and looked up at me.

'While we are on this topic,' she cleared her throat and lowered her tone, 'there have been some ... concerns ... shared with me about some of your social media posts.'

In the space of a few seconds, thousands of my social media posts flashed past my eyes. Was it when I mocked my girlfriend for loving the Pussycat Dolls? Was it the time I posted a selfie of a man who had been sending me pictures of his dick whilst posting about his wedding anniversary? Was it the post I uploaded of me wearing that rubber rhino head at the karaoke bar?

I tried to play it cool. 'Oh? Which ones?'

'Just, um . . . the, um,' she stumbled over her words, 'the posts about . . . being a "council estate academic" have been brought to my attention.'

'What's wrong with me saying that?' I laughed.

I was relieved it wasn't anything more controversial; I didn't fancy explaining the rubber rhino head to her. Especially as my friends had only told me later that it was from a latex fetish website for people who pretended to be animals to have sex. Who needs enemies, eh?

I still can't believe they had me going to the bar to order drinks dressed as a sex rhino. Charming.

But I was annoyed that 'concerns had been raised' about me talking about being an academic who had grown up on a council estate, especially as I still lived on one. What concerns could there be? I couldn't change where I came from.

'Oh no, no. There's nothing wrong with it!' Laura frantically back-pedalled.

I frowned.

'So why would concerns be raised?'

She looked down.

'It just . . . it doesn't . . . look . . . very good . . . for you.' She picked over her words like she was carefully selecting each one from many as she went along.

I stared at her in silence. I waited for her to elaborate.

'You see, there are concerns that you becoming a psychologist . . . would . . . look bad . . . on the rest of the discipline . . .'

My eyes widened. My jaw fell open. She must have known the gravity of those words as they glided out of her finishing school mouth.

'Me saying I came from a council estate, and have grown up to become an academic, would look bad on our whole discipline? Are you being serious?'

Malcolm looked away, but Laura sighed.

'Jessica, I think you need to realise that in order for you to make a difference, and become respected and accepted as a psychologist and an academic, you must have a certain level of behaviour and decorum. Talking about your council estate and your . . . lifestyle . . .'

She said the word 'lifestyle' like it disgusted her. Like she spat it out on the floor. Like it tasted like shit in her mouth.

It was the first time I had ever seen her talk like that. She was such a warm and easy-going person towards everyone else. As far as I was aware, there were no rules which stated that a young woman from a council estate couldn't be a psychologist. Although come to think of it, I had never heard of one before.

'What do you mean by "lifestyle"?' I prodded, annoyed. If she was going to say it like it revolted her, I wanted to know what it meant. Did she think I lived in a pig sty, rolling around in my own shit? Did she think I went out on the evenings tooled up, attacking innocent passers-by?

She shifted uncomfortably in her seat and looked across at Malcolm. There was more. My heart sank.

I tried to steel myself for whatever was coming next.

I started to pep-talk myself in my head. Whatever comes out of her mouth next, do not fucking cry, I told myself. Do not show these fuckers that it hurts. I dug my thumbnail into the side of my finger, to focus all my pain somewhere else. The pain seared up my finger.

'We . . . have had some complaints about an article you have written. It's about . . . you living on the council estate . . . and you becoming a teenage mum, and keeping your baby . . . and you know, we don't judge you for being a teen mum, Jessica, but we have to consider whether it is suitable for you to be training to be a psychologist whilst writing about things like this.'

She trailed off as the hot tears filled my eyes quicker than I could control them. Fuck's sake.

'I understand this must be upsetting for you, Jessica, but we must always ensure that we separate ourselves from those we help. We are the professionals. As a psychologist, it is not advisable to also be seen as a victim – because then – what sets you apart from the victims you help? You are just the same as them . . . vulnerable.'

I felt my face flush with utter embarrassment. I felt like slatting my notebooks at her.

My mind whirred. Why couldn't I be a psychologist and a victim? Why couldn't I also be vulnerable? Why were we pretending that psychologists had their shit together, when Malcolm got drunk and set his kitchen on fire last year, and no one questioned his suitability?

Were they all perfect with no histories and no complexities? Why did I have to lie about where I was from and who I really was?

I wanted to ask her all of those questions, but I was consumed with shame. I had never been embarrassed about being a teen mum before, and I had certainly never felt ashamed of it.

Even when Simpo pulled up next to me in his lowered Seat Leon, revved his engine at me, and called me a slag for having a baby, I felt no shame. In fact, all I could think was how on earth Simpo had passed his driving test before I had. The boy who chewed his sleeves until they were soggy, was only allowed to use the plastic safety scissors, and pretended to walk with a club foot until a doctor finally confirmed he was putting it on for attention; had a fucking driving licence. And there he was, using that driving licence to pull up alongside a seventeen-year-old girl with a pram to yell, 'Slag!' and then drive off whilst blasting Akon.

I was just about to tell you that I had never been embarrassed or ashamed about living on a council estate either, but that would be a lie.

I had been desperate to escape that estate. So desperate in fact, that me and Isabelle had sat in English and devised a plan to leave school to become strippers so we could rent a flat together in Manchester and buy as much Lambrini as we wanted.

My estate terrified me. It stripped me down to nothing. It humiliated me and mocked me. It exploited and abused me. It suffocated me. It hardened me. It desensitised me. It threatened me. It forced me to grow up too quickly. It taught me. It nurtured me. It broke me. It made me. It destroyed me. It rebuilt me.

When I finally did run away at eighteen years old, I never wanted to set foot in that place for as long as I lived. I blocked it out. I tried to never think of it again. If I was honest with myself, I would say that I had hated my council estate, until that very moment, when all of a sudden, all I wanted to do was defend it. It was a peculiar urge, and one I never thought I would ever have.

I wanted to tell Laura that she didn't understand. I wanted to shout at her that my estate was the making of me. I wanted to tell her that every fucked up experience I had ever been through had brought me to sit in front of her and Malcolm in that stuffy closet office, doing my PhD in forensic psychology at a top university.

But all I did was cry.

2

I've got one hand in my pocket

Spring 2002

Just as we got to my little wooden gate with the squeaky hinges, Demi took a bite of her Wham bar and then said the weirdest thing.

'My mum says you don't live in a real house. Is this your house then?'

She grinned at the other girls whilst I looked up at my semi-detached house, puzzled.

What did she mean?

The other girls giggled and shuffled, their school bags rattling and bashing together.

'Umm, I dunno what you mean. It's a real house. Got walls and doors and windows and everything else all the regular houses have got. Dunno what else you want. I don't live in a tent . . .' I tried to make light of what she was saying, but I felt my face burning.

The other girls stopped giggling and stared at me. It was like being a comedian with a tough crowd.

'No, stupid. You live on this estate. This is where the families live who can't afford real houses. My mum bought her house, but some people can't afford their own real house, so they get given one of these . . . cos . . . they're poor!'

Demi and the others burst out laughing as I looked sheepishly back at my house. I didn't understand anything she was saying.

I knew she lived with her mum in another part of town. And I knew her mum had thrown a cocktail party one time and hung butterfly fairy lights all over her house, but could never be arsed to take them down for the next fourteen years, so we called her house 'The Butterfly House' until we were well into our twenties.

But I didn't know what she meant about buying the house. I was eleven, and I realised that I had never considered how we got our house, or how anyone got a house. I guess I thought that humans needed houses, and they were free.

Suddenly, I felt very naïve.

I thought about the letter under my bed. I often wrote letters, but the previous weekend, I had written a letter to my future self. On the envelope, I had written in my best hand-writing, 'Dear Jess, DO NOT OPEN UNTIL YOU ARE 18!'

Inside, I had written detailed instructions and plans of my life, and everything that was going to happen under subheadings: House, Car, Occupation.

I had daydreamed about my adult life. I envisioned myself as an adult, and then instructed myself to buy a car for no more than £200 and make sure it was big enough to put the shopping in. I suggested a Peugeot 106, or maybe a Vauxhall Nova. Failing that, my third option was a Ford Fiesta. I figured £200 would be more than enough, especially as Dad had recently bought a much larger car and that was £300 from a weird man up the moors.

Under 'occupation', I had told myself that there were three jobs to aim for. The first was a social worker, the second was a psychologist, but failing those, the third was to become Prime Minister. I did write a note to myself that it was possible to become all three. I assumed those jobs would pay similar amounts, and would give me enough money to buy the little car, too.

But now I was questioning my instructions about the house. I had instructed eighteen-year-old me to get a little two-bedroomed house where I could have my own space, a bookshelf, my own bedroom, and maybe even a little dog. But I had only budgeted £5000 to buy the house and all the furniture. Maybe that was not going to be enough?

I felt stupid.

'We are not poor!' I shouted at her, but she just chuckled and shook her head at me. The other girls carried on eating their Space Raiders and grinned.

'So why do you live here, then?' She pointed at my house like she was pointing at a slimy hole in the floor.

'I . . . don't know.' I looked at my squeaky gate, and wondered if that meant we were poor, because Demi's big metal gates didn't squeak at all. I put my hand on it to stop it from moving.

I didn't know why I lived there. We had lived there since I was one. When I was born, Mum and me lived at Nana's little house with her and Grandad, and all my uncles, and my dad, but it got too much. I didn't remember much about the house, except the weird-patterned bricks lining the back garden, and the black and white collie called Susie.

Mum was nineteen and Dad was twenty-three when they had me. I'm not sure anyone was too thrilled by that, but both sets of grandparents felt strongly that my dad should have to move in with my mum and be an active parent, which meant I always had them both, and I guess we all grew up together.

Mum's religious and traditional parents had insisted my dad marry my mum as soon as I was born, and they got married a fortnight after my arrival. How my teenaged mother motivated herself to get out of bed, let alone wear a wedding dress and get married, two weeks postpartum is beyond me. Not long after, we moved into our first house together and we had been there ever since.

'Maybe you should ask your mum and dad, scrubber!'

'Shut up, I am not a scrubber!'

My face felt hot and sweaty.

'What make are those trainers, again?' she laughed, remembering the conversation from PE earlier.

I glanced at my PE kit.

I didn't know. I realised that I didn't know trainers had a 'make'. They were just whatever we could afford from Windsor's World of Shoes. I picked mine because they were silver. I really liked them. And they were only £5, so Mum had said I could have them. Joanne had told me they looked like shit space boots, and then called me 'Knock Off NASA' for the rest of the day.

I was being humiliated, and all I could do was turn, and run away.

I avoided swinging open the gate so it didn't squeak to further expose me, and instead trampled across the left flowerbed my mum had lovingly created as a remembrance for my little brother, and ran inside. I slammed the door and stood at the bottom of the stairs, chest heaving, trying not to cry, and praying Mum didn't see me run through her tulip bed. I looked around my house, and up the stairs. I thought it was a real house.

The spiky artex walls were definitely real. If you scraped past those, you would know about it – and the school would be on the phone asking where you got those purple scratches from.

The floor was real, too. Stacey had gotten some pretty serious carpet burns from our favourite game where we slid down the stairs as fast as we could, like it was a bumpy slide. Although Mum did eventually ban us from that game when we learned that it was even faster in an old sleeping bag and we both ended up crashing into the shoe rack.

'Jess! Is that you?' My mum's voice rang out from somewhere. She didn't sound too angry, so I guessed she hadn't seen me after all.

'Yeah.'

'Oh, good. What's seven times eight?' she snapped.

'What?' I frowned, dumping my bag on the floor.

'Seven times eight!'

I shrugged.

'Fifty-six. Why?'

She went back to whatever heated conversation she was having with Dad, and didn't respond to me any further.

I walked through to them both and realised that Dad was not only home, but wasn't in his overalls. He was stood in the kitchen with his head in his hands, leaning against the work-top. Mum was in the exact same position but on the opposite side of the tiny kitchen. Mum was stood exactly where I had fallen off the worktop as a four-year-old, and bitten clean through my bottom lip. I still have that scar to this day.

I always did think that side of the kitchen was bad luck, as a few years later, I earned myself yet another lifelong scar by attempting to cut myself an apple with a meat cleaver. Come to think of it, that would become the exact same place my previously sober Dad launched into a violent drunken rage at me and fractured my wrist many years later, but I guess we'll get to that.

I looked at them both.

'I already told you it was fifty-six, Kim,' Dad sighed.

'Right, well she's good at maths, int she? So I was just checking!' she snapped back at him.

'Uhhh . . . Mum, Demi said summat to me outside, saying we live here cos we can't afford a real house . . . and that families get given these houses who can't afford their own house. Is that . . . true?'

'Don't be stupid. Tell her to piss off next time. Cheeky little shit. I know her mum, too. Just ignore her, she doesn't know what she's on about.'

Mum folded a tea towel and slapped it down.

'Next time she says shit like that, tell her I saw her mum on the street corner on Friday night . . . and we all know she's on the game!'

Dad nearly choked on his brew.

'Kimberley!' he gasped.

'What?' she bit back.

'Mouthy little bitch . . .' she mumbled under her breath.

'They're just kids,' Dad mumbled back.

And with that, Mum went back to arguing with Dad about seven times eight.

I didn't know what 'game' Demi's mum was playing.

I did know that I didn't want to answer any more angry times tables, so I slowly backed out of the kitchen and slipped upstairs to take my school uniform off. I definitely was not going to tell Demi to piss off either, because I had a flawless behaviour record at school, and I wanted it to stay that way. If my teachers caught me telling someone to piss off, I would probably not be able to become a prefect, and then my entire life would likely spiral, and I would never become Prime Minister.

Stacey and Alfie were upstairs, clattering about with Action Men and My Little Ponies in the plastic toy box from the charity shop.

'What you pair doing, then?' I leant in the doorway as I pulled my green stripy tie off and finally undid my top button.

'Mum said go upstairs to play before we go out. We been waiting for you come home from school,' Stacey said whilst she brushed her white pony's tail with a tiny lilac brush.

'Yeah, you was agessss!' Alfie chipped in, his tiny chimp-like face beaming at me.

Dad buzzing all his hair off the other night had only made him more chimp-like in a family where all the men already looked like Gollum or cute but gangly chimps.

Alfie had seen a footballer on TV and said he wanted slits in his eyebrow, so Dad had attempted it and accidentally shaved most of his right eyebrow off. I had cried with laughter as Dad had tried to calm Mum down, who was stood over him as he tried to stick Alfie's tiny bits of eyebrow hair back on with a homemade mixture of glue and V05 hair wax. I laughed uncontrollably, full tears rolling down my face, wheezing from not being able to catch my breath at the sheer sight of Alfie and Dad sat on the living room floor at 9 o'clock at night, trying to fix the mess they were in before school the next day.

Mum had snapped at me to shut up, but I only lasted until Dad had sheepishly, but seriously, walked into the kitchen and suggested shaving his other eyebrow off so they matched. I even heard him say the words, 'he might look permanently surprised for a few weeks, but I'm sure it will grow back . . .'

He came back into the living room smirking, having been told in no uncertain terms, not to be so fucking stupid, and I hadn't realised it was possible to laugh so much. Eventually I was sent to my room, where I had to work hard to calm my breathing and not to begin the cycle of giggling all over again every time I pictured Alfie with one eyebrow.

'Shush you!' I grinned at him, lunging down to tickle his skinny ribcage. 'It takes me ages to walk home now cos I'm at middle school. I'm not at baby school like you two no more!'

'It's not baby school! I'm in Year 2 now!' he protested.

'You could have just gone to Crawley, that's closer. You wanted go the posh school. It's your own fault. When we're big, we are just gonna go Crawley. Aren't we, Alf?'

She might have been nine, but Stacey was right. I could have gone to Crawley School, which was just up the road.

But I had chosen, no, I had fought to go to the posh school. I wasn't in the catchment area for it, but I was hellbent on going to the school on the posh estate, even before I had realised why. It had meant that girls like Demi had sniffed me out pretty early, and realised I wasn't from their ends, but I had decided that I would endure pretty much anything to go to the better school – even a two mile walk to school every day, come rain or shine.

It was especially important to me to go to the posh school, because I hadn't been able to take up the scholarship I had won at a private all girls' school in Alderley Edge when I was nine. Mrs Brown had said that she had sent my work, and the work of another girl, off to somewhere; and they had come back with an offer of a scholarship. She had told me that I needed to go to a school that would challenge me and support my potential, but my parents didn't agree. Instead of encouraging me, they had moaned about the school being too far away from home, about the extra driving, and started to make comments that I would never make new friends there. I still drive past that school and wonder where I would be today if I had been able to take up the scholarship.

My next best option was Redtree, the old grammar school on the outskirts of town. I thought it was incredibly posh. It had a much stricter, and much better reputation than Crawley, on our council estate. They rejected my application at first, and I had sat in the living room sobbing for hours. Mum had then done her best to argue that I should be given a place at Redtree, on account of my grades and awards. After what felt like weeks of hanging around, we got the letter to say I had been accepted.

Whilst the walk was exhausting, I had quickly been picked out for being different, and I often arrived to school soaking wet or freezing cold; I was doing brilliantly and loved my school.

My mum's voice came ringing up the stairs: 'Jess! Are you ready? We're going out in a minute!'

'Where we goin'?' I whispered to Stacey.

She shrugged and put her ponies back in the box.

In the car, I did my favourite game of imagining a dramatic song in the charts whilst staring out of the window at the terraced streets, the main roads and then the countryside, and pretended I was in a music video. It was better when it was raining, and it was even better if I was on a bus.

Dad drove the narrowing roads to the reservoir, and I thought about Demi saying we didn't live in a real house. We drove past her house on the way, and I thought it looked just like our house. If anything, her house was smaller and newer than ours, and ours was older but bigger, with a huge garden. Dad had built a patio, a play area, a summer house and a little cherry tree garden over the years. At the front, he and Mum had planted a weeping willow tree in remembrance of my brother, who had died a few years earlier. Dad had built a rockery and Mum had created perfect flowerbeds around a tiny lawn. We had enjoyed hundreds of barbecues, picnics, water fights, snowball fights, games of hide and seek and hours of make believe in our garden, but Demi didn't even have one.

At some point, every kid on our street had been in my house or garden. We lived on a street filled with families, and drama. There was Bella and Danni, two sisters who I loved going swimming and playing hide and seek with. Nice girls, but viciously beaten by their dad. Sometimes they couldn't come swimming because of the black bruises sprawling from their calves up their backs. The Rodgers family lived at the top of the street, a large Christian family with seven kids ranging from nineteen to three years old. Quiet, god-fearing and neighbourly, they were the real-life Flanders Family from *The Simpsons* – and the rest of the street regarded them as naïve and mollycoddled.

The Wilshaws lived at the bottom of the street, and one of their daughters was in my class at primary school. They were just your average family on the council estate. Mum, dad, two kids and a dog. Mum worked on the fruit and veg market stall, and the dad worked at the supermarket. The Hulmes were a strange looking family over the road, and I had spent many years convinced they were pirates. Both the mum and the dad looked like a cross between Captain Hook and Marti Pellow from Wet Wet Wet. Both with long thick hair, shirts and waistcoats, boots, and earrings. Every time I went to play with their only daughter Jayde, I would listen out for any evidence that they were indeed pirates, hiding out on our estate.

As proof that memory is indeed reconstructed, and the brain is not a literal video camera that records things as they are, I can only recall them nowadays with a parrot on one shoulder and an eye patch – when I know for a fact they had neither. I always picture the mum with a bandana on too, which I am pretty sure she never wore. Sadly, the reality of that family was much more grim, and one day when the door was ajar, I walked into Jayde's house to find her mum crouched on the floor, blood pouring from her ear having had her gold hoop earrings ripped out by her abusive pirate husband in an argument over dinner. Jayde was curled up under her desk in her bedroom, shaking and crying, and he was never seen again.

Then there was the Bowlers next door to them. Their dad had a modified Subaru and insisted on putting bigger and bigger exhaust systems on it, so it woke the whole street up every time he went out in the morning, or at night. I will always remember the thud as Nicky was hit by a speeding car whilst we were playing (admittedly in the road) when I was nine years old. One second, we were talking, and the next minute he drove his bike right into the centre of the crossroads and was hit so hard that he was thrown over the car, whilst his bike crumpled underneath it. I was the last person to talk to him as he lost consciousness on the tarmac, whilst the driver screeched in horror and banged on our neighbours' door to use a phone to call an ambulance.

Miraculously, Nicky survived because the driver of the car behind was a paramedic on the way home from work, who ran over to help us.

It was Nicky being run over, and then our friend Pippa being run over a few months later, that led to the local council finally putting speed bumps and traffic calming measures in place.

One of the measures they implemented was to stop John from parking his huge HGV truck on our street, four doors up from us, because it would block the street for days at a time. He was always getting into trouble, and Mum said he thought he owned the street. One year he decided he was going to host a firework show on the grass verge in the centre of our street with some knock-off fireworks he had acquired from somewhere. His wife had knocked on everyone's doors, inviting them to this spectacular display, that they could watch from the comfort of their own front yard.

Unfortunately, none of us saw any fireworks that year, because John put the huge cube of fireworks upside down, lit them, and they blew a crater in the grass verge, sending a tonne of grass, earth, stones and tree roots hurtling into the air instead. That incident also led the local council to ban firework displays on the grass verges, and order John to repair what I can only describe as a scorched meteor crater in the middle of our street.

That caused years of fights and chaos between him and the two families on our street who were volunteers for the local Village in Bloom Committee. They were horrified that their chance at winning the competition for the best street had been scuppered by his firework stunt, and reported him repeatedly to the council in an attempt to get him kicked out of the street.

There was never a dull day.

As we pulled into the reservoir, I thought about the time I was playing 'potions' with Stacey in our garden. She was only three, which could have only made me six. Potions was our favourite game. We used to take a small plastic bucket and collect berries, leaves, grass and flower petals, mix them together into a magic potion and use it to cast spells, or heal our imaginary life-threatening injuries. That time, I decided to feed her the 'poison berries' from the bird bush, and Mum had come rushing out of the kitchen to stop her from swallowing another mouthful.

I hadn't really seen what the big deal was, especially as I had cleaned them in a puddle before handing them to her. They didn't have any mud left on them. And I had polished them up to be a lovely shiny red, too. Apparently rolling them in a shallow puddle on the driveway and polishing them with my sleeve did not negate their toxicity – and Mum rushed Stacey to the hospital.

We walked halfway around the reservoir and stopped at Mum and Dad's favourite viewing point. It was a warm April night, and we skimmed stones whilst they cuddled on a log behind us. They said they had something to tell us all, and the little ones ran up to them to sit in their knees. Alfie sat on Dad, and Stacey sat on Mum. I continued skimming stones, sensing something was wrong. Mum asked me to stop, and come to sit with them so we could talk, but I didn't want to.

After much cajoling, I settled about five feet away from them all, on another log. I picked up a stick and poked the sandy shore of the reservoir. I listened as Mum's voice wavered.

She reminded us all that they both loved us very much, but said that they had decided to get a divorce. I had been having nightmares about this moment for years. I had been having them for years, but I still can't tell you why. They were more like predictions than nightmares, really. I always knew it was coming. The nightmares were always the same. Something would happen, then Dad would look at me, silently pull on his black coat, wrap a turquoise scarf around his neck and walk up the street into a raging blizzard. He would move away and I would wake up with tears streaming down my face.

Instead of feeling utter devastation at the news, I felt nothing. Mum's words blurred out as I was consumed with emptiness: the same feeling I felt when they told us our little brother had died a year earlier. The same feeling I had when they told us that my great-grandma had died, just three months before my brother died. It was always the same – the deep, empty, numb nothingness.

They sat behind me crying and holding each other. Alfie couldn't have understood what was happening, but I think he just burst into tears at the sight of his parents and his sister crying.

I stared at the calm water, and the way the soft afternoon light bounced off the ripples. I watched the ducks dive, and bob back up somewhere else. A dog launched into the water to chase a stick.

'Jess, dya want a cuddle?'

'No.'

'Come here, come on sweetheart . . .'

'I said no,' I snapped.

Visions of the text messages I had found on Mum's phone popped up in my mind like some unwelcome emergency alert system. A few months prior, I had become suspicious of a man who was decorating Nana and Grandad's house. Well, that's what they said he was doing, except he didn't seem to be doing anything at all. Whilst Mum was downstairs talking to her parents, I had asked to go to the bathroom, and gone upstairs to do some snooping. I had always fancied myself as the amateur detective, and spent a lot of time watching and listening, instead of talking. I always found you learned a lot about people and their intentions by watching them, and listening carefully to them. Many times, I found that the words didn't match the body language, or the eye contact, or the mouth.

I didn't know who this man was, and he seemed nice enough, but even at eleven years old, I didn't believe he was living with Nana and Grandad so he could decorate their house. I sifted through his things, all in black bin bags, and I wondered if he had been kicked out of somewhere, or maybe even ran away from somewhere. I didn't find a single clue as to who he was or where he was, and was about to give up and go to the bathroom, until a dim green light shone out of a trainer.

I picked out a phone that had two unopened text messages on the front screen. I opened the inbox to find a stream of explicit messages from a woman called Kimberley. My mum. Part of me didn't want to believe what I was seeing, and another part of me sarcastically shouted out, 'I knew it! I was right!'

I sat on the bed in the guest room where the man was staying, and tried to piece together why Mum was texting the man who was living with her parents, whether Dad knew, and whether my grandparents knew. The next day, I checked Mum's mobile phone whilst she wasn't looking and found the same text messages in her deleted items. Everyone was in on it, except for Dad. Mum had been seeing the guy for months, Nana and Grandad knew about it, and had offered him somewhere to live for a while.

I couldn't hug Dad at the reservoir, because I couldn't bear the guilt of knowing something was wrong for months. I couldn't hug Mum because I knew she had been lying, and I was angry at her for sitting there and saying that she loved Dad, and that they had mutually agreed to end their marriage. I might have been eleven, but I wasn't unaware.

But Dad was hardly innocent anyway. I will never forget the screech of the karaoke microphone and the deafening bang of it hitting the floor and rolling away the moment I literally dropped the mic as I watched my dad duck out of the pub to snog a woman he just met. It was already late, Alfie was fast asleep in his pram, and Stacey was hidden under a pile of coats, trying to sleep through the pounding bass and the warbling karaoke.

Dad had been chatting to the woman with the big frizzy blonde hair for an hour, and I was bored out of my brains. The smoke was hurting my throat, and Uncle Jax was getting confrontational again. At least six men had already refused his offer (read: demand) for an arm wrestle. I had already asked to go home, but something had happened towards the end of Mum and Dad's marriage, and we seemed to be forever in pubs and working men's clubs until closing time. We were surrounded by other pub kids, who spent years surrounded by pissed up adults, pool table competitions, violent brawls, and lonely old nicotine-stained men who gave you 20p for a pick n mix from behind the bar just so you would sit and talk to them.

I was young enough to still be distracted by something I loved, and after the fifth time of pulling on Dad's sleeve and shouting over the music that I wanted to go home, he leant down to me, smiling.

'Sweetheart, you haven't had a turn on the karaoke yet. Ya know how much I love hearing ya sing. Why don't ya get up and sing the Alanis song ya did at the show?'

I looked at Dad, excited. It was the first time he had spoken to me in hours. The blonde frizzy woman smiled kindly at me, too. I had been singing at shows for months, and was getting pretty good.

'Ummm yeah okay, Dad! I'll go request my song.' I jumped up to find a chewed up biro and a little slip of paper to submit my song to the karaoke guy. Not for one single second did I consider that I was being distracted.

All I could think about was doing Dad proud. I would get up there on that stage at the end of the pub and sing my absolute best.

I went to hand in my little slip of paper. The plump old guy took my request without even looking up at me.

As I walked away, he shouted me back.

'Eh! Scuse me!'

I spun back around. He looked at me briefly, realising I was no older than eleven. And it was almost midnight, in a dirty little pub on the estate. He frowned, and then smiled at me.

'There's no one else in the queue, little 'un. You can get up now, I'll load the track.'

He handed me the mic, and I stood awkwardly on the stage as people started to look up from their drinks and their conversations to find the reason why the music cut, and the introduction to Alanis Morissette's 'Hand in my pocket' was starting.

I wasn't frightened. I sang in public any chance I got. I loved singing. I loved Alanis. I focused my mind, and looked at the screen with the little bee and the title of the song. Instrumental. Counting myself in. I didn't even need to look at the lyrics. I would face the crowd, sing to them, and pretend I was a star.

'I'm broke but I'm happy, I'm poor but I'm kind, I'm short but I'm healthy, yeaaaaah!'

One hundred people stared up at me, instantly singing along to a pub classic. The dancefloor was packed. I relaxed into the song.

'I'm high but I'm grounded, I'm sane but I'm overwhelmed, I'm lost but I'm hopeful, baby!'

People swayed and yelled the lines back at me. I smiled at them. I was a superstar on that little wooden stage.

I looked for Dad. I always looked for Mum or Dad when I was singing, so they could smile at me and I could feel encouraged and safe. But I couldn't find him. Keep singing, I told myself. Don't stop.

'And what it all comes down to, is that everything is gonna be fine, fine, fine . . .'

But where was he? I scanned the room. He wasn't at the bar. He wasn't at our table. Alfie was still fast asleep in the pram, with his dummy half falling out of his little mouth. Not that he needed a pram, or a dummy, at six years old – but I was often envious of his comfy seat-on-wheels where he could fall asleep whilst we were stuck in these pubs. Stacey was slipping off the ripped red leather pub seat, asleep with her leg and arm flopping down by her side, covered in strangers' coats. It was a wonder someone hadn't sat on her yet.

'Cause I've got one hand in my pocket . . .'

I gasped into the microphone. I saw the blonde frizzy woman and Dad duck out of the back of the pub, kissing, holding each other, laughing.

I stood there in silence. Frozen. The backing track played. Anger coursed through me. He had tricked me. He wanted to distract me.

I dropped the mic to the floor and jumped off the stage. The deafening noise bounced around the pub as everyone flinched and covered their ears. People groaned and shouted at me. I shoved through them all on the dancefloor whilst they stared at me in shock, giggled at me, tried to hold me back, or tried to calm me down.

'MOVE!' I screamed at a drunk man who was telling me to calm down.

'Get off me!' I peeled a drunk but concerned woman's hands off my arm.

Suddenly, Uncle Jax appeared again, absolutely bladdered. He crouched down to talk to me, trying to stop me from pushing through the dancefloor to the door I saw Dad go through.

'Come on, Jessica. Get back up there and do ya song. What's up with ya?'

It sounded like a threat.

'I want me dad!'

'He's busy!' He laughed at me, but his eyes were angry.

I could see that, and said so as I shoved him out of the way, and ran to the back of the pub.

I ran into the fresh air of the late summer night to find absolutely nothing. There was no one there. I was baffled. I know I saw them. I could have sworn I did. I ran back into Alfie and Stacey but they were still alone and asleep. The karaoke man was apologising to everyone and calling for people to finish the song. A drunk couple clambered up on the stage to a round of cheers.

I dodged Uncle Jax again, and ran back outside. I stood in the carpark overlooking the estate, and felt totally lost. I ran to the left, round the back of the pub, and stared into the darkness of the wasteland and fields. I panicked. What if something terrible had happened to him? What if he was out there in the wastelands? He didn't usually drink this much. I could count on one hand how many times I had seen him drunk in my whole childhood up to that point.

Ever since stuff fell apart between him and Mum, he had been drinking a lot. I had overheard Mum convincing him to get out, go drinking, meet new people, join sports teams, and get his own life. At first, he had been reluctant, but over time, they had both been doing the same – and I guess that's how we ended up Pub Kids.

As I stood staring into the darkness, imagining finding his unconscious body face down in the grass, I heard a woman's

31

voice. I looked around, but saw nothing. I crept around the corner, still nothing. My heart raced. I felt it in my throat. I slid down the walls of the pub, terrified of what I might see around each corner.

'Dad!' I exclaimed, clapping my hand over my mouth.

My dad and the woman with the frizzy blonde hair jumped apart and cried out in terror.

'Jess! What . . . are ya doing out here?'

'You!' I scowled at him. 'You told me to go up there and sing to get me out of ya way, didn't ya?'

The woman, still up against the pub wall, giggled at me and smoothed her clothes down. Dad fumbled over his words and sighed. He was a terrible liar. He often didn't even bother. He couldn't get his words out.

'Stacey and Alfie are in the pub alone, Dad. You made me sing . . . to shut me up!'

'Come on darlin . . . it's not like that. And the kids are . . . fine in there, your Uncle Jax is . . . lookin' after them,' he stumbled.

'Uncle Jax is smashed! He is not lookin' after them at all, he keeps offerin' arm wrestles to strangers!'

The blonde woman swayed and giggled at me again.

I saw red.

'Shut up!' I roared at her, launching my whole body at her in rage.

She hit me with her little white handbag and ran away from me into the carpark.

'Get away from my dad! Who even are you? Get away from us!'

'Jessica!' Dad gasped in utter embarrassment and shock that his little daughter was trying to chase his love interest around the pub carpark.

I ignored him and outran them both, to find her in the dark.

Dad tried his best, pleading with me to stop, telling me Kerry was just a friend, they were only talking. But it was too late, I had already found her.

Just as I went to throw myself at her for a second time, Uncle Jax appeared out of nowhere and restrained my arms.

'Calm down, right now,' he growled into my ear. 'Her husband is in there, and you're causing a fuckin scene. Shut up. Now.'

His fingers dug into the soft tissue of my arms. I was writhing and kicking to make him let go of me, but suddenly, I slowed as it all clicked in. She was married. Dad was out here with her. Uncle Jax knew about it. It was pre-planned. I was the distraction.

'Jessica. Calm down darlin, it's fine, everything is fine. She's just my friend. She's lovely,' Dad slurred at me whilst Uncle Jax held me back. I wasn't looking at either of them. I was glaring at the woman. Then I looked at Dad. Then up at Uncle Jax. My anger spread through my body. I heaved. A crowd was forming. People were coming outside, pretending to spark up cigarettes, but coming to be nosey at the little girl having a tantrum.

Suddenly, the rage came up from nowhere. I hated them all.

'You're married!' I screamed at my dad. 'You're both married!'

The crowd whispered, laughed, gasped, and people nudged each other. Dad stared at Uncle Jax.

I lunged at the woman again, but both men grabbed and held me tight.

Suddenly, she ran. She just turned, and ran. Through the gap in the wall, out on to the wasteland, out into the night. Dad took a few steps after her, and then stopped.

Uncle Jax abruptly let go of me, and I dropped to the floor.

'Someone check she's okay! She can't run out there on 'er own!'

She disappeared into the darkness, and I smirked a little. Good. She went away. I wanted to go home. I didn't care about her.

Uncle Jax dropped down into a crouch again, swaying, stinking of lager and cigarette smoke, and stared at me. He was a huge man. He was known for being extremely violent, and he loved his bad reputation. He bragged about his past all the time, and was the first into any drama or fights – just for the kicks.

That stare was terrifying. His eyes were dead. I thought he was going to knock me into next week. I braced myself for the impact.

Instead of being punched as I suspected, he gripped the top of my skinny arm and dug his fingers in.

'Look what you've done! This is all your fault. Now Kerry is out there in the wastelands alone, in the dark, with no one. And I've gotta go and explain to her husband. You think you know everything, but you don't have the first fuckin clue what you've just done!'

He let go of me, and stormed off.

'The fuck are you lot lookin' at?' he hissed at the crowd and lunged at them as he stormed past. They scattered, and then came back together to gossip about the unfolding drama, the drunk man, the little girl causing chaos, and the woman who had run off into the pitch-black wastelands.

I turned around to find Dad sitting on the carpark wall, looking like he was about to burst into tears. He looked lost.

'I didn't even want to come here tonight. I'm only here cos your mum and Uncle told me it would be good for me to meet someone else. Your mum is out with a guy. I didn't even want to come. I love your mum so much. I would give my right arm for her. You know that. She knows that . . .' He started to cry. I just stood there, watching him sob.

Mum was where? Mum wanted him to meet other people? Uncle Jax knew about this?

My head spun. Dad looked like he was going to throw up, but I remembered that Stacey and Alfie were still in the pub, alone. Dad wiped his tears, and sniffed. He looked up at me like a broken little boy looking at his mother.

It was in that moment that I realised I was the only sober person able to get the little ones home safely. I looked up at the stars in the sky. Why was this my life?

I took a deep breath and walked back into the pub. It was closing time, and most people were leaving, laughing, hanging off each other, shouting about getting a kebab, and singing Chumba Wumba at the top of their lungs. Men walked down the street clutching their stolen pint glasses and women took off their shoes to run barefoot through the estate.

I pushed through them, against the current, and got back to the kids.

'Stacey. Stacey. Stacey. Stace. Stace . . .' I shook her awake, gently at first, and then more vigorously as I lost my patience.

'What?' she moaned, looking around her, confused.

'It's time go home, Stace. We need get home, it's bedtime. Put your coat on.'

I helped her into her little jacket, as she sleepily yawned and rubbed her eyes, red from the smoke. I tucked the blanket back around Alfie for the walk home. I picked his dummy up off the floor and cleaned it off on my T-shirt. I found Dad's coat, and checked the pockets for the house keys.

'You not gonna finish off your song for us?'

I turned around to see the karaoke man tidying up and packing his kit away.

'You have a lovely voice you know. You could be a singer one day, if you keep practising. You're good on stage, aren't you, duck?'

I knew he was trying to be kind, but I didn't even have the energy to respond. I wearily looked down at Stacey, the pram cradling my crunched up little brother under a blanket, and then imagined my dad outside, undoubtedly slumped next to his own sick – and sneered at the possibility that I would ever be anything more than I was on that night.

Famous singers don't grow up round here, I thought.

I looked at the floor, grabbed the handles of the pram, hung Dad's coat off one side of it, and guided a wobbly Stacey to the door. The fresh air hit me as I sighed into the night, glancing over at my dad, awake, but still sobbing on the wall next to the pub.

We all walked solemnly home, until we were just steps from the front door. After twenty minutes of silence, Dad became agitated.

'You know how much I love your mum. Don't you? I never even wanted to meet someone else. She's everything to me. She made me do it. I told her . . . I didn't want to . . .' He started sobbing again.

I stared at him, leaning against the door as he stabbed the lock with all the wrong keys.

'You are not going to tell her what happened tonight are you?'

I thought about it.

'She should know the truth, shouldn't she?' I challenged, 'We are not allowed to lie.'

He stumbled through the door, but turned quickly around to me. His eyes were different. I had never seen him this angry at me before. He was usually so laid back, my mum used to call him horizontal. He seethed, but I couldn't understand why.

And then, seemingly out of nowhere, he went from standing perfectly still, to swinging his open hand towards my face. I ducked and felt the air rush over my hair, as he missed me. He lost his balance and went stumbling into the spiky artex of the hallway wall.

I gulped, and suddenly found myself entangled in a struggle. I tried to break free and get away from him, but he grabbed me, and started apologising profusely. I didn't want to hear it, but he wouldn't let go. His hands were tight around my wrist as he tried to stop me from wrenching away from him. He pulled me back towards the kitchen cabinets, and I felt my wrist crunch as it slammed against the cupboard door.

We stood in heavy silence, staring at each other, both in disbelief and horror. I held my throbbing wrist with my other hand, as Mum crashed through the door and almost into the pram where Alfie was still fast asleep.

Initially giggling and jolly from her own night out, even she wasn't too drunk to sense the tension she had fallen into.

'What's going on here, then?' she slurred, her eyes moving back and forth between us in the tiny kitchen.

Silence. I watched my parents look at each other in the twilight.

'I think you'd better go bed, Jessica.' Mum pointed up the stairs and I quickly made myself scarce, and eventually fell asleep whilst they drunkenly argued until the small hours.

Looking back, it was those moments that totally broke me. The arguments. The affairs. The drinking. The divorce. Mum leaving and disappearing for weeks. Dad going off the rails and losing his job. Mum turning back up. Dad leaving and disappearing for weeks. Dad turning back up. Avoiding each other at all costs. Selling the house. Watching strangers walk around our house, asking what would be thrown in. Curtains? Carpets? Furniture? It was like living in a nightmare.

I spent months writing threats and abuse on the walls of my house in invisible ink. It was the only way I could cope with what was happening to my family home. I got my little invisible ink and UV light kit from under my bed and started graffitiing all over every room in the house. Sometimes in huge bubble writing. Sometimes repeated twenty times down one wall.

'YOU DON'T BELONG HERE'

'FUCK OFF'

'GET OUT OF MY HOUSE'

'THIS IS MY BEDROOM'

'FUCK THE NEW OWNERS'

And on the final day, when the house was being cleared of everything, I lay on the bare wooden floorboards in my little box room and wrote a message on the skirting board, under the radiator.

'This bedroom belonged to Jess Taylor. She was here until 2002, when her life fell apart. This will always be my room.'

I checked it with my UV light, angry cried, and walked away.

3

Just say fuck all

Autumn 2003

Nothing says life is moving too quickly for you like spending your morning asking your mum's new boy-friend how old he is, what his surname is, and what he does for a living.

Over breakfast. Because you're living with him now. Yay.

I ripped at my dry piece of value white bread and looked up at Mark. My appetite had packed up and fucked off since my life got turned upside down, and I lived on a couple of pieces of bread a day, and some knock-off smart price super noodles occasionally.

'So . . . how old are you?'

'Same as ya mum. Thirty-one,' he smiled back.

'And what do you do for a living?'

I felt like I was interviewing him for *Blind Date*. I was like Cilla Black but without the canned laughter and sexual innuendos.

'I work in an office,' he smirked.

'What kind of office?' I ripped at the dark crust at the top of the slice, my favourite bit.

'The kind with computers that spit paint at me all day,' he gestured to his paint-covered overalls. And then tipped his head to one side and raised one eyebrow at me.

I rolled my eyes. He had been trying to make me laugh for weeks. He didn't know I knew about him staying at Nana and Grandad's house. Mum didn't know I knew either. No one knew.

'So, you don't work in an office then? You work for yourself?'

I tried to carry on interrogating him and pretending he wasn't funny. But he was.

'I've got my own painting and decorating firm,' he smiled again.

I stayed quiet. I already knew that. Not that he actually did any painting or decorating at Nana's house. I ripped off some of the white bread and rolled it into a ball in my hand, and then ate it. He watched me, probably disgusted. He sipped his mug of tea.

He suddenly looked up at the clock, and jumped out of his chair. He grabbed his pack of Golden Virginia, his Rizlas, and a Twix, and rushed out of the kitchen.

'Uh . . . one more thing!'

He stopped and turned back to me.

'What is your surname again?'

'Scanner, why?' he grinned.

'Because I thought your surname was Scammer, and I was wondering how on earth you get any work with a name like that. Scanner makes more sense.' I kept a straight face, but inside I was giggling at the fact that I had thought his surname was Scammer for three whole weeks.

He laughed at me, 'Yes, that wouldn't be very good for business now, would it?'

I stuffed the last bit of bread in my mouth, and as he turned to leave, he hesitated at the door.

'I tell you what, I will decorate the bedroom for you and Stacey this weekend. You name the colour, and I can do it. Anything at all. What do you reckon?'

I smirked. Challenge accepted.

'Fine. I want it to be light blue like the sky at the top of the wall, slowly going into a gradient blue, that then goes into a purple, which then goes into a pink at the bottom of the wall. Sort of like how sunsets look after the sun has gone down. Reckon you can paint that?'

He shook his head and chuckled, 'Yep, easy peasy.'

I gave him a thumbs up, and he rushed out to work. There was no way he was that good. He would have to use wallpaper.

I heard Mark greet someone as he left the house, and in his place, Kalen appeared. He stood at my door, huge smile, a blond mohican bleached down one side of his brown hair, uniform immaculate, cubic zirconia earring in his right ear lobe.

'Ready?'

'Always!' I smirked.

He knew what that meant. He rolled his eyes at me, adjusted his rucksack on one shoulder, and let out a sigh to mock me.

'For fuck's sake, Jess . . .'

I wasn't ready, of course. I was never ready. I'm thirty-two as I write this, and I am still never ready, when someone asks me if I am ready. Ever.

I scraped together the basics for school, threw on my rucksack and ran back out to him.

Kalen lived four doors up from my new tiny, terraced council house on Trent Grove. If the other house wasn't real,

41

then this was a mirage. It was a sliver of a house, stacked in a row with thirty other houses. There was no dining room, but there was a small living room as you first walked in which led into a small kitchen. The back garden was just some rough grass, but Mark had built us a small pond on the weekend, which I'm not sure he was allowed to do in a council property. He said we could have some fish in there, and maybe we would get some newts too.

The new street was a dead end. On the posh estate over the brook, the kids called them 'cul-de-sacs', but on the estate, no one used that language.

Kalen's mum, an uncompromising but popular matriarch, had insisted that her son would look after me as I settled into the estate. She didn't have any daughters, but she knew I wouldn't have survived long without a decent guy friend. I wasn't naïve, and I wasn't resentful. It's not like I hadn't lived on the council estate my entire life, but she knew, and I knew, that we had moved to the roughest end of the estate. It's probably a weird thing for some people to understand, that there were different areas within the council estate. Some of them were quite pretty, I thought. The houses were kept tidier, the little front gardens had marigolds and poppies. The old couples sat outside playing dominoes.

But there were areas of the estate that were like walking into another area. Another realm. Another world. The atmosphere changed. The people were angrier. The streets were dirtier. The houses were falling apart. The noises were scarier. The gulleys were darker. The parks were shitter. It was like Scooby Doo and the Mystery Incorporated Team running down a repetitive corridor. Candlestick. Mirror. Portrait. Creepy door. Candlestick. Mirror. Portrait. Creepy door. On the estate it was slightly different. Broken down car. Overgrown garden. Piles of black bags. Sofa on the pavement.

Broken down car. Overgrown garden. Piles of black bags. Sofa on the pavement.

I was grateful that Kalen was there to walk me to the bus stop and back every day for a year. He was in my class at school, but other than acknowledging each other, we had never really talked until his mum brought him to our house the morning after we moved in.

At school, he was quiet, and teachers didn't pay him much attention. He was polite enough, but I think teachers had written him off as a bit slow. I have absolutely no idea how Kalen got into Redtree. His mum was a very proud woman, and there was no way she would have had him in a bad school. The one on the estate was only a stone's throw away but had a terrible reputation. I never asked how he got in, but she must have pushed for him to go there too. On reflection, there were about six of us from the council estate who went to the school on the posh estate. I guess I was just lucky that I had moved in right near a boy who was in the same boat as me. On the council estate, he was my friend, and my guru. Despite being almost a whole year younger than me, he kept me safe, gave me advice, listened to me, explained what words and references meant, kept me away from the dodgy people, and kept an eye on me.

Interestingly, despite being very much sidelined at school, I hear he is now a very successful and wealthy businessman with a company in education, and has a beautiful, successful wife who is also in business.

I only have positive things to say about Kalen, and I doubt he will ever know how much he meant to me back then. It was hard enough being bullied for being a 'swot' before moving to the rough end of the council estate, but being a swot and trying to survive on that council estate was hard as fuck. If you can survive that, even if you come out the other end clinging on to dear life, I reckon you can survive anything.

I was so out of my depth, it was laughable. I was smart, but not the right kind of smart. I was good at fractions, but I was too naïve to know not to get into the back of a van with those girls that were pretending to be my new friends. I knew the periodic table, but I didn't know which of the taxi drivers locked their car doors and forced you to give them a blowy instead of paying in cash.

It was like falling into an underworld you didn't even know existed. A world that everyone else walks or drives past every day, unaware of the darkness around them. Mummy and Daddy aren't around to save you. Well, they are, but they are often wrapped up in their own shit – just kids themselves, trying to figure life out whilst raising the next generation. Each of us, a new level of fucked-up.

To survive, you have to learn another form of intelligence. One that can't be taught at school or university. You have to learn about people, and you have to learn quickly. You have to learn new words, new codes, new body language. You have to learn about power, violence, and poverty. Most of the time, you learn by failing, and failing dangerously.

You're all doing it together. Hundreds of you navigating the concrete jungle, trying to dodge STIs, drug overdoses and car crashes. At least I had Kalen to give me the heads up when I needed it. It might sound like something Shane Meadows dreamed up for a Channel 4 Lottery Grant Funded film, but it was just our day-to-day life. If you haven't lived it, you'll never understand it.

'Morning, Mr Tompkins! How are you doing today?' Kalen sang at our elderly neighbour as we made our way out of the dead end.

'Morning, lad. Busy.'

'Why you busy?'

Kalen smirked at me and raised the eyebrow with the two slits in. His oversized diamante earring sparkled in the early morning sunlight.

'Lost me golf balls, ant I?'

'Not again, Mr Tompkins!'

I stifled a giggle. Mr Tompkins' purple hands shook as he pulled a handkerchief from his pocket, wiped his nose, put his handkerchief back in his pocket, and opened his little metal gate to join us on the path. Together, the three of us continued down the street and towards the junction.

'I bet I know what ya thinking, lad. I know I shouldn't. They just go too fast for me.'

He searched for his handkerchief again.

'I know. Not as young as you once was, were ya?' Kalen mimicked back.

'Eh? Speak up, lad.'

We both giggled.

'Anyway, not as young as I once was, lad. Can't catch up with em,' Mr Tompkins repeated, unaware Kalen was able to script this conversation.

We both laughed and Mr Tompkins smiled at us.

This conversation had been happening almost word for word every single morning, and it was only getting more amusing. Mr Tompkins was a tiny man in his late seventies, and ever since his beloved wife Valerie had died a few years ago, he had developed a peculiar and hilarious habit, to keep himself active, or perhaps, just temporarily distracted from his grief.

Every morning he would wake up early, make himself the same breakfast, and then go and stand at the junction that led onto the top of Church Road. One by one, he would simply roll his large collection of golf balls down the steep main road that sloped all the way down and through the council estate.

The balls would gain more and more momentum, speed, bounce and crash down the road until they finally got stuck in someone's privet hedge, flower bed, or maybe even on the big roundabout with the huge glowing blue lanterns the council installed with a fund they won to improve our estate. Needless to say, they didn't provide anything useful with the £200k they were given, but instead built four 50ft tall metal miners' lamps with mammoth light bulbs in them.

They said they would honour and pay homage to the miners who lived and worked in our little town. What they actually did was cause rampant insomnia and delirium in everyone who lived in the houses facing the roundabout, because they glowed bright blue all night, every night, for fifteen years. I still can't tell you why they glowed blue. Like giant bug zappers. In fact, I give you full permission to go and Google 'electric insect bug zapper lantern'. Go ahead, do it.

Okay, are you back? That's what we had on our roundabout. How that pays homage to mining communities, I will never know. Moths who lost their lives to grizzly electric zappers, maybe. Miners who lost their livelihoods and were plunged into poverty by Thatcher, no.

Many years later, in 2021, a huge town argument broke out over the lanterns being allowed to rust, rot, fall into disrepair and finally, stop glowing. For most, the final death of the glow was a huge relief after years of humming, glaring neon light. But the town council have reassured everyone that they will be repairing and reinstalling the lights so they can shine forever. Terrifying.

Mr Tompkins would spend all day, every day, hunched over in the street, searching for his golf balls and putting them back in his pocket so he could do it all over again the next day. The whole estate knew him, and would often collect his golf balls for him as they saw them roll by their feet on their way to work, or as they took their kids to school.

In fairness, golf balls had become quite the feature of this estate since I moved there. Just the weekend before, I had been down the road at the little park when a kid a couple of years younger than me had strolled confidently up to me and invited me to play golf with him. I had never played golf before, so it didn't occur to me that we would need a golf course. Come to think of it, I have no idea where Reece got that huge golf club from, or the plastic bag of golf balls slung over his shoulder.

I wondered for a moment if he had been swiping Mr Tompkins' balls.

I followed him to the highest hill on the playing fields of the park, overlooking hundreds of Schindler houses, the Barley Mow pub, and the main road through the estate. I didn't know what a Schindler house was until I had overheard my elderly next door neighbour explaining it to my mum. He was telling her that you can't get a mortgage on them because of the way they were built for the miners. They were not meant to last. They were built by the National Coal Board from prefabricated concrete or metal panels, and were built to last around ten to thirty years. They were filled with red ash, which had been causing the houses to crack and bulge for years. Thousands of people on the council estate still lived in them then, and indeed still live in them today, over eighty years later. Barely anyone even knew they were Schindler houses, as no one owned them. How would anyone have known they were uninsurable and un-mortgageable if they were all council owned?

There are all these problems before you even begin to consider that areas of Stoke are built on an endless rabbit warren of mine shafts that often collapse and cause mayhem. Only that month, Katie had woken up to a sinkhole instead of a garden. Her whole street had to be evacuated whilst the council figured out if her house was going to disappear down the canyon that had opened up overnight. I had spent many sleepless nights imagining the dark mineshafts below me, propped up by old wooden beams and metal rods, just waiting for a shift in the earth or for something to rot and crack, sending us all tumbling into oblivion.

It certainly didn't help my fear any when our old next door neighbour told us that he had swapped shifts with his brother one day when he couldn't be bothered to go in, and sent his brother to his death. The shaft had collapsed and killed several men instantly whilst he had gone back to sleep, something he still talked about after a few too many pints of Guinness.

Maybe one day, all the mine shafts will collapse underneath us, and Stoke will just become one deep hole in the ground where a forgotten town used to be. I guess it will save the government from having to explain why we are still suffering from the decimation of our communities in the eighties, if we simply disappeared one day.

It's already happening, bit by bit. When I was nine, panic ensued when a 40ft hole opened up in a field near my house, and in 2013, we all woke up to find that Tunstall lake had disappeared down a 13ft hole caused by a mine shaft collapsing. I spent weeks wondering where the water and fish had gone. Did it all just slosh down abandoned mines whilst the fish flip-flopped and suffocated to death underground? Did it create a new underground lake?

Did anyone ever plan for the future of a town built on holes? Not just holes, of course, but most people don't know that Stoke on Trent is build on top of a volcano, and for that reason, it is one of the only cities with a volcano strategy.

In a weird twist of optics, I remember reading a few years back that Stoke on Trent City Council had decided to try to bore down the two miles to the volcano, and use it to lift everyone out of fuel poverty by harnessing the power of this volcano to heat our water.

Ambitious for a council that have left potholes for so long that they can be used for public swimming, but I guess we have to let them dream. Maybe we could fill the potholes with water, let the volcano heat them up, and use them as hot tubs?

'What's ya name?' The kid asked.

'Jess.'

'Jess what?'

They always asked your surname on that estate. It was the quickest way to size you up, and figure out which family you were from. The wrong surname given, and you were instantly in trouble. The right surname given, and you were instantly untouchable.

'Taylor.'

He raised his eyebrows in disbelief.

'Related to the Taylors on Baker Street?'

The Taylors were as solid as they came, and several of them were running drugs in the area. He must have looked at me and quickly realised that I didn't belong to them.

'No. My family are from Stockport. But we moved from down near bottom shops up to the top of the estate a few weeks ago.'

He relaxed again. I wasn't a threat to him.

'Ooh, bottom shops! Posh girl.'

He mocked me whilst he pulled a pouch of baccy out of his boxers.

'Not posh,' I muttered back.

'Well you don't go Crawley School cos I would know ya, and I don't know ya. I know everyone round here. And. You talk funny.'

On account of my parents, grandparents and countless aunts and uncles being from Stockport, I had never picked up the full Potteries accent. I said 'book', 'cook' and 'look' like my family, with a deep 'uh' sound instead of the 'oo' sound that everyone else pronounced round here. I said 'bus' but the kids on the estate said 'buzz'. I said 'kid' but they said 'duck'. All this meant that local kids looked at me sideways on the regular.

'Me mum and dad are from Stockport.'

He frowned again.

'Near Manchester?' I offered.

He smirked.

'Posh, then. What school you go?'

'Redtree,' I mumbled, realising what was coming next.

He burst out laughing, 'See. Told ya you was posh! Only posh little twats go over there . . .'

He licked his Rizla and rolled his fag with disgustingly dirty fingers. I stared at him, concluding that the only way a boy could have such dirty hands and fingernails was if he had been digging in the mud like a dog for hours. His fingernails were bitten down to the skin.

He sparked up, and inhaled deeply. He relaxed, and blew the exhaled smoke slowly onto the end of the roll up until the embers glowed orange.

'How'd you get in there, then? You're on the wrong side of the brook for that school.'

'Dunno,' I lied. There was no way I was going to tell him that I was a straight A student who begged for a place at Redtree as a second best, because I couldn't accept a scholarship at a top private school. Better to keep that shit to yourself.

He sensed my worry.

'Don't worry posh girl, I'll keep ya secret safe for ya.'

He flashed a huge cheeky smile at me, and scratched at his bright ginger hair, whilst I wondered how a kid of that age could have lost so many teeth at once.

'Anyway, I'm Reece. I used go Crawley School. Got kicked out. Don't go nowhere now. Just hang around here all day. Wank. But better than fuckin school, innit.'

He dragged on his roll up and stood up next to me. He pulled a golf tee out of his pocket and stuck it in the grass. He carefully placed his first golf ball on the tee, roll up hanging out of his little mouth. You would be forgiven for thinking I was describing a forty-five-year-old golfer on his Saturday morning golf round, not an eleven-year-old boy on a council estate park.

'Want first shot?'

He thrust the golf club at me, but I shook my head. I had no idea how to use one of those.

'Fine. I'll show ya how it's done anyway.'

And with that, he smashed the golf ball as hard as he could. I was impressed. The ball whistled and sailed through the air, landing in the overgrown grass just near the bus stop.

'Fuck's sake!' Reece raged.

He slammed the golf club into the ground, and sent a chunk of grass and mud flying over my head. I froze, wondering why he was so angry, but mostly hoping I wasn't about to get clubbed to death by this little kid I just met.

Instead, he calmed down quickly, smiled back at me, and took another deep drag.

'Right. I missed that one. Let's call that me warm-up shot. Not gonna miss any more!'

I stared across the playing fields. What was he aiming at? The only thing in front of us was the houses, the road, the pub and the cars.

He flicked the rest of his fag on the floor, stamped it out with his foot. He focused intently, practised his swing, and then suddenly stopped. Stricken with epiphany, he tipped up his plastic bag of balls and lined them all up in the grass. He looked at me like he had just realised that he was a genius, and I smiled back, totally confused.

With that, he bounced back into position, and made light work of smacking each and every golf ball as hard as he could whilst the horror of what he was doing slowly dawned on me.

Windows shattered, car alarms screamed, cars braked in the road, people came out of their houses in terror as he licked off shot after shot. It was utter chaos. Senseless, ridiculous, shocking . . . and yet I couldn't look away. I couldn't stop watching the unravelling destruction whilst Reece jumped up and down in delight.

'Hundred points for that one!' he cried in glee.

My jaw fell open.

'Did you see that shot? Did you see it bounce off that car roof?' He whooped and yelled in sheer delight.

A man bravely came out of his driveway and started yelling about phoning the police.

'Oh, shut the fuck up, you daft old prick! Go back in ya house right now before ya get my balls in ya face!'

Reece thrust and gyrated at him, and the startled old man hurried back inside.

I lay flat on the grass, terrified that someone would recognise me with this crazed, ginger kid causing thousands of pounds of criminal damage.

One by one, confused residents and traumatised pensioners came out of their houses and cars, searching for the origins of the missiles that were destroying their streets. They looked up to the sky, scratched their heads, and watched as their neighbours picked up glass, metal, wing mirrors and smashed plant pots.

And all I could do was lie in the grass on the hill, and laugh at the absurdity and horror of it all.

I suppose I should have known better. Kalen had already warned me about Reece and his family. But in my defence, he had warned me about so many families I could barely keep up.

There was the Masseys, of which Reece was the youngest. Every single one of them had been excluded from school or sacked from jobs and they were totally feral. Kalen said they would rob you blind and not give it a second thought. He told me to be kind to the big brother Massey because his mum had told him he wasn't quite right in the head.

'He's obsessed with little girls though,' Kalen had hesitated one afternoon, 'so maybe not be so nice to him actually. In fact, probably best to avoid him, Jess.'

Then there was the Kirbys. An entire family of violent, ignorant and dangerously confrontational people who would start on you for looking at them as you passed them in the street. There was the Taylors, who everyone knew were controlling the drugs on the estate but no one ever said it out loud. The Rigbys, I think I already mentioned those to you. The Rigby mum chased Hannah up the street with a meat cleaver for knocking on for Chris when he was grounded. Not sure what else you need to know about them.

The Bradwells were something else. There was the mum who was housebound, and couldn't move out of the living room chair, so she screamed through the house if she needed anything – day or night. If she wanted a yoghurt, or couldn't find the TV remote, the whole street knew about it.

The husband reminded me of a portrait of a neanderthal. There was the son who talked with a lisp, and walked with a limp, but could knock out anyone who mocked him. Then there was the daughter who was nice enough, but she got in trouble for covering up some serious crimes for her boyfriend who later escaped from prison, and the police made us all stay in our houses for nearly two days whilst they called out helicopters and dog teams to comb our gardens and sheds looking for him.

There was only one family I had encountered that were more peculiar than the Bradwells, and that was The Wrong Turns. I didn't know their names, and neither did Kalen. He told me that their dad took them out into the back garden every Thursday night to hose them down because they had no bath in their house. I had doubled over laughing, assuming it was a joke. Still to this day, Kalen swears down that was true.

As we approached the gully, Kalen suddenly quietened and put his head down. Under his breath, he said to me, 'Whatever he says to you, you say fuck all.'

'What?' I panicked.

'I said,' he whispered, barely moving his lips, 'whatever he says to you, say fuck . . . all.'

I looked up and saw a tall, thin, strange, dark-haired man in trackies that were too short for him, and a faded Fred Perry jumper that had shrunk, and now showed the bottom of his pale, hairy belly. He walked towards us with his body at an angle. He was limping, causing one arm to swing.

A few years earlier, Kenny had been hit by the 6A bus whilst he was high. No one knew how he had survived. The bus driver had screeched to a halt whilst twenty-odd people had been thrown from their metal seats. People had come out of their houses at the deafening noise, and the thud of Kenny slamming into the flat front of the bus to Hanley.

Imagine the shock of the balding, tired, middle-aged bus driver as he nervously went to check if he had killed a crackhead, only to find him spring to his feet and call him a bald cunt.

Now he was stood in the entry to the gully, blocking our way to school.

'Say fuck all,' Kalen nudged me, urging me to follow his lead.

'Yalrite mate? Listen can either of you help me? Could ya borrow me 20p? I need 20p for the payphone, mateys.'

'No, Kenny. Sorry mate. Can't help ya today,' Kalen calmly and confidently disarmed the man who was either staring at me, or through me, or maybe behind me.

Kalen linked my arm and tried to get us around Kenny, but he blocked our way again.

'Have you got 20p, duck? Just 20p? Me sister had a baby and it died on the bus and I need to call her right now!'

I panicked. I stepped back, and he stepped closer to me. A baby? Died on a bus?

'Come on, duck. I'm tryin' be nice here. Me sister died! I just told ya. I need to ring me mum . . .'

I frowned at the inconsistencies in his story, and he became agitated with my hesitation.

'Come on. I need ring me sister. It's emergency. She's dying, matey . . . I just need 20p, mate . . .'

I panicked.

'Fuck all,' I remembered.

'What?' Kenny snapped.

'Fuck all!' I repeated, louder.

'What did you just say to me?'

'Fuck . . . all . . .'

Kalen stared at me.

'What the hell are you doing?' he whispered to me, eyes wide.

He didn't even give me time to answer before he took control of the conversation again.

'Look Kenny, she is sorry, didn't mean anything by it. Sorry, Kenny. We've gotta go school mate. We haven't got 20p to give ya. You know me dad, tight as fuck int he? And she's broke. Parents split up and all that . . .'

Kalen tried everything to keep him calm, whilst staring at me in disbelief.

Suddenly, Kenny calmed.

'Oh, yeah mate. I know ya dad. Good bloke he is. Top bloke . . .'

Kalen grabbed my arm and took the opportunity to slide right past Kenny and drag me with him.

'Okay then Kenny. Better go mate. See ya!'

Kalen hurried us both out of the gully, past the graffiti, past the leaves and the crisp packets, and past the three girls sat on the floor having a sneaky fag before school.

'What in the fuck were you thinking?'

'What?'

'Why did you keep saying that to him?'

'Saying what?'

'Fuck all!'

I was baffled.

'You said, no matter what he said to me, I had to say "fuck all" . . .'

Kalen stopped in his tracks. Turned to me. Jaw open.

'No.' A grin spread across his face.

'What?'

'You didn't actually . . . think . . . you fucking idiot!'

He burst into uncontrollable laughter, and hung on to me as he bent over giggling, tears filling up his eyes.

'I meant say fuck all, like nothing. Say nothing. Not literally say fuck all like a prick on repeat till Kenny batters us over 20p . . .'

I immediately realised, and felt thoroughly ridiculous.

'Ya gonna get us both killed you are, Jess.'

At the time, we continued the walk to the bus stop whilst Kalen tried to control fits of giggles, and then hiccups, whilst I shrank in utter embarrassment.

I had a lot to learn if I was going to survive on this part of the estate, and I already had enough going on at school.

It is safe to say that things had gotten a little rocky at school since Mum and Dad divorced and sold our house. Mum was pregnant with a new baby, Dad was off his face every day, and had sunk into a world of drinking, one-night stands and unemployment.

School had always been my safe place. I could do the tasks with ease. I understood what was expected of me, and I was frequently rewarded for excellence. It suited me just fine.

I was less skilled at the social stuff. Kids perplexed me. One minute they were best friends, and the next they hated each other. One minute they were asking for my help, the next, they were telling everyone I was a swot.

One minute the boys were scratching my name into tabletops, the next they were spreading rumours that I stuffed my bra with tissue. It was not cool to fancy me. I was pretty, but I was too much of a nerd. If you fancied me, you got bullied too. Nerd-fucker.

I never did understand the lack of consistency or loyalty. The years had taught me to never get in deep with a clique, or a friendship group. This led to years of playtimes and breaks reading books, writing, doing homework, or setting up projects for the school.

However, since Mum and Dad were both busy focusing on their respective crises and new lives, everything had become meaningless to me. I wasn't interested in positive praise. I wasn't interested in awards. Stickers. Class charts. House points. I already knew I could do the work. School had become a place I tolerated, until my toleration slipped into resentment.

I pretended to need the toilet and hid in the music store-room. Racks from floor to ceiling of beautiful violas, violins and cellos. My own violin among them. I took it out and played it sometimes. Only pizzicato, so I wouldn't be dis-covered. I lay on the cold hard floor with my bag as a pillow, plucked my violin like a tiny guitar, and contemplated life. The universe. The stars. The lunar cycles. The meaning of it all. The vastness of it all. The beginnings and ends of the universe. The place where it stopped, and what was on the other side of the stop. The purpose of life. The way we learned a different version of world history all over the world, depending on what the government wanted you to believe. The way the cartographers would draw Great Brit-ain bigger and Africa smaller. The arrogance and audacity of us calling ourselves 'Great'. Wondering why other coun-tries don't name themselves with an adjective. Fantastic Italy. Brilliant France. Powerful Russia. Beautiful Australia. I marvelled at how many things were things 'just because' – and how many things we didn't know. What happens when we die? Where was my dad? Was my mum going to have a boy or a girl? Why was my hair always greasy no matter how much I washed it?

When the endless, mind-bending introspection began to bore me (or more often, gave me existential dread that caused my heart to race), I had started to hide in the toilets, writing poetry on the walls.

They either never suspected me, or I was so unnoticeable that teachers took nearly two weeks to notice that I was missing.

They found me late one afternoon, huddled in the small gap between the old wall and the frosted glass, sitting on the floor, playing snake on my Nokia.

Mrs Hudson was horrified. Her thin hand clapped over her equally thin mouth.

'Oh my word, child! Is this where you have been hiding?'

I shrugged. 'Looks like it.'

'Excuse me!'

She was stunned. And truth be told, I was stunned at my own attitude.

'Get up off that filthy floor right now!'

I sighed, and stumbled to my feet, brushing myself off as I stood.

'What the hell has gotten into you, Jessica?'

I rolled my eyes. Oh, so now they notice me.

'Look at the state of your uniform! Tie too short. Shirt untucked. Skirt hitched up your behind . . .'

She trailed off as she began staring at the collection of marker pens in my shirt pocket, and then turned around to see the walls, covered in my poems and doodles. Some funny. Some smart. Some cute. Some disgusting.

Next to the mirror where the girls checked their hair, popped spots, and put on some more lip gloss, I had written the words:

Mirror, Mirror,
On the wall
Who's the fairest of them all?
The mirror sighed and then it cracked,
It sure ain't you, you ugly twat

Mrs Hudson lowered her glasses in utter disbelief.

'Get to the headteacher's office. Right. Now,' she shrieked.

I had never been in trouble before. I suppose that should have been the moment that I burst into tears and realised the error of my ways, but instead, I just laughed to myself. The novelty. The excitement. The adventure. The comedy. The absurdity of rules and social expectations.

Laughing in the face of just about everything had become my default response of late. Life felt like it was upside down. No one was who they said they were, and no one was looking after me. I had stopped caring, and I had stopped expecting others to care about me.

I detached. Everything had become entertainment, a way to pass the time until something else caught my attention, or until I died.

Outside the head's office, kids whispered that I was probably going to be made Head Girl. That I had been called there for the mythical mountain bike that it was rumoured they give the best child in the school. I thought about the mountain bike, just falling out of my reach forever. Then I cringed when I remembered the last time I used my own bike at home, and the swift, painful lesson I learned when I decided to go as fast as I could down the street and then practise going no-handed.

The perfect girl was sat outside Mr Cooper's office, daydreaming and smirking instead of shaking and crying. It caused much confusion to kids passing by.

Mrs Billings from the science department rushed past and frowned down at me before stopping, swinging back around, and doing a double take.

'Oh Jessica, what are you doing here? Has someone hurt you?'

I shook my head.

'Are you being bullied again?'

I shook my head, and she got down on one knee to convince me to tell her what was wrong, and what had happened to me. Mr Cooper's door swung open, and he stood in the frame. He was a small, thin man with grey hair, round glasses and a sharp navy suit.

'She's here, Mrs Billings, because she has been missing lessons to deface school property!'

She turned to look at me, baffled.

'Jessica, in my office, now please.'

I stood up, walked past Mrs Billings, and sat down on the chair opposite his shiny desk with the ornaments and pictures of his grandchildren.

'Just like Mrs Billings, I am shocked to have you sat here today, Jessica. In four years, you have never been in here, and now here we find ourselves, in your final weeks of Year 8, and you have caused us great concern.'

He was right. I was sitting in what should have been my worst nightmare, and yet I felt nothing. Well, I felt something. Something unusual. Unfamiliar. A sense of not caring, of mockery, or amusement. A feeling of having lost every shred of patience I had ever had, with anyone. With everything.

I tried not to smirk, but I have always been incapable of controlling my face. If my mouth won't tell you, my face will.

'Are you . . . laughing at me?'

Oh shit, I thought, don't ask me that, it will only make it worse.

'No,' I smiled, and my voice cracked into a laugh.

'How dare you!'

'I'm . . . I'm . . . sorry . . .' I stifled more laughter, trying to cover my face with my hair and then my hand. The more I told myself to stop, the more it came. No amount of panic could have contained my laughter at the meaninglessness of these rules within my upside-down life. Mum had moved in with a stranger and got pregnant. Dad was drinking himself to death. I had been offered drugs or asked for 20p so many times I had lost count. I was living on an estate filled with people who could punch me with no warning, and I had spent all week dealing with Fun Time Frankie, an old man on a mobility scooter who chased girls through the estate with his dick out. School just paled in comparison.

Nothing meant anything to me any more.

'I have no choice, I am afraid. With that behaviour and attitude towards me, and towards our school, our rules and our property, you will be banned from the end of year trip to American Adventure Theme Park.' Mr Cooper was a mixture of confused, annoyed, and hoping to get some sort of response from me.

A year earlier, I would have broken down. Cried. Pleaded. Apologised.

I shrugged.

His eyes widened at my indifference.

'What on earth is going on with you, Jessica? You have been a model pupil for all these years. Top of your classes. Perfect grades. Orchestra. Prefect. Pupil mentor. Reading tutor to the little ones. You sit in front of me today, a completely different girl!'

I stopped smirking.

A completely different girl.

I pondered on that. I looked out of his huge single-pane window with the metal frame. I watched the breeze play with the grass outside the music block. A child skipped to the art block, holding their wet painting to carefully place on the huge drying racks.

'Hmm. Maybe you're right.'

He tilted his head, his expression softening. He looked at me with confusion, and kindness.

I was a completely different girl.

I couldn't argue with what he said. I wasn't the same as before. All these people, all these harms, the lies, the betrayal, the uncertainty, the danger; it had written upon me a new person. Overwritten the old me like a file on a floppy disk. I was a new girl. I had a new way of seeing the world. A new disdain for everything.

Maybe that's why, the day before the trip, I went to the dodgy shop at the bottom flats and bought a small bottle of knock-off Russian vodka with the red and black label made to look like Smirnoff. Another two girls had been kicked off the end of year trip. Lexie had been banned for telling everyone that Mr Wheeler wore a toupee, and Rosie had been banned for saying her big brother had witnessed his toupee flapping off in a rage as he threw a science lab stool at a kid.

Everyone knew it was a toupee, but no one was allowed to talk about it. Telling really, that you got in more trouble for talking about the toupee than the metal stool being launched at a kid.

Like the time that Mr Bridges punched a boy so hard in the face that they had to call an ambulance, and we were all told that Mr Bridges was having some time off to go on a lovely holiday when he was most certainly suspended. We were never allowed to bring that incident back up, even when Mr Bridges turned back up at school like nothing happened six weeks later, and despite forty lads being in the sports hall when he did it.

It was me who had suggested that we spend our last day in Year 8 smashed. We had been forced to help take down all the displays in the science labs, which I had betted would be much more interesting if we shared a bottle of vodka. And I figured, they couldn't give us more detentions as it was our last ever day in the school.

We poured the vodka into our bottles of Fanta and Lilt, and drank them right in front of the teachers whilst we climbed up and down ladders to take the display about photosynthesis down. We were laughing, wobbling and stumbling more and more as the day wore on.

'You girls are very happy considering all your friends are out at the theme park on this lovely sunny day!'

'We just love taking displays down, miss,' Lexie had cracked.

We all exchanged looks and burst into echoey laughter in the empty science lab. I wobbled on my ladder as the teacher frowned at us all and walked away, shaking her head in disbelief that even kicking us off the school trip hadn't been enough to break our rebellious spirits. But I was relaxed, tipsy, and caring even less than before. If only I cared this little all the time, I thought, as I pulled a diagram of a Bunsen burner off the display.

The bus of rowdy, excited twelve- and thirteen-year-olds arrived back at school from the theme park, and they poured out of the bus, hugging each other, singing, and even crying at their last day of middle school. I watched some of them cry and hug their favourite teachers as I boarded the bus home.

Kalen swaggered on in his shorts and T-shirt, carrying his new American Theme Park spiral drinks bottle and sat down next to me. Suddenly, he stopped.

'Why do you smell like fuckin booze?'

'I don't!' I laughed.

'You fuckin do! Have you been . . . drinking . . . at school?'

I grinned at him, my eyelids heavy.

'You little fucking legend! Ha! You just keep surprising me!'

I leant against the window as the glass vibrated my forehead. I felt sick. I was just closing my eyes when my pocket vibrated twice.

A message from some lads from the estate.

'R u still comin the party 2moz?'

'Yh corse,' I stabbed back.

'7pm. Bring drink.'

'KK.' I smiled at my phone. At least it was going to be interesting.

Kalen nudged me at our stop, the last stop, and I stumbled home with him. As we meandered the estate and the gully, he pulled out a packet of Tic Tacs.

'Eat some of these. You fuckin stink of that vodka!'

I breathed into my hand and sniffed it.

'No, I don't. Drama queen.'

'You do, eat these.' He thrust a handful of white Tic Tacs at me.

'I don't like minty stuff . . .' I slurred.

'You don't have a choice!'

'If I wanted to eat toothpaste, I'd carry some Aquafresh around with me,' I laughed at him.

'Your life. Dickhead.'

We both sniggered, and Kalen linked my arm. He was a good dude. He was raised well. He understood the estate. He watched the people. He knew how to keep himself safe, and he tried to keep me safe. He just didn't always succeed.

4

It's only experimenting

Summer 2004

The sleepover was pretty dead until the booze came out and the parents fucked off. Kaz lived on the posh estate. Her parents spoke with an accent. I don't know which. They weren't Stokies, that was for sure. There were six of us in total. Her parents had done that thing where they had tried to be cool, and bought a worktop full of Lambrini.

It was the first time I had ever drunk Lambrini. I usually drank the knock-off shit. £2 for 3 litres. Lambrella, I think it was called. I had been drinking Orange Reef for a while, but when they pulled it off the shelves, I had to find something bigger and cheaper to fill the void. Lambrella was utterly grim in comparison to Reef, but it did the trick.

I wasn't close to the girls who had invited me. I only really went for something to do. It was Kaz's thirteenth birthday, and it was a hot summer evening in July. She was one of the youngest in our year, and most of us had been thirteen for months already.

The house was massive. Beautiful. At least three bedrooms, with a wooden handrail all the way up the curved stairs. The doors had chrome handles that matched the plug sockets and the light switches. The carpets were thick and felt fuzzy on my bare feet. Kaz's room looked like it was fresh out of a teen girl magazine. I marvelled at her double bed with the ornate white metal bed frame.

Since we moved to the new house, I shared a small room with Stacey and my new ten-year-old stepsister, Maddie. Three of us in one room meant having a bunk bed on one side, and my cabin bed on the other, with a walkway just wide enough for us girls to walk down and climb the ladder each night. Alfie had his own tiny box room. Mum and Mark were in the double room, and were planning on keeping the new baby in there in a Moses basket.

Mark had kept his promise though, and I had been frankly mesmerised by the paintjob he had achieved one day whilst I was at school. I didn't think it was possible to achieve a gradient of three different colours using paint, and had stood there scratching the walls, looking for evidence of a wallpaper join. He smiled proudly, as he explained that he had created the perfect gradient from blue to pink. I just wished we could see more of it, as every wall had been promptly covered by bunk beds, cabin beds and some old drawers. There was no question of his talent, though, and he had gone up in my estimations immediately.

Kaz had more room in her one bedroom than I had in my entire house. Her bedroom wall was plastered with posters of her favourite artists, and beautiful framed photos of herself from a makeover photoshoot her parents had bought her for Christmas.

I admired her room as we stayed up late, ate snacks, drank more of the fizzy piss, and talked. The Lambrini was disgusting, but I downed as much as I could, and at least I was getting that warm, comforting, don't-give-a-fuck-about-the-state-of-my-life feeling again. No wonder Dad spent years smashed. You can't say it isn't effective.

We sat around a bowl of snacks, and I realised that Kaz had invited all of the most popular – and sought after – girls in our year group. They were all dating the most popular boys, and they all lived on the posh estate.

I realised I was the odd one out whilst I pushed my finger into the carpet to see how deep it went. Way past my fingernail. Past the first joint in my finger, too. Must have cost a fortune.

I wondered why I was invited to the sleepover.

I prayed it wasn't going to end the way the last one did. I hadn't really been a fan of sleepovers since I was invited to one when I was ten years old and I nearly died. Three of the popular girls had invited me, waited until I was drifting off, shoved me deep into my sleeping bag, closed the end and then sprayed an entire can of Impulse spray through a tiny gap. I choked, struggled to breathe, and became more and more disoriented. One girl held the end of the sleeping bag as tightly as she could whilst I suffocated and struggled for air. But eventually, I did what I found I always do in trauma. I begged for them to stop, and then accepted I was not in control of the situation, and awaited my fate. Either they would continue until I died, or they would stop. I had no power over three people holding me down. I was like the cat in the bag, being thrown into the canal to die.

As I lay in there, gasping for air, listening to them shriek with laughter, I simply gave up. I wanted to suffocate. My stillness must have surprised them, as they let go of me.

'You all right in there!?' They laughed even harder as they saw my tears roll down my face.

I shuddered as I remembered the way they smiled sweetly at breakfast when Rosie's mum asked if we had all had a lovely time together. I watched them lie when she asked them what all the laughing and shrieking was about, and Rosie told her they were doing impressions of *Trigger Happy TV*.

It taught me to never underestimate the posh kids, and it taught me that rich doesn't equal good, as I had always been led to believe. Maybe that meant that poor doesn't equal bad?

The conversation took an interesting turn, and my attention was back in the room.

Emmy had started talking about sex, and I watched the faces of the popular girls light up at the prospect of some dirty, graphic gossip, and endless conversations about sex and boys.

I was sat opposite Natalie, the best artist in our year. Her mum was on the PTA. Next to her was Sasha, the student head of the library. Her mum was a pharmacist. Next to Kaz was Emmy, who was from the posh estate and owned not one, but two horses – but had somehow found herself neck deep in sex, drugs and alcohol at the same time as me.

We had chatted a few times, and I could tell she wasn't bluffing. You could always tell the kids that were exaggerating, like that time Matty told everyone he had an eighteen-year-old girlfriend who wore a waterbra.

I don't know. You'd have to ask him. I think he had tragically misheard 'Wonderbra' from somewhere, and then made himself look a total bellend whilst kids tried to interrogate him about what a waterbra was, and why an eighteen-year-old would be fucking a twelve-year-old boy. He said he met her at a club. And that a waterbra was like a waterbed that she wore to make her tits look bigger. He was full of shit, but it was entertainment nonetheless.

Sat next to me was the most popular girl in our year. Top of everything. Captain of the girls' sports teams. The girl every boy fancied. The girl everyone wanted to be best friends with.

Despite being rich, pretty, clever and having everyone fall at her feet, Vanessa was actually a really well-raised kid. She was probably only at that sleepover to be polite and kind to Kaz, who was a bit weird at times. As far as I could tell, Kaz had never even spoken to Vanessa. Nor had I, really. We were in the same netball team for years, but I tended to keep myself to myself, play as well as I could, and get on with it. I wasn't in the 'netball crowd', despite being their best Goal Shooter for three seasons, but then again, I had never been the type to chase friendship or belonging.

'Have you lot ever had sex then? Any of you lost ya V-Card yet?' Emmy pushed everyone.

Natalie, Vanessa, Sasha and Kaz all shook their heads. They all turned to me.

'Yeah . . . Yeah, I have,' I mumbled into my cup.

They didn't need to know that Lewis and Jay had got me stoned and forced me to have sex with them on the mattress on the floor. They didn't need to know that I had lost my virginity at twelve years old, crying in pain, asking them if it was supposed to hurt, whilst they complained that I was being frigid. They told me that they would tell everyone what a fridge I was if I didn't shut up.

I felt my thighs tense with the memory of the pain. I pushed that out of my head and took a drink.

'Ooh you dark horse, Taylor! It's always the quiet ones innit!' Emmy laughed, her drink sloshing up the side of the glass and on to the beautiful carpet. I winced as it soaked in.

'What positions have you done?' she prodded, eager for a graphic reply. I felt myself blushing, but the way Vanessa looked at me in awe made me shake it off.

'Ah, only a few to be honest,' I lied, trying not to think of lying on my back with Jay above me, kneeling on that disgusting mattress.

Emmy hadn't noticed my lie.

'So, Ash fucked me on his dining table right? He was like standing up, and I was sitting on the edge of the table . . .'

The room gasped and giggled in excitement and horror at her confession.

'Fucking hell. I hope you wiped it afterwards. Fuckin grim that is!' Kaz mocked before falling about laughing.

I sniggered, sipping at my glass of now-flat fizzy piss, which tasted even worse than before. I imagined Ash's mum serving them all a midweek roast on the table just hours after he had fucked his teenage girlfriend on it. Vile.

'He wanted to do anal but I told him to fuck right off. That is an exit not a fucking entry, you know what I mean?' Emmy laughed as the posh girls turned crimson.

I watched the embarrassment and laughter spread around the room as Emmy recounted more and more graphic details of what her fifteen-year-old boyfriend had been doing with her over the last few weeks.

'You lot know what monkey is?'

'No!' I giggled at her, the drink hitting me in waves. My lips and nose had started to tingle, and my eyes had relaxed. She was thoroughly entertaining me. It was positively disgusting to listen to. It had been a while since I wasn't the roughest kid in a room, and she was flooring me with her unashamed honesty and humour.

'It's like when a guy is fucking you and he's like stood up, and he holds you up, and you wrap your legs around his waist, and put your arms around his shoulders or neck. He puts his hands under your arse and you ride him . . .'

This caused uproar.

'Wouldn't you just fall over?' Natalie questioned.

'Don't his legs get tired?' Kaz threw her enquiry in, too.

'What . . . what if his dick isn't long enough to like . . . go in?' Vanessa cried out, laughing so hard she could barely get her words out.

That was what broke the room, and all six of us crumpled into the most painful fits of laughter I had felt in a long time. My stomach hurt, my chest hurt. I couldn't control it. It just kept coming. Every time I thought I had calmed down, I caught the eye of another girl and it started all over again.

Just when I thought we were all getting it under control, Kaz piped back up, pointing out that Emmy was the tallest girl in our year, and Ash was around 6 inches shorter than her. The image of Ash trying to hold Emmy up whilst they had clumsy, terrible, adolescent sex was utterly hilarious.

I begged for the giggles to end, and as my stomach and my breathing finally returned to normal, Kaz gestured to us all to come in closer to her.

'But have any of you . . . ever . . . ever wanted . . . to . . . you know . . . experiment . . . with . . . a girl?'

I felt my temperature rise. My heart pounded in my throat. My hands clammed up. It felt like she could see right through me. I put my head down and avoided any eye contact.

'Ugh! No! That's fucking gross!' Natalie snapped back.

'Same!' Sasha laughed, as if the question was preposterous.

Emmy, taking on some weird new role as Sex Guru, kicked back in.

'Uhhh, hang on you two! Loads of girls experiment, and it doesn't mean a thing! It doesn't mean they are . . . well you know . . . a lemon! Trust me. I know I'm right. I read it in *Mizz*.'

My mind raced. Please do not ask me. Please do not ask me. I can't lie. Please. Please.

'Taylor, have you?'

Emmy gestured to me, as the only other girl in the room she considered to have any sexual knowledge.

Lie, Jess. Lie. Do it. Just lie. Say no. Say ewww! Copy Natalie and Sasha. Make a joke. Laugh. Change the subject. Anything.

'Well . . . uhhh . . . yeah . . .'

Oh. My. Fucking. God. Why did I do that? My heart raced. I felt sick.

But Emmy just nodded in agreement.

'So have I,' she shrugged.

'Me too,' Kaz added.

'And me . . .' Vanessa smiled, looking up through her eyelashes at me. My pulse skipped.

'Would you snog a girl then? Like proper get off with her?'

'Yeah, why not?' Emmy chuckled, taking a swig.

'Taylor? Would you?'

'Uh . . . yeah . . .'

'Vanessa?'

'I guess!' She giggled into her glass.

That was when Kaz, bold as brass, turned to Emmy on her left and said the wildest shit.

'Would you let me kiss you? Just so I know if I'm bi, or whatever?'

I gasped. Surely not.

'Sure!' Emmy said, unfazed.

Natalie and Sasha recoiled in horror, sat there in stunned silence, grimacing as Kaz excitedly leant into Emmy and kissed her. And then kissed her again. And then touched her hair and her face while they fell into a snog like they had done it a hundred times before. I watched them in shock and wonder.

'Wow!' They both exclaimed, looking at each other in surprise.

'That was a lot better than kissing Ash!' Emmy laughed.

Kaz tucked her long blonde hair behind her ear. 'It was so soft. Your lips are so soft. And gentler than boys. Boys never kiss like that . . .'

I downed what was left of my warm drink and poured another from the bottle we were told to leave downstairs because we had all had enough. Just keep drinking, I thought. Whilst the rest of the girls were tipsy off a couple of small glasses, I was on my second bottle already.

'You two should deffo try it!' Kaz pointed directly at us.

I turned to look at Vanessa, expecting her to be revolted, but instead, she was grinning and looking at me expectantly.

'Do . . . do . . . you . . . wanna?'

Inside, I was gobsmacked. On the outside, I was desperate to stay cool.

'Yeah . . . do you?'

We both looked at each other in silence, blushing and laughing.

'Oh, shut up and just try it. God it's not a big deal. Fucking Christ!' Kaz interrupted.

I looked at Vanessa. The prettiest girl in our year. In our school. She was just there. Looking into my eyes, waiting for me to kiss her. I felt dizzy.

Was it the Lambrini, or the adrenaline coursing through me?

She touched my knee and leant in to kiss me, taking the decision into her own hands. She closed her eyes. I closed my eyes.

As our lips touched and moved together, a small kiss turned into a snog, turned into her hands in my hair, and my hands on her waist. My body and mind exploded. I floated.

I died. I lost track of everything. Time was meaningless. I was no longer in a room of tipsy, confused teenage girls. It was just me and her.

Emmy's voice cut through the bliss.

'Fuuuuuuuuuuuuckin hell! You two! What is this? A fucking love story? Jesus, why don't you just scissor each other, and get it over with?'

I had absolutely no idea what that meant, and we pulled away from the kiss, dazed, embarrassed, shocked.

She smiled at me.

I had to say something. Something. Anything. Break the tension in the room.

'Well, it's definitely better than kissing lads!' I managed.

Vanessa chuckled in agreement.

'Well, you lot can just do lezzer shit all night, but me and Sasha have got boyfriends and ain't gonna be doing that! We are just gonna go sleep. Weirdos!'

I shot a look at Emmy, and she frowned back at me. Kaz visibly panicked. I didn't even dare look at Vanessa.

I was not a lezzer.

'Well, we need to just all agree right now that we never tell a soul about this . . . um . . . well . . . what we just did. And it deffo doesn't mean we are . . . we are . . . lezzers. Okay?'

We all nodded. Pinky promised. Hell, I would have cut my finger and sworn in blood if it helped.

I didn't know any real-life lesbians. Lesbian was just a word that got yelled at you if the boys thought you were frigid. Or if the hairdresser had cut too much off. Or if you wore dungarees. There were no lesbians on TV, and there were certainly no lesbians on the estate.

What is it they say? 'You can't be it, if you can't see it'?

The only place I had ever seen two women kissing was in some porn Ben Baker showed me on the school computers at morning break right before we both got given a week of detention.

Lesbians didn't really exist at all. 'Gay' was a much more common insult than 'lesbian'. Everything was gay. If the lesson was boring, it was gay. If the weather was bad, it was gay. If you didn't like the teacher, he was gay. If the rules were unfair, they were gay. Boys were gay if they weren't dating or shagging yet. They were gay if they weren't raging misogynists. They were gay if they were nice. They were gay if they smelled clean and combed their hair. They were gay if they were polite or kind, for god's sake.

Natalie and Sasha fell asleep, and the rest of us laughed the whole thing off. We shuffled up next to each other and flicked through all the new albums Kaz had been bought for her birthday. We decided to put Usher's *Confessions* album on, which on reflection, is an album about shagging, and then confessing to shagging a woman. Never mind.

The four of us chatted about everything from who the woman was that Usher was clearly leaving his wife for, to what the new high school was going to be like, and whether aliens existed. Vanessa cuddled up to me as the night turned into the small hours of the morning. Emmy fell asleep across Kaz, who fell asleep a few minutes later.

'Maybe we should get some sleep?' I whispered to Vanessa.

'Yeah. Maybe we could . . . share my sleeping bag?'

My heart pounded.

'Yeah, okay.' I tried to stay calm. Cool. Collected. In control. But my mind was doing backflips.

As the skies got light again, we slipped into her sleeping bag together and continued where we had left off earlier, while the others slept and snored.

The next morning, in the cold light of day, Kaz's mum and dad made us all a bacon butty and joked about where the Lambrini went from the kitchen. We all laughed nervously, played with our hair, looked at our mobile phones, and pretended we were all shattered.

Shattered from talking about girly stuff and making prank calls, they assumed. Certainly not shattered from hours of making out with the most popular girl at school. Who had a boyfriend.

I smiled reassuringly at Vanessa, who smiled, blushed, and looked down at her lap. I had gently lifted her head off my chest, sneaked out of her sleeping bag and stumbled to the bathroom just before anyone else woke up. No one knew that we had been awake all night together.

What did any of this even mean?

Emmy said the magazines did loads of articles about it being completely normal. Common, in fact. It doesn't mean you're gay.

Nothing but some teens experimenting, I guess.

None of us would have survived the humiliation of our friends and families if we admitted what we had done. Better kept a secret. Better just forgotten about. And anyway, Vanessa had a boyfriend. Emmy had a boyfriend. Maybe I should get a boyfriend?

I walked home, all the way back to the council estate – and thought about the fact that my face never lies. I practised keeping a neutral expression so I could survive my mum's questions when I got home.

As I walked back up the steep side of the valley to the council estate, the houses changed shape and colour. Gone were the detached houses with the driveways and the beautiful double-glazed windows. Gone were the new cars, the pristine gardens, the UPVC doors, and the block paving. Across the valley, those houses were acutely, quickly, harshly replaced by huge rows of terraced and semi-detached Schindler houses, built for the miners and their families when the local pits were still open. It was like walking back in time. The cars were old. The paint was peeling. The gardens were overgrown. The atmosphere was different. The people were different. The smells of everyone's cooking merging into one smell.

A little boy no older than five marched past me, covered in transfer tattoos. He had stuck black tribals all over his face, neck and arms. He had a white candy stick hanging out of his mouth like a cigarette, and he looked like he meant business.

Where does a five-year-old even go, with such conviction? He looked like he was going to collect debt from some dude who hadn't paid him back on time.

As I walked back past the bottom flats, a group of young girls I vaguely knew from school stood around with their prams, discussing which of their babies would grow up to marry each other.

Nicky's dad drove past me at double the speed limit, almost lost control at the roundabout and then disappeared in a plume of blue-black smoke. The backfire echoed around the flats like gunshots, but no one even flinched. The babies in the prams didn't even cry.

We lived two different lives, in two different worlds, and all that separated us was a tiny trickle of a brook.

The road home from the posh estate was a steep downward climb to the brook, over a little bridge, followed by a steep upward climb to our new house which was right at the top of the estate. One long hilly road ran through the centre of thousands of families.

As I passed the Jehovah's Witness Hall on the right next to the playing fields, I questioned for the millionth time why they built that thing in the centre of one of the most intolerant and atheist areas I had ever known.

Religion barely played a role on our estate. The churches were used for mums and toddlers groups, weight watchers and children's clubs. If you were god-fearing like the Rodgers at the top of my old street, you'd be branded a Bible-Basher and chased home by kids yelling, 'God isn't real!' and 'There is no heaven!'

One kid threw a Bible at Ethan on his way home once, and screeched, 'The Bible-Basher just got Bible Bashed!'

I do wonder why God didn't feature in our lives on the estate. If anything, people were deeply cynical of anything and everything. Where was God whilst we struggled to make ends meet? God wasn't going to answer your prayers by paying the gas bill, but my Uncle Jax could bypass your gas meter for you for thirty quid and a four pack of Stella Artois.

God wasn't there when my brother died, and Mum cried into the bathroom mirror every morning, searching for a reason as to why God would kill her baby son. God wasn't there when Ben drove his car off a cliff edge and his body didn't wash up for months. Or when Helena's mum drank petrol in the living room and then set herself on fire when we were ten years old. Or when Sara gave birth to a tiny underweight baby after telling the school nurse she had stomach ache.

Where was God when Thatcher shut the mines and plunged Stoke into a depth of poverty it has never recovered from?

People believe that the most oppressed, disadvantaged and traumatised communities turn to God and faith for meaning and purpose – but what happens when you've already realised that there is no meaning, there is no purpose and there is no greater good?

What happens when those people realise that there is no cosmic justice balancing out the world? Good things don't happen to good people. Bad things don't happen to bad people. There is no good. There is no bad. There's just this shit. Day in. Day out.

No one cares if you live or die. No one is coming to rescue you. No Disney Fairy Godmother is coming to give you three wishes. No TV competition is going to make you a millionaire. No Christmas miracle is going to put the latest toys under the tree for your kids at the eleventh hour.

Having said all this, the older generations on the estate were certainly more likely to be what I call 'casually religious'. What I mean is that they would always pick a fry up over Sunday service, but they would backhand you for 'taking the Lord's name in vain'.

My nana was one of those. She is one of the least Christian Christians I have ever known. She spoke of God like she knew him personally, but only to punish and judge us.

For her birthday, I always wrote her a poem in her card. One year, I wrote her a lovely little poem in my very best cherry smelly gel pen. My handwriting was perfect, I had double checked my spelling, grammar, rhymes and punctuation, but when she opened the card, she glared over her glasses at me.

'How dare you?' she asked me.

I froze, frantically thinking of all the possibilities of bad behaviour I could have committed in the poem.

'I cannot believe you would do this. To your own nana. On her birthday!'

I had glanced at Mum, who looked just as frightened as me. For a moment, I thought Nana was going to explode, but instead, she took a deep breath in, then out.

'You should never write in red ink, Jessica,' she started calmly, 'and you never write a person's name in red ink, either!'

'Why?'

'Don't question me, child. Just never do it.'

I hesitated. The question burned on my tongue. Mum looked at me as if she was telepathically pleading with me to stop.

I wanted to stop, I really did.

'But . . . why?' I couldn't resist.

Nana turned back to look at me from the kitchen and stormed towards me, disgusted that I had continued to quiz her.

'Because it wishes death on the person. Red is the blood of Christ. Do your schools teach you nothing?'

I frowned at her.

'But, it's just my new smelly cherry . . .'

'I don't care one iota what it bloody smells of! Never write in red ink to me again!'

She glared at me over her gold-framed glasses. She thought she was going to have the last word. That I would back down like her own daughter does.

'It was a poem for your . . .' I started again.

'Kimberley! Get control of your child, right now!'

Mum shuffled, visibly uncomfortable. She regressed to somewhere in her childhood around her own mum, so I knew she wasn't going to jump to my aid. However, this also meant that she didn't get control of me at all. She was frozen to the spot.

'For god's sake!' I muttered, turning to walk back into the living room where Stacey and Alfie were sat quietly watching *Fireman Sam*.

Nana bellowed at me down the hall, 'How DARE you! You do not utter God's name in my house, under my roof!'

I rolled my eyes at her as my siblings jumped.

Mum stared at me.

I'd come too far to stop.

'I don't believe in God. So. There.'

'Well!' Nana laughed, outraged. 'You'll believe in hell when you get there!'

I smirked.

'I don't believe in that, either!'

Nana raged on, but I switched off.

She could threaten me with hell, the devil, the demons, God, Jesus, Mary, Joseph, the three wise men, and the little donkey, I couldn't give a shit.

What is God to an atheist? What is the threat of hell to a little girl already living in it? Those abstract concepts meant nothing to me, and nothing to the thousands of us on that estate.

Justice and consequence were much swifter and harsher here than in heaven and hell. The phrase 'fuck around and find out' pretty much summed up living here. You didn't have to wait until your judgement day to be judged, that was for sure.

Since I had moved to the rough end, I had learned quickly that you either learn to hold your own, or learn to hold your tongue. And I was never any good at the latter.

I finally got to our little gravel entrance, where the old front garden had been converted into a space for two small cars. The cars came right up under the front window and within a couple of feet of the front door. But it was better than parking them on the street for Chris to carve BICTH and FOGGAT into the side of them with a rock.

When he had done just that to one of the neighbours' cars the month we moved to the street, I hadn't known whether to laugh or cry. How do you tell the hardest kid on the street that he's illiterate?

Answer: you don't. You stand there and feign interest, and pretend to look impressed whilst he explains that he only did it cos she has the same car as his social worker. He was lucky FCUK never sued him for using their brand everywhere, put it that way.

'I'm back!' I shouted through the door.

I heard Mum stop what she was doing and come through to me, but I suddenly flushed red with the memories of last night. I shrugged my jacket off and tried to escape up the stairs, opposite the front door.

'Uh. Where do you think you're going?'

'Toilet!' I lied.

'Uh, I don't bloody think so!' She sensed I was trying to escape.

'I'm bursting though . . .'

She raised one eyebrow and tucked her bleach blonde hair behind her ear. She put one hand on her hip, and gritted her teeth.

I took my chances, and ran for the bathroom door, slammed it and locked it shut behind me. I sat on the toilet, desperately willing my bladder to push a wee out so I could somehow back up my lie.

She stormed up the stairs after me.

'Get out of there now. You'd better not be stoned again, I swear to God, Jessica!'

I sighed with relief. She thinks I'm high. Not a lezzer who just got off with the popular girl all night.

High was definitely the lesser of two evils. The lezzer of two evils. Ha.

'Jess! Answer me now! Are you high again?'

'Uhhh . . . no . . .' I deliberately hesitated.

'You little shit. Where have you had weed from? You're not telling me those posh girls had weed, so who gave it to you?'

'No one.'

It was weird being told off for something I knew I hadn't done. I wasn't even arguing back. I was just letting her believe I was high. Much easier than the reality of trying to figure out what I was. Just experimenting. Probably. Everyone does it. Emmy said.

'If I find out Lewis and Jay have given you weed again, I'll be at their door. I know his dad you know, and he's not gonna want me kicking off and making a scene. Don't think I won't do it, cos I fucking will!'

I wasn't even listening to her empty threats. She wouldn't do it. She would probably just give me the silent treatment for a week. I didn't care. I was wondering how Vanessa would look at me on the first day at high school. We had gone to school together for years, but we were all moving up to the high school in a few weeks' time. Ironically, no matter which estate or school you were from, there was only one high school that served our entire area, and it was just outside the council estate, through a gulley from my house. Rich or poor. Crawley or Redtree. Posh estate or council estate. You all ended up at the high school that had been labelled 'inadequate' for so long, I think OFSTED had given up.

I wondered whether I should text her. I was imagining the whole canteen rippling with controversy and rumours whilst everyone called me a lezzer. A queer. A lemon. A dyke. A rug muncher. A freak.

Oh god. What had I done?

'Are you even listening to me in there? I'm starting to wonder if you even went to that fucking sleepover!'

That got my attention. Mum carried on shouting through

the thin bathroom door, accusing me of smoking weed with Lewis and Jay all night.

'I wasn't, Mum!'

I sat with my head in my hands. This was a nightmare.

'Well, a word of warning. You get yourself a name for being easy, and you'll never get rid of it. Don't end up Biddulph bike!'

I sat on the toilet seat, nothing coming out, listening to her scathing advice. I had nothing to say. I wasn't Biddulph bike. Far from it.

Jay had already told everyone I was frigid cos I cried when he forced it in. Only minutes earlier, I had been high as fuck, laughing and feeling all grown up whilst playing strip poker and passing around the resin. The world had gone wavy and funny. Strip poker was just a laugh, but somehow, I kept losing. I was down to just a pair of knickers, and one of the lads had given me his old Man Utd shirt to cover up a bit.

I'd met Jay and Lewis on the street. They were best mates. Lewis lived with his dad and Jay lived on the next street, but mainly got high and crashed at Lewis's every day. Jay looked like a Nice 'n' Spicy ginger NikNak in comparison to Lewis, who personified the phrase 'built like a brick shithouse'. At 6ft 5in, 18 stone and nineteen years old, he towered over both of us. Jay was sixteen years old, and had been smoking draw for so long that his teeth had turned dark brown and his finger-nails were stained yellow. He was kicked out of school when he was eleven, and they just never came looking for him.

I had been wandering around the street, looking for something to do.

'New are ya?' Jay had asked as I passed him.

'A bit.'

'You been up the garages yet?'

'What? Them old ones down there?'

'Yeah.'

'They're just a bunch of old garages aren't they?'

He shook his head.

'Come with me, I'll show you how to get up on the roof. We always chill up there.'

I looked around for the 'we' he referred to, but saw he was alone. He showed me around to the edge of the garages, to a small gap between the garage exterior wall, and the concrete barrier to the side of the next set of council houses. I watched as he pushed through the overgrown privet hedge, and showed me where to put my feet to propel myself up without getting caught on the old rusty nails.

Within a couple of minutes, we were both sat on the roof of the block of eight garages, overlooking the street. I loved it. It was instantly my new favourite place.

'See, told ya,' he smiled at me, rolling a spliff.

I asked him his name and when he told me it was Sally, I said that was a girl's name and asked for his real one.

'Fuck off, bitch!' He laughed, holding his roach between his thin lips, trying not to spit it out 15 feet to the ground.

'Are you gonna tell me or not?' I prodded.

'Everyone calls me Sally, so you can call me Sally.'

'Well then, I won't tell you my name.'

'I already know your name, Jess,' he smirked.

'How?'

'People talk. Anyway, I like you. So I will tell you my name. It's Jay.'

'Why does everyone call you Sally, then?'

'You ask a lot of questions. That'll get you banged out around here, posh girl!'

'Why does everyone call me that?' I frowned.

'Cos you are.'

'I won't stop until you tell me why people call you Sally . . .'

'I can't tell you.'

'Why?'

'More questions . . .' He sparked up his spliff. 'Maybe have some on this, and chill ya beans!'

He took a huge drag and coughed, before exhaling through his mouth, then nose, then mouth, then nose. I laughed at him.

'Want twos?'

I didn't know what that meant, but I knew better than to let on that I didn't understand something. If people figured out that you didn't understand something, they smelled blood.

I nodded, and he passed it to me, watching me carefully. Too carefully. I was being tested.

I took a small drag, inhaled, held it for a couple of seconds, and then exhaled as smoothly as I could without coughing. I passed it back like it was nothing, but my head spun out. Jay didn't seem to notice, or maybe I was convincing enough, but he took the joint back and carried on talking.

As he launched into conversation about his big brother being an annoying prick, we were interrupted by one of the biggest men I had ever seen. We were sat up on the garage roof, and yet he seemed tall enough to just hop right up to us.

'Thought I heard your voice, Sally,' he growled, and flicked his roll up on the floor, not even looking at it.

'Alrate marra.'

'Alrate, shag. Who's this? New girlfriend?' He gestured towards me, but didn't look at me.

I shook my head anyway.

Jay laughed and blew out more smoke. 'Maybe.'

I stared at him. I looked back at the big guy. He looked scary. Dark short hair, dark piercing small eyes, three hoop earrings in one ear, huge black combat boots. Bruised knuckles. Slit in one eyebrow. Black jumper. Black trousers. He was 15 feet below me and yet he still felt like he was towering over me.

I took another drag of the spliff and my whole body felt like it was melting. I laughed at the sensation.

'What are you laughing at?' He looked up at me for the first time.

The answer was the weed. It had hit me like a train. But for some reason I said something very different.

'Your outfit.'

'You what?'

'What are you wearing? You look like you just came from a funeral!' I giggled. Jay choked as he inhaled and laughed.

It went silent, and I laughed into it.

'I did, actually.'

'No, you did not!' I burst out.

'Yeah I did.'

'Get off!'

'Is this some sort of joke?' He scowled at Jay, as if he was making me mock him. Pulling my strings. Winding him up.

Jay looked at me like I was tying my own noose.

I gulped, 'Are you being serious?'

'Yeah. My Uncle Pete died in a bike accident a few weeks ago. Horrible crash. He was only forty-one. We were dead close like. Cruel bitch, you are.'

I searched their faces. Were they winding me up? Was it the weed? How did I find myself in this situation, stoned on a garage roof with two guys I didn't know, trying to figure out if a dead Uncle Pete was real or not?

I could have sworn I saw Jay smirk. A tiny bit of the corner of his mouth turned up.

'Nah. You're lying! Why you really dressed like that?' I laughed. Idiots. Thought they could fool me.

The guy gritted his teeth. 'Is she being fucking serious?'

Jay nodded, shrugged, and took another drag of the spliff. The more awkward and uncertain it became, the more I laughed. Small laughs at first, chuckles almost. But it got weirder. And more silent. And I just laughed and laughed at the uncertainty.

Suddenly, a deafening crash filled the garages as the big guy punched the garage door next to our dangling feet and stormed off. The bang seemed to hang in the air, the echo bouncing around the other garage doors. I jumped out of my skin.

'Fuckin hell posh girl, you know how to make a first impression don't ya?'

I shook. My heart pounded. The high disappeared, replaced with a feeling of dread. Jay shook his head and rubbed his forehead.

'His uncle just died, you dickhead. He just got back. And you have just pissed yourself at him!'

'I . . . I thought he was having me on though.'

'What? Why in the fuck would he lie about that?'

I was stunned into silence. I panicked. I didn't know.

'He's either gone to roll himself a joint, or gone to get a baseball bat . . . so, we will see how much you laugh when he comes back!' Jay chuckled to himself as he pulled his phone out of his jeans pocket.

'What?!' Suddenly, I felt very twelve. I took a smoke from a stranger, mocked a grieving giant, and now I was going to get battered on a garage roof. I was losing control of the situation I was in, and there was nothing I could do about it. No one knew I was there. My heart was in my throat.

'I . . . it . . . was . . . just a mistake. I . . . got . . . confused . . . He's not gonna come back here with a baseball bat, is he?'

'Dunno.'

'An actual baseball bat?'

'Dunno.' Jay seemed unfazed. Maybe even . . . enjoying it.

'You'd tell him though. Wouldn't you? That it was just a joke. A mistake?'

'I've only just met you!' he snapped.

'Please. Please. I didn't mean anything by it. It was the weed or something. I don't know . . .' My eyes filled up, but I was desperate for him not to see me cry. My breathing changed.

'I can't keep this up, she's having a fucking breakdown here!' Jay shouted and then burst into laughter and put his arm around me, rubbing my back and grinning. Lewis peeked back around the garage wall, red in the face from holding in his own laughter.

I guess with a first experience like that, I shouldn't have expected anything better to happen when they rolled another joint, passed it to me, and asked me if I wanted to go back their place to chill out, but I was determined to act like it hadn't bothered me, and that I wasn't too scared to go to their place.

Ironically perhaps, I was way too scared to say no anyway. And no good time for a twelve-year-old girl starts off like that. Does it?

5

Don't you want people to like you?

Spring 2017

'Miss. Miss. Scuse me. Miss.'
    I turned around to see a short young white guy with his tattooed hands in his boxers stood behind me. I grimaced. Why do men do that? I always wondered if it would ever become socially acceptable for women and girls to just walk around with their hands in their knickers, playing with their pubes or their vulva whilst talking to their friends or walking around the supermarket. Clearly, playing with their genitals was a privilege reserved for the male of the species.

'You okay? Can I help you?'

'I've got a medical. I just need get through this door, miss.'

I smiled at him, but I gripped my prison keys tighter. They were chained to my waist, but a fat lot of good that would do if he decided he was going to drag me to the nearest door to unlock it.

'You know I can't let you through here, mate,' I replied, smiling sympathetically. I was under strict instructions by the head of security not to let any of the guys off the wing.

'But, I've got a note. I need to go to my medical.' He waved an obviously forged note in front of me, and I tried not to think about the fact that he had just been playing with himself with that same hand. Vom.

The note was almost falling apart from how many times it had been folded, shoved down his pants, or into his pockets. I didn't take the note, or look at it. I knew I was being played. It took two different keys to get off the wing, and I was becoming more aware that this young guy was pushing his luck with me because I was alone, I was small, and I was female. Not just that, but I was also new to the prison, I was untrained, I had no alarm, I was unchaperoned, and no one really cared whether I was there or not.

All I had was my personality, and years of experience of bluffing my way out of dangerous situations by pretending I was confident and in control, when I knew I wasn't. These kinds of situations had been common since I had begun conducting the research at the category B prison. It was a contract that had been suggested by one of my university professors. He said it would be good for me to build experience, and broaden my knowledge of forensic settings, since I had only ever worked in forensic settings with victims of crime – never the perpetrators.

I had been there for six months, and already a convicted rapist had tried to get me to go into his cell, another guy had pestered me for my number, and one guy had trapped me in a small room where he tried to intimidate me by graphically recalling the way he stabbed his ex-wife with a machete he had bought off the internet. I could see him getting off on retelling the story, hoping I was terrified, hoping I was fearing for my own life.

Instead, I ignored his gory story and told him I had a pack of really nice biscuits with me, if he wanted to share some.

Interestingly, he stopped his gory tale of murder and ate half the pack whilst telling me I was 'one of the good uns'.

Sometimes, diverting someone's attention is the only thing you have. Especially when you have been accidentally backed into a small room, and the convicted lifer who stabbed his ex-wife is blocking your only exit, and you both know it.

In those six months, I had already established that there was no amount of systemic or cultural change I could make to such a toxic, corrupt and dangerous prison. Everyone knew it was a hellhole, but the Governor didn't want to hear my findings unless I was coming to massage his already inflated ego about what a stellar job he was doing. It had caused arguments when I had reported how dangerous the wings were, not only for the prisoners, but also for the officers, who were frequently passing out from inhaling the spice smoke. Several officers and prisoners had been electrocuted by stripped wires, and prison officers were making a mint from using drones to get drugs inside to sell on.

Prisons are like little empires. If they are not well managed, the Governor becomes something of an emperor, or higher, a god-like figure. Staff and prisoners alike walk past them shaking like a leaf, or hoping they will nod at them, or maybe even raise a smile. They become untouchable, and depending on who they are deep down, they will either become a tyrannical dictator who rules with fear, violence, corruption and punishment, or they will seek to move away from such behaviour. Unfortunately for me, I was working for a Governor who couldn't give a fuck about my research, but knew it would look good come inspection date if he could claim I had been working with them to address the issues in his prison.

On top of that dynamic, every time I was in there, I worried I was going to bump into someone I knew from my old estate. So many people I knew were in prison, but at twenty-seven, and having left the estate almost a decade ago, it was hard to keep up with who was where, and for what. I knew Smithy was in there somewhere for taking a load of coke and deciding to bring GTA to life. I was pretty sure Declan was in there for nearly killing that window cleaner a few years back, too. I had my suspicions why Baggsy was in there, and his literal partner in crime, Greeny. Fuck only knows what for this time, but they had become frequent guests.

All I knew was that I could do without being recognised.

'Go on, miss, don't be tight!'

The young guy gestured towards my keys, and the door. I instantly thought of the weary chuckle the Head of Security had let out when I asked him why we didn't have any emergency alarms. He laughed, and then told me they were pointless, because no one would get to me in time anyway. I thought he was being sarcastic, but turns out, he was being completely serious.

It didn't help that he looked like Beaker from *The Muppets* – and this whole prison sure did feel like some twisted puppet show. Nothing was real. People were terrified of the rank structure, so no one said anything. Everyone knew how the drugs were getting into the prison, but no one said shit. Prisoners had prison guards under their thumb: they were gathering information on them from the outside, to use to blackmail them on the inside. It was common for prisoners to get you into conversation, and then ask you about your wife's white BMW, or your son's school fete last Saturday.

'I really can't let you out mate. I'm sorry. You might need to go and talk to whoever is on duty today over at the office . . .'

'Okay, miss. Understood. Sound. Will do. You have a good day now!' He turned on his heels like it was nothing, and started walking away.

'Bitch.' He whispered under his breath, just audible enough so I could hear it, but no one else could. Charming.

I turned to check he was definitely gone, quickly opened the door, shut it behind me, and locked it again with two different keys. The thick metal door slammed and squeaked shut as I pulled it tight. The locks creaked and whined as I secured them both. It would have been a lot easier to do if the doors were not so warped.

It was a long walk back to my office, another long walk, and many more double-locked doors down to the exit, and then yet another long walk back out to the car. I had my monthly research meeting to get to with Laura and Malcolm, and wanted to make sure I had enough time to grab some lunch on the way.

I got to the car, took off my belt and chain. It dropped to the footwell of my car, and I glared at it. It was so alien to me. A prison belt. I shuddered. Weird.

I never would have pictured myself walking around with a set of keys chained to my waist, surrounded by guys that were either eyeing me up for sex, or eyeing me up for the keys. Or both. I resented the lack of safety around my role. I was an experienced professional by that point, but I was very new to the prison environment. I had been given a short tour, and that was pretty much it. The place was vast, the wings all looked the same, the design was like a maze, and no one seemed to know what anyone else was doing.

I asked the prison officers whether they trusted that if they were involved in an incident or emergency, their colleagues and management would rush to help them. They laughed. They told me that was one of the reasons you didn't piss anyone off there. If you wanted help when a prisoner had got hold of you, and was trying to drag you to the floor, you had better hope you hadn't annoyed your teammates recently, otherwise they would let you suffer a while before 'rushing' to your aid.

The prospect of that toxic culture, plus the fact that absolutely no one knew me, meant that I felt constantly at risk.

Even when I had reported the guy trying to get me into his cell, the response was less than encouraging. Barely raised eyebrows, and a shrug. 'He's not usually like that . . .' didn't exactly fill me full of confidence. But then again, nor did sending me to go and work with him alone, without telling me he was a convicted rapist.

In some ways, life hadn't changed that much, I guess. I used to be surrounded by perpetrators with their hands in their boxers on the estate, and now I was surrounded by them in a prison. Same dangers. Same risk. Same misogyny. Same feeling of being prey. Same games. Same manipulation. Same drugs. Same tension. Same uncertainty. Same poverty. Same desperation.

In other ways, life had changed drastically, and I was still coming to terms with that. No matter how much I identified with the guys in the prison, I wasn't one of them. I was the psychologist who was doing the research. I was the woman with the nice sweater with a name badge on. One of the screws with the keys chained to my waist: I was in the prison, but I wasn't in prison.

I was almost three years into my PhD, I owned my own small company, and I was a million miles from where I started out. Despite that, I couldn't shake the feeling that I didn't fit in anywhere. I certainly wouldn't be accepted back on the estate – and arguably I had nothing in common with the struggling families who still lived there. On the other hand, I didn't fit into the world around me. I was noticeably working class, and I stuck out like a sore thumb when surrounded by wealthy, successful, educated academics and consultants.

I pulled away from the prison in the special edition VW Golf GTI Sport that I had treated myself to, and started my favourite playlist. I swiped to my self-curated 'Strong and Successful' playlist, and pressed shuffle. The bass in the upgraded sound system kicked in, and I relaxed into my bucket seat. No one really expects the PhD scholar to turn up to work in a lowered sports car with the sound system up.

I was a walking (driving) contradiction.

I was in uncharted territory, and I knew it. Was I a serious academic psychologist with a prestigious career ahead of her, or an unlikely, undeserving council estate chav whose luck streak was eventually going to run out?

I had a foot in both camps, and kind of in none.

It was thoughts like these that plagued me whilst I was driving long distances alone in my car. It was, and still is, the only place I can truly think, reflect, dissect, and feel completely safe doing so. Most of my greatest discoveries, epiphanies, ideas, inventions, designs and decisions happened in my car, usually at 70 mph, and usually after many hours of driving.

My mind was always whirring, but there was something incredibly effective about the focus being on my car, my driving, the road, the sound of the engine, the feeling of the gearbox and the movements of other drivers – it allowed another stream of consciousness to step in and do all of the hard work for me.

Whilst I was busy overtaking that annoying lorry on the M6, eating a bag of crisps, and singing my lungs out to anything from Missy Elliott to Lily Allen, my mind did its magic, and it was always elsewhere. Solving problems. Strategising. Writing. Synthesising. Theorising. Criticising. Analysing.

Linking. Remembering. Playing devil's advocate. Forcing me to look at that one tiny thing from fifty different angles. Replaying conversations and incidents, and deciphering what someone really meant when they said that thing four years ago. Imagining solutions to big problems. Wondering about the purpose of life on earth. When the meteor would finally hit us. Why it was taking so fucking long.

On reflection, my car had become the new version of the floor of the music storeroom at Redtree.

As I neared the university campus, I thought about the last time I was there. Those conversations about my 'lifestyle'. Ugh. It made me shudder. I had tried to put it to the back of my head as I had been buzzing around working fifty hours a week, and then studying at night when my kids were in bed – but it had been nagging at me. Somewhere deep. Somewhere injured.

Surely they didn't think that my childhood, and my background, were legitimate reasons why I couldn't be a competent psychologist?

I shook it off. Fuck it.

If that's what they thought, I would only go on to prove them horribly wrong, I decided. The last thing anyone should do is tell me that I am not capable of something. It's game on from the moment it leaves their mouth. I loved nothing more than letting people watch me succeed and surpass them.

I had already done it many times over, and I was determined to continue. No one expected me to escape that estate. No one expected me to do anything at all. I was supposed to be trapped there forever. I had already won.

I smiled as I remembered the conversation I had with my Uncle Cameron in my mum's kitchen at a family party. The house buzzed. The walls shook with that hybrid of singing and shouting that only karaoke can produce. People danced, jumped, and fell into each other. Mum had put a disco ball on the mantelpiece and turned the lights off. The kids of the family ran around at top speed after loading up on sweets, occasionally being yelled at to calm down when they were bright red in the face. Eventually, one of them would run into a wall and they would all be told that they deserved it for not listening.

I was stood in the kitchen with a group of my aunts and uncles. My three-year-old was one of the red-faced children zooming around the house, having the time of his life.

'So what are you doing then, Jessica? Anything?' He sneered, obviously gesturing towards the fact that I was nineteen years old with two children. My similarly unplanned three-month-old baby was being looked after by my close friend for a couple of hours.

I smiled at him, a smile that said, 'Go fuck yourself, Uncle Dickhead.'

'You were always so smart at school, weren't you? What happened, eh? Remember when you said you wanted to work in medicine? In biochemistry?'

Still, I just smiled at him. He was probably high anyway, I figured. The last time I had seen him, he had tried to sell stolen steroids to my friends.

He continued to push me though, and I realised there was a purpose to this conversation. I had turned to start a conversation with someone else, but he tried again.

'Your mum said you have applied to go to university!'

I looked over at my mum, but she took a sip of her drink and rushed off to busy herself over near the snacks. I sighed. I was the first person in my family to apply to university and no one really knew what it was. To some extent, that included me too.

'Yeah, I have.'

'What are you gonna do there, then?' He put his arm around the shoulders of his new girlfriend and sipped his beer. I looked at her. She was probably the tenth one I had met. She was pretty, petite, long dark hair. Like clones. I often wondered if each of them knew about the exes before them, and whether they knew they were on some sort of production line. One of the old ones taught me to ride and jump horses, which was pretty awesome. We used to listen to the All Saints album and ride around on her tall dark horse, Benji, and the little sandy horse she let me ride, Jezebel. This new girlfriend seemed friendly enough, but they never lasted long.

'Psychology degree,' I fake smiled again and passed my son his sippy cup of water as he ran around my legs.

'Oh. Right. Well . . . I mean, you don't actually think you are going to be a psychologist, do you?' He sniggered.

I sighed.

'Yes, I want to be. One day. I will have to do a PhD too. But I have to do the degree first . . .'

He cut me off.

'Oh, don't be so stupid. If you even finish it, everyone knows that psychology is a bullshit degree!'

Says the man with no degree, I thought to myself. I dug my thumbnail into the side of my leg for a distraction from my bubbling anger.

'If you are going to do a degree in science, at least pick a real one. Biology. Chemistry. Physics. Summat that will actually lead to a job . . . You may as well be studyin' a degree in fuckin horoscopes!'

His girlfriend slapped his arm and gasped, 'Eh! Rude! I have a degree in psychology you know!'

'Yeah, and look at you, are you a psychologist?'

It went quiet.

'No . . .' she conceded, looking embarrassed.

'There you go then. She isn't going to be a psychologist, Nicola. She will probably end up a teaching assistant or something. No point lying is there?'

I rolled my eyes. Prick.

'Which university did you get into then?'

Oh god. I knew what was coming.

'The . . . um . . . Open University.' Now it was my turn to concede. I glanced at Nicola, both of us having our arses handed to us by this idiot. She shifted uncomfortably and looked into her drink.

'The Open University! Ha! Is that even a real university? What do you get at the end of it? A little certificate and a pin badge? Brilliant! Told you so!'

He grinned at his successful destruction of me in front of everyone, and waltzed off to get another beer out of the fridge.

I walked into my campus thinking about how deflated he had made me feel that night. How embarrassed and ashamed. How I had made my excuses and told everyone I needed to get my son to sleep, and I had found a dark, quiet room upstairs, cuddled up with him, and we had both fallen asleep on a pile of cushions. I had stroked his tiny head of blond hair and thought about the way everyone in my family always sought to cut me down. I would never do that to my kids, I thought as I drifted off to the sound of someone murdering 'Sweet Caroline'. I would be so proud if you ever made it out of this shit hole and to a university, I said in my head to my baby, softly breathing into my arm.

Back on campus, I wondered how Uncle Cameron reacted when he heard I got my degree five years later. When I got accepted on to my PhD at a top university. When I overtook him. When I overtook everyone. I knew I was being watched in my family, but I was also being performatively ignored.

At first, it hurt. No one cared when I got my first excellent mark during my undergraduate degree. No one noticed when I was doing my final exams. No one wanted to come to my graduation. I had started many arguments whilst trying to get to the bottom of their apathy. I begged them to tell me why they didn't care, or why they never remembered anything I was doing. I asked them why I was never good enough, and why I was always overlooked, sidelined or excluded. None of my questions were ever answered, and I had to accept that I was alone.

Over the years, I had had to learn how to be my own cheerleader. I had to be the person who sat down with myself, and said, 'Right, what do you need to focus on today?' I had to be the person who did the work, and then I had to be the person who congratulated me when I did well. I had to give myself my own pep talks when it got too much. I had to be the person who gave me a good talking to when I wasn't putting the effort in. I had to wipe my own tears. I even bought myself little gifts and rewards to motivate myself (although on reflection, I probably should have gone easier on the Terry's Chocolate Oranges . . . or at least bought shares in them).

I walked from the carpark past the music department. Every huge sash window gave me a different gift. A woman with a beautiful voice singing an Adele song to herself as she played with some different chords on the piano. A young guy blasting out a deep solo on the saxophone.

I was less than a year from becoming Dr Jessica Taylor. I had the stamina. I knew I could do it. Uncle Cameron making me feel two inches tall didn't deter me. My family blanking years of my life didn't deter me. Some petty comments about my childhood were not going to stop me, either. I shook it off, and picked up my pace.

The centre of the campus looked stunning. Students of all ages and backgrounds rushed to their lectures and meetings. Groups sat on the grass reading books and eating their lunches. The clocktower peered over us, ringing out to keep us all on time. The old red brick buildings and long sash windows. The endless library. The solemn statues. The wonderful old domed ceilings and the ornate tiled floors. Every time I set foot in this place, I was reminded of how lucky I was to be there, surrounded by inquisitive minds and limitless learning.

As I neared the forensic department, I fumbled around for my ID card. The forensic corridor was locked, and we couldn't access it without one. Mine had been playing up for a few weeks, only working intermittently. I knocked on the main doors, hoping someone would hear me and let me in.

Malcolm heard me knocking and popped his head out of his office.

'Hey Malcolm, my ID card isn't working! Could you let me in please?' I shouted through the thick glass, pointing at my useless swipe card.

I thought he was going to come and open the door, but to my dismay, he looked at me, stood there for a few seconds, and then simply went back into his office. I stood there, baffled. Why would he leave me outside like that? Was he just going to grab something? Did his phone ring? Was he confused? Could he hear me?

I knocked again. Nothing. I looked at my phone, I was one minute late for my meeting with them both.

I knocked again. Silence.

I started to write a text message to Laura to explain I was stuck outside the corridor when she came out of her office to look for me. She instantly saw me at the end of the corridor and came to open the door.

'Hey! Are you okay?'

'Yeah, I got stuck again.'

'Ah I'm sorry, I hope you weren't there long?'

'Only a few minutes . . .'

Malcolm emerged from his office as we made our way down the thin, dusty corridor.

'Oh, hello Jessica! Good timing!'

I frowned at him. He smiled at me. What was going on? Laura was clearly oblivious, but Malcolm and I knew what he had done. He kept holding eye contact with me, like he was goading me to ask him why he ignored me. I decided not to give him what he wanted, and instead chose to be sickeningly polite to him.

'It was indeed good timing! How are you today? How are your projects going?'

He was thrown. Good.

'I saw your undergrad student the other day, Emily, I think. She is exceptionally bright, isn't she?'

He squirmed. He didn't know who I was referring to, of course, because he didn't remember any of his undergrad students.

'Yes, she is,' he lied.

I smiled. He smiled.

Laura watched on with a third fake smile. What a weird conversation this was.

Eventually, she interrupted. 'So, Jessica, how have you been getting on this month?'

'Good, thank you. I have completed the literature review chapter. Data collection and analysis is finished. Findings are written up. I have structured the discussion chapter. I gave two speeches about my work this month, and I have been busy on the prison contract. Oh, and my new national evidence review on exploitation has been published, so that's been brilliant.'

They never really did know what to say to me in these meetings. They would often reflect back interesting observations, or signpost me to some new literature every now and then, but I think they were both taken aback by supervising someone who was so self-motivated and efficient. My PhD was supposed to take me five to ten years part-time around my job, but two and a half years in, I was almost done.

'Wow, you've done a lot. That's great. Could you keep us updated on your progress with the discussion? And could we see copies of the chapters you have completed so we can both give you feedback?'

'I sent them to you last week, do you have them?'

She turned to look at her computer.

'Ah . . . yes, probably. Sorry, I must have missed that. I will have a look later on.'

'Thank you.' I looked through my notes in case there was anything else I needed to ask, but I felt tension rising.

'Um. Actually, do you have ten minutes you could spare to discuss something else with us, Jessica?'

'Absolutely, fire away.' I looked up, thinking it was going to be about my work, but the look in her eye had changed. She shifted slightly in her seat. For the first time, I noticed she was holding a few pages of white A4 paper with printed black text on. She noticed me looking at them, and tilted them back towards her.

'I am afraid to say that we have had several more complaints about you in the last month . . .'

My heart sank. What? Who from? What for?

'Oh, right?' I managed.

'There was also a research position I had suggested you would be perfect for, but the response was that they didn't want to work with you because of these complaints . . .'

That one hurt. My work had always been excellent. All of my contracts were done efficiently, accurately and I was often recommissioned and asked back to do further lectures or work. I glanced at Malcolm, whose bravado had packed up and fucked off, and who was sat there like a sheepish little boy.

'Who are the complaints from?'

'I'm afraid they have asked to remain anonymous.'

'Can I see them?'

'No, you don't need to see them. I am raising them with you.'

'So how do I know they exist?'

'They do exist,' Laura sighed, quickly exasperated.

'Who were they sent to?' I pushed.

'They were sent directly to me, because I am your supervisor.'

I pondered. Who would send a complaint about a student directly to their academic supervisor? Not a member of the public, that's for sure. It had to be someone in academia. Or someone known to me. Or to Laura.

I scanned her face. Nothing. I hesitated.

'Are these complaints being investigated by the university?' I asked, my mind putting together different possibilities.

'No, it is not a formal complaint,' she explained carefully.

'So, it's an anonymous person, and it's not a formal complaint? Then I reckon we just ignore it. I get all sorts of abuse online simply because of being a woman on the internet. If you add that to the fact that I post information about abuse, violence, victim blaming, feminism and patriarchy then it's not exactly a shock that some anonymous idiot troll on the internet would start sending false complaints, is it?'

'This person is not an idiot, nor are they a troll.'

Ooh, defensive. My eyes narrowed.

I chose not to respond to that comment, but it set off alarm bells in my head. Sirens. Red flags. Loud and clear: this was someone she knew.

'Do you want to hear the basis of their complaints?' she asked me.

Not really, I thought. But I nodded.

'So, there are several. In fact, one of the complaints is over three pages long . . .' she sighed.

I rolled my eyes. What on earth could someone have to say that took three pages?

Laura watched me roll my eyes and I watched her bite her tongue. She cleared her throat and tucked her hair behind her ear. She started reading, and paraphrasing from the emails in her hands.

'So, they are raising that you are very critical of the use of films that are being shown to children who have been abused. That you started a campaign to have them banned. That your campaign is aggressive. That you keep using bad language on your social media. They have also raised that they feel you are misrepresenting the effectiveness of the films, and how they help children . . .'

I was laughing and shaking my head by this point.

'Sorry. Sorry. Do you know anything about these films, Laura?' I interrupted.

'Well, actually, after I got the complaints, I went to read more about them and I looked at your campaign. They are films made for children, about sexual abuse and exploitation. They are shown in schools. Your argument, if I understand it correctly, is that they are graphic, that they are abusive to the children and to the actors, and that they traumatise children instead of helping them . . . Is that about right?'

I was impressed. At least she had gone to read my work, which was a damn sight more than most people did. Most people who criticised me had never actually bothered to read a thing I had written. They had seen the word 'feminist' and spiralled into a tirade of insults.

'Pretty much. Those films contain rape scenes of children. Who even makes a rape scene of a child and then shows it to children? Not just children in their schools, but to children who have already been raped? It's unethical, it's untested, it has absolutely no evidence base, it is done for shock tactics and tick boxes, and we are harming tens of thousands of kids all over the UK . . .'

She frowned. Malcolm twiddled his pen.

'I can tell you are very passionate about this, Jessica,' she started, 'but the fact is, you seem to be upsetting a lot of people. Others may have a different perspective on this . . .'

'That showing rape scenes to eleven-year-olds is good?' I quipped.

She paused. She knew she couldn't agree with that. She knew there was no defence for the films. I raised one eyebrow at her.

She took a breath, reset herself, and started another angle.

'I know you care about this, Jessica, but no one is going to listen to you, if you carry on like this . . .'

'Like what?'

'Being so . . . so . . . loud about it. So confrontational. So relentless. Some people feel it is unprofessional.'

God, I was so bored of the same old ways women were framed for having a voice. I expected so much better from successful women in academia, but I was slowly and painfully realising that women in academia were often right near the bottom of a very large, very patriarchal power structure. Whilst I looked up to them as women in brilliant jobs who had earned their doctorates, they had found themselves slotted in, as a tiny cog in a huge billion-dollar machine. Publishing or perishing. Frantically pulling as much grant funding in as possible. Teaching hundreds of students and marking hundreds of dissertations a term. Playing office politics to stay alive. Being nice. Being polite. Not ruffling feathers. Being friends with everyone. Remembering everyone's birthdays. Sitting on tokenistic boards on their lunch breaks. Desperately trying to achieve promotion and tenure. Writing twenty-five emails just to book a meeting room for an hour.

They were the ones making sure the shared kitchen wasn't a state, and the student having a breakdown was okay. They had studied for a decade to end up mirroring the role of women in society, whilst their male counterparts had quickly become Professor, then Head of Department, and then Head of School, whilst ignoring everything around them, stabbing anyone in the back who got in their way and simply focusing on their own goals and desires.

I couldn't be like that. It irritated me that so many of these conversations came down to 'be nicer'.

'If you want change, you have to chase after it,' I started. 'People don't stop doing things by just raising it politely with them. We have to keep fighting. Women need to find their voices. People are making huge amounts of money from those fucking films. More and more being churned out every year. What about those girls, those child actors? "Oh, hello, could you just lie there and cry whilst we get this forty-year-old man to simulate rape on top of you for this new film we are going to show to eleven-year-olds between maths and geography?" Come on, Laura, it's a scandal that they even exist!'

They both sighed and rubbed their heads.

'I think this is what Laura is trying to get at. You take a sledgehammer to everything. You won't make friends this way, and people won't listen to you . . .' Malcolm tried next.

Oh god. First it was 'be nice', now it's 'make friends'. What was this, nursery?

'I don't want to make friends, I want us to stop showing rape films to children – predominantly girls by the way – and I want us to stop pretending that they are effective interventions for child sexual abuse. If those films were in the cinema, they would be rated 18. We are showing them to kids of eleven years old. Girls are crying in assemblies. They are going home and cutting themselves with razor blades. They are having panic attacks in their classrooms. I don't care who I piss off. This has to stop!'

Laura straightened up in her chair.

'Could you watch your language, please? Many people are noticing that you frequently swear when you talk . . . and as I said, that was also included in this complaint.'

'I didn't swear!'

'You did,' Malcolm muttered.

'When?'

'Just now!' Laura protested.

'What did I say?'

'I'm not repeating it.'

I frowned at them both. I tried to wind myself back in time, to remember what I had said, but the truth was, I didn't notice when I swore. I had always sworn. It was just part of my vocabulary. I had never understood the obsession with swearing. They were just words. Fuck. Piss. Dick. Twat. Bastard. Who gives a shit?

The world was literally upside down. Governments were gaslighting, exploiting and oppressing their own people, and global corporations were grooming and controlling the world. People were killing, raping, abusing and harming each other every second of every day. Kids were growing up without enough food to eat, or safe houses to live in. Schools couldn't afford felt tip pens. The military were deliberately targeting the poorest areas of the UK to convince sixteen-year-old lads to sign up, promising them a life of adventure and riches only to dump them on a street corner or into a life of addiction and trauma.

Women were having their children removed from them for reporting their ex for domestic abuse. Rich white people were exploiting poor women in other countries to carry their babies for them, so they didn't have to suffer stretch marks. People were being sectioned and diagnosed (for the rest of their lives) with made up mental disorders for being different. Countries were executing women for being raped, and men for being gay.

We were polluting the ocean, the skies and the land so fast that even Usain Bolt couldn't escape the shit floating in the sea at Skegness. We were burning and crushing the rainforests in chunks bigger than football fields every second. Millions of people were being trafficked for profit across the world, for everything from organ harvesting to slavery (which we all pretend has ended).

Bloodthirsty egotistical men having a midlife crisis were paying to shoot endangered animals in Africa and pose with a bleeding zebra on Twitter. Airhead influencers were claiming they were animal rights activists and then paying to pose with an abused, sedated tiger on their Tinder profile.

And. We were now showing little kids videos of other little kids being raped and sexually abused, and pretending it would 'prevent sexual abuse'.

We were disgusting. We were abhorrent. We were swimming in our own filth.

But whatever you do, don't say fuck. Because it's bad.

All of that whirred through my brain in a millisecond, like a superhero monologuing at the end of a Marvel film.

'Really?' I scowled.

'What do you mean?' Laura asked me.

'Like, are we really going to police how I talk? The words I use? Are we going to pretend that academics don't swear? Who is this even for, this charade?'

Malcolm, who swore more than I did, stayed quiet. I stared at him, especially.

'Is no one allowed to swear in this department, or is this special rule just for me?'

'I think you are taking this quite personally now, Jessica . . .' Laura tried.

'Maybe that's something to do with the fact that you are getting mysterious anonymous emails about me. I would say that was pretty personal. Wouldn't you?'

'Like I said, this isn't a formal complaint. I was just raising it with you, so you can reflect on what they have said. Maybe think about your approaches, your language, your attitude. You won't make any change if you put people off you. No one will like you.'

I bit the inside of my lip, seething. No one will like me? Ha!

'I'm not scared of that,' I told her straight. 'You might be. But I am not.'

She stared at me, but I continued.

'There are bigger things in the world than being liked. I'm not here for a popularity contest. I have a job to do. I don't do cliques. If people want to dislike me for saying what I need to say, and doing what I need to do, that's up to them. I'm not here to make everyone else happy,' I said, flatly.

Firmly.

At twenty-seven years old, this was the third time in my life I had been threatened with not being liked.

The first time was when I was twenty-two years old, by my CEO in my old job, on the night I won an award for my work in sexual violence. As I returned to the table at the glitzy event, excited, shaking, shocked, emotional, she slowly stirred her drink with her straw and warned me that people would not like me very much if I kept being so 'arrogant'. The ice clinked against the glass as she calmly told me that everyone at work thought I was arrogant, and people were beginning to dislike me.

Back then, I had no idea what she was doing, but with the wisdom of another ten years under my belt, I now know exactly what she was doing, and why she chose that precise moment to do it. But at the time, she had the desired effect on me. I sat there, still clutching my glass award, heart pounding, face flushing with embarrassment, fake smiling to everyone else congratulating and hugging me whilst my head spun with the new reality that my boss hated me, and everyone I worked with disliked me.

Funny how quickly someone can reframe you. Reshape your identity. Reposition you amongst your peers. One look. One comment. One sentence, and you don't see yourself as the same person you were just moments before their venom sank in.

Isn't it alarming how much of our self-perception is based on what other people say about us?

The second time it happened was after I had written several critical articles about the use of failing risk assessment tools in child safeguarding. I called for them to be retracted, and for effective research to be completed before any other tools were used. My articles were being shared, and were causing a lot of conversation. The toolkits were dangerous. They were missing children. They had never been validated or tested, and they were being used to blame teenage girls for being abused by men. Some professionals were thanking me for them, and telling me I was right. Others were not so supportive.

An influential professional emailed me and asked to meet me to discuss my article. I was of course thrilled. I was twenty-five years old, and I thought I was networking, meeting new people, and making the changes that were vital to protecting children.

When I got to the meeting, she was cold.

'I am here to give you some advice, Jess. You don't want to be unpopular, do you?'

'Sorry?' I sat up straight. She had my attention. This wasn't a nice coffee and a chat at all, this was an ambush.

'You are ruffling feathers. You are upsetting people. You don't want people to dislike you now, do you?' She played with her rings and bracelets casually.

Oh, I see where this is going, I thought to myself.

I grinned at her.

'Is this what you have driven 80 miles to say to me?' I performatively chuckled at her utter waste of time, making sure she knew that I was laughing at her.

She held my eye contact, but said nothing.

Be brave, I thought. Stand your ground.

'I think you've got me mixed up with someone else.'

'What do you mean?' She scowled.

'Oh, I just mean, you must have me mixed up with someone who gives a fuck about popularity!'

I held her eye contact, and smiled at her whilst she searched my face. She was confused.

I stood up from the little round table in the busy coffee shop, and gathered my things.

'People won't listen to you,' she sang obnoxiously, and then sipped her foamy latte.

'Oh, they will,' I mimicked back as I walked out of the coffee shop and back to my office. I didn't even look back at her.

This conversation with Laura and Malcolm was no different to that one.

They both stared at me.

I was becoming accustomed to being told that no one would like me, but it was jarring to hear it come from professors and academics. In a psychology department, no less. It seemed that no matter where you were, the same tactics would be used.

The school playground. Your family. Your friends. Your job. Your relationship. Your community. Your university. Society.

That oh so familiar threat to women.

You don't want to be alone, do you?

You don't want to be disliked, do you?

Unpopular? Isolated? Ignored?

Hated, even?

Maybe it didn't frighten me because I had already been there. Done that.

I'd already been alone. Disliked. Unpopular. Isolated. Ignored.

Hated, even.

They couldn't frighten me with a potential outcome, when I had already survived it in real life.

6

Bad news he is

Summer 2005

The summer before I turned fifteen was a hot, heavy, hazy few months of late nights and experiences that would shape me forever.

The estate came alive in those summer months. Hi-fi systems had been pointed out of open front room windows, for five hundred different house parties and barbecues. The Masseys had dragged their faux leather sofa out into the front garden, and in some weird one-upmanship, the Kirbys had set out all of their deckchairs in a row on the pavement where they sat drinking a crate of beer and yelling abuse at passers-by.

'Jess! Jess! Jess! Come sit on my dick!'

Roaring laughter.

'Fuck off, Simon,' I shouted back, not even turning my head towards him and his family.

'Aww don't be mean to me, you're breaking my heart!' he yelled back.

I shook my head, and carried on down the street. The best thing you could do was to keep moving. Any hesitation, replies, eye contact or validation of what they were saying would result in confrontation or worse.

'Ignorant bitch! Go suck ya mum!' he shouted and then launched a crumpled can of Carling at me. Again, I ignored the can as it sailed by and landed in front of me. I ignored the laughter and shrieks for my attention. I just wanted to focus on getting to the party. It was far too hot for that shit.

That summer, if you couldn't find me, I was usually half-cut at one of those garden parties, or in the back of a car somewhere. I took a long drag on the joint and passed it to the girl next to me.

Sinead? Sian? Sarah? Steph?

I couldn't remember. Bren had a new girl every week anyway. There was no point getting too familiar with her when she would be replaced by another blonde girl soon. I was always friendly to them, but there was no point in anything other than small talk and passing the joint. Truth be told, I couldn't be bothered to keep up any more, and had started calling them all 'duck' or 'babe', so I didn't have to remember their names.

I giggled to myself as I watched a guy I barely knew pour another crate of Carlsberg into the paddling pool and hose the cans down with cold water. They bobbed up and down like little ducks on the water as the current hit them, spun them and bashed them into each other. Keeping the beers cold in the paddling pool was the stuff of a top tier house party on the estate.

I rested back into my white plastic chair, the legs becoming bendy in the hot August sun.

'Fuck! Take cover!' Ginge screamed as he ran full pelt past me and into his house.

I didn't have time to process what he was saying, let alone take cover before the explosion sent the barbecue 25 feet into the air, shattering it into pieces that then scattered the back garden.

All around me, people fled, ducked, screamed and gasped; but my body wouldn't move. I froze. Everything slowed down. I watched part of the barbecue sail into the air and then smash down on the roof tiles. I saw shards of the metal and plastic wheels rain down, still on fire. I couldn't move.

I felt the heat, and the shock of the explosion. I smelled the burning and the sharp acid of the smoke, but I was eerily, and confusingly, still.

As the chaos died down, and my friends crept out from their hiding places around the garden, they laughed and patted me on the back for being hard as fuck. Staying still. Being unmoved by the huge explosion and the resulting miniature fires all around me.

'Jess didn't even flinch!' one of the lads laughed.

I smiled, masking the inner confusion at my inability to flee. It had been happening a lot lately.

Suddenly, a woman's voice screamed from inside the house.

'What have I fucking told you about putting your fucking Lynx collection in the barbecue? Fucking moron. That's three fucking barbecues, you little cunt!'

I glanced down at the mangled metal on the floor near my feet, and recognised the front of a can of Lynx Africa.

'Sorry Mum!' Ginge yelled back, still stifling his laughter.

'You're not fucking sorry though, are you?' A glass smashed against a wall. Ginge shrieked.

'Fuck's sake, Mum! I said sorry!'

'Get the fuck out of this house now, and clean up the fucking mess you have made of my garden again!'

He ran out of the back door and out into the garden, stamping on a few remaining smouldering fires.

'Cunt,' I heard her whisper to herself as she poured another whisky and went back to watching the *EastEnders* Omnibus in bed.

This family was wild. The mum was a forty-something primary school teacher who had been sacked for drinking on the job. The dad was ... come to think of it, I don't know what he was. He always dressed like he was working on a building site, but I had never seen him work another day since the driving ban. It was as if he was stuck in an endless loop. He got up at 6am, got ready, put his work gear on, slid his rigger boots on, and then ... well ... he just stayed in the house.

They had been together since they were at high school themselves, and had six teenagers. Their house was one of many on the estate that was a total free-for-all. I could turn up there at 10am or 2am, the front door was always open, and someone would always be in the kitchen having a drink or a smoke.

With five sons and another twelve nephews, they were a huge family of men and boys – all involved in their own murky shit. A couple of them were known for buying and selling stolen cars. Two of them dealt drugs. One of them was on pub watch, and banned from every bar in town. One of them did hired hits on the quiet for a couple of hundred quid, and one of them was a serial womaniser, with a string of abused and heartbroken women with STDs trailing behind him, begging him to call them back.

They weren't the most dangerous family by any means, and Kalen was friends with a few of them, but they were tight enough, and rough enough, that they were useful friends to have on the estate. The lads all decided that me and the new blonde girlfriend had to walk to the shop for more Rizlas, so I went without question.

My shoulders burned in the hot sun, and the tarmac went soft and gooey under my battered trainers.

'He's so good to me you know, it's almost our six-week anniversary . . .' Bren's girlfriend swooned on the way to the shop.

I smiled, said all the right things, remained polite, but had to bite back what I really wanted to say, which was that there is no such thing as a six-week anniversary, and that Bren goes through girls like he goes through Rizlas. And we were on the way to the shop to buy him some more.

The lowered, modified cars hummed past as they cruised the estate streets. Young men drove past us at a few miles per hour, windows down, seats laid back, the sweet smell of draw always creeping just behind them.

Out of the cars, men shouted slurs, wolf-whistles and offers of anything from a ride to the nearest Maccys, to a ride on their dick.

As a fourteen-year-old girl, you couldn't even walk from your own house to the bottom shop without at least two cars stopping next to you and trying to get you inside. The only way to survive was to befriend them, know them all, learn who they were, and whether they were particularly dangerous.

That may sound strange, but there were differences between the guys inside the cars. Whilst the cars were all modified in the same ways – second hand alloys, body kits they had pulled off another car, induction kits from Halfords, exhaust tips, pearlescent paint jobs and huge bass speakers in the boot – the men inside were all looking for something different.

Kappo was a slim, brown-haired twenty-six-year-old factory worker who had a thing for teenage girls. If you got in his car, he was going to expect sex, simple as that. He often gossiped about the girls he had sex with, and even pitted them against each other. He would spread rumours about them after he got what he wanted, and leave them at the mercy of the entire estate. He was popular and well-liked, and yet the two hundred teenage girls he had shagged in his Subaru and immediately binned, were demonised as sluts and whores.

Drew was a twenty-two-year-old loner who used his Volkswagen Golf to make friends. He was harmless really, if you ignore the fact that most of his friends were thirteen-year-olds, of course. He held down a nine to five in a train station, lived a pretty normal life, came from a pretty normal family, but from what I knew of him, seemed not to have any confidence around other adults. He didn't know too many adults other than his own parents and family, and it was an open secret that he spent all of his free time with kids from the estate. I had met his parents plenty of times, and they treated me as if I was also twenty-two years old. Or as if Drew was also fourteen years old. To them, I was just 'one of Drew's friends'.

Gray was just using a car, any car, for dealing and moving drugs around. If you were in his car, you were on drug runs all night. He was generally safe, but everyone knows that drug dealing isn't for the faint-hearted, and you can end up in some pretty dangerous situations pretty quickly. Conversely, you also ended up at some of the most beautiful houses you had ever seen, in areas you didn't know existed, worlds away from any council estate. The guys at the top were doing very well for themselves, usually professionals and business owners with a sports car, a coke habit and a trophy wife.

Guys like Birchy on the other hand were terrifying. If you got in his car, anything could happen. You could end up wrapped around a tree in it, dying from some dodgy pills, raped by him on the backseat, or waking up somewhere you had never been in your life. A huge tower of a man, he was twenty-five years old and weighed at least 25 stone. He didn't date girls, he just took what he wanted from them and kept them in a permanent state of fear.

'Bad news he is, Jess,' Kalen had warned.

I was in the back of the car the night he ran his 'girlfriend' over. I say 'girlfriend' because she had tried to dump him at least five times, but he refused to let go. Every time she tried to leave, his rage intensified.

One night that summer, he had driven me and Jase to pick up a McDonald's. I had met Jase several months earlier on the estate, and he had become controlling very quickly. Kalen didn't like him, and he didn't like Kalen.

A few years older than me, and friends with Birchy, Jase had somehow convinced me that none of my friends were true friends, and they were all jealous of how much he wanted me. He was increasingly violent, intermittently charming, forever sleeping around, and one of the most manipulative liars I have ever known. I didn't know it then, but I lived in a web of lies he had meticulously weaved his entire life. Nothing was real.

I hadn't noticed that on the way Birchy had driven past three other McDonald's to get to the one we were at. I also hadn't noticed that we had long finished our fries and still Fanta and we were still sat in the carpark. I'd been taking shots of vodka all night, so I wasn't exactly in my most observant state.

I didn't even notice when the blonde-haired woman in the coat had finished her shift, slung her handbag over one shoulder and walked across the carpark and out on to the street. I didn't notice when Birchy's eyes narrowed, his breathing sped up, his mindless conversation about getting some new alloys slowed to a halt.

All I remember was the sudden force of the acceleration slamming my body into my seat, throwing me to the side, and banging my head on the door handle as Birchy sped, swerved, mounted the kerb and knocked his girlfriend to the floor with his Peugeot 205.

He gleefully laughed in those final moments as she froze, open mouthed, to gasp into the headlights before he mounted the kerb. I heard him slam his foot on the brake deliberately just before he hit her, which threw me face first into the back of the passenger seat.

Maybe he wanted to hit her with his car. He did mount the kerb, and the grass verge, after all.

Maybe he braked because he was just trying to scare her, intimidate her, and wanted to send her a warning that he would kill her if she tried to break up with him again.

I saw her go down, in front of the bonnet. I didn't know how hard he had hit her. I didn't know if he had hit her at all. Maybe she fell? Maybe she was dead?

I looked around, desperate for a way out of the car. I just wanted to run and run and run. I drunkenly reached from the footwell to the door handle, but it was locked. I started hyperventilating as my mind played show reels of us being arrested and questioned about Birchy killing his girlfriend outside McDonald's.

I looked up at Jase, equally as abusive, equally as violent, and yet terrified by what Birchy had just done.

'We need to get out of this car,' I silently mouthed at him, tears creating streaks in my orange foundation.

But I knew he wouldn't help me escape. I knew he would let Birchy do whatever he wanted, just like the night we were stood in the PC World carpark and Birchy kept challenging me to a fight.

On Thursday and Friday nights up at Festival Retail Park, hundreds of cars would meet, race, drift and cause utter chaos. Police had absolutely no power there. They were outnumbered, and outpaced. It was no man's land. The only businesses that stayed open were the McDonald's and the KFC, who were making a killing every car meet. Managers of Morrisons, PC World, Carpetright, B&Q and ToysRUs barricaded their doors and windows, desperate not to come in to yet another smashed window, or an upside-down burnt-out wreck in aisle 4.

Older men hung around their midlife crisis BMWs and Audi A3s, smoking weed and challenging each other to drifting trials. The younger men sat in their clapped out modified Corsas, Fiestas and Novas, teaching each other how to rewire their rear lights, build in NOS systems, and talking about where to buy stolen fibreglass body kits.

Festival Park (or Fezzi, to the Stokies), was where I learned to drive, race and handbrake turn. I had quickly learned how to race like everyone else, and at a time when *Fast and Furious* was only on its second movie, I adored the illegal racing scene. I was 'surprisingly good for a girl', they said, so I had earned some respect by being one of the only teenage girls up there who could drive as well as the adult men.

By the end of that summer, I had been in at least five car crashes, and I remember proudly telling everyone that I was not the driver in a single one of those crashes. I was always the passenger.

One was when we spun out on a roundabout during a race and crashed sideways into metal railings. One was when we spun out in a multi-storey carpark during a race, and went into a wall. The only crash that left me with long-lasting injuries was when a woman who was racing lost control of her car and ploughed into the back of us at 60mph when we were parked up, stationary, flicking through pirated CDs.

The woman in the crash was infinitely sexier than me, so Jase abandoned me to care for her for hours, and left me barely conscious, with my face on the dashboard. The only time he came over to me was to tell me to get out of the car because someone had called the police, and he didn't want a fourteen-year-old in the car when they turned up. A kind couple at a hotel nearby took me in and looked after me whilst I vomited and cried from the pain, and whilst Jase got the number of the woman who had smashed into his car.

'For insurance purposes,' he had assured me, like I was born yesterday.

Fezzi was a volatile place. Some nights were hilarious fun, some nights were taken up watching exciting races and drifting competitions, and other nights were life-threateningly dangerous. I came to know the other teenage girls there. We were all in the same position. Drugs, sex, abuse, drinks, cars, lies, secrets.

Birchy was up at Fezzi a lot. He had a big group of friends, and he had modded his car to include a NOS button, which caught the attention of everyone he met. Loads of the men up there lied about having NOS injections, but Birchy actually had one.

As an 8 stone fourteen-year-old girl being offered a fight with this monster of a man, I nervously laughed, and declined multiple times. I carefully backed away, as everyone watched this exchange. Some of the men were grinning, and some of them looked on in concern. I should have known he wouldn't take no for an answer. My polite decline didn't faze him at all, and instead, he sucker punched me as I turned around, instantly knocking me unconscious in front of all of his friends.

Much like most times I had been punched in the head, I don't remember feeling the impact of the punch, but I remember the agony of waking up on the cold, gravelly carpark floor. I remember the searing pain in my head and my neck, and the confusion of looking up at him laughing above me, wondering how I got on the floor. My face was pressed to the gravel, and as I slowly came round, I lifted my hand to my mouth to check my teeth were all still in.

Jase did nothing. Again. He smirked and laughed along whilst Birchy told everyone that I had deserved it for being a little slag.

I guess that was why, a few weeks later, him and Jase drugged me with something and did something that left me horrified. Sometimes I wish I knew what they did, but most of the time, I am glad I was unconscious. I am glad I have no memories of that experience, and I hope I will never recover them. I hope I was totally unconscious, and unable to create any memories to recover. I don't want them to poke through one day in my fifties, whilst I am sipping on a cocktail somewhere, or in my sixties whilst I am at my grandkid's birthday party, or in my seventies, watching something on my TV that triggers me back to that moment.

Such are trauma memories. Sneaky, protective, secretive, until the day they decide you need to process them. And then they are just there. With their flashing neon sign. Hitting you over the head with it. Hello! Remember this traumatic experience? Time to process it!

Maybe I will never remember some of the details, but I will never forget the smile on Birchy's face when I woke up and asked why I was naked from the waist down. That grin. That vile grin. The way Jase put his head down. The way they both walked out of the room whilst I scraped around for my underwear. The feeling of being totally exposed was only trumped by the feeling that it didn't matter, because they had already done much worse than looked at me.

The dawning realisation.

The way I looked around the dirty room, desperate for a shred of a clue as to what happened.

Nothing came.

3 Missed Calls

3 New Text Messages

> *12:39*
> *Y U Being a moody bitch? Come down, me and Birchy are going to pick up some beers.*
>
> *12:41*
> *Y u ignoring me?*
>
> *12:45*
> *Jess. Answer me. Y u being a dick?*
>
> *12:57*
> *Ur embarrassing u know that? U were loving it last night. Fukin Slag. You better come down here now*
>
> *13:33*
> *Only jokin babe. Luv you xxxxxxx*

I sighed. He was a monster, and he would flick from threatening and abusing me to telling me he wanted to marry me like it was nothing. Looking back, I find it hard to remember what I was thinking at the time. I know I didn't think he was a good person. I know I was scared of him. I knew he was dangerous, too. He just had such a psychological hold over me. I'm not sure people understand that dynamic. They think they can just teach women and girls about abusive men, and they will have some sort of lightbulb moment, realise their boyfriend is an abusive dickhead, pack their shit and leave. But the power they have over us is such that all the education in the world won't protect you from the mental and physical control they assert.

To everyone else, he was still an angel. A committed boyfriend, a devoted partner. Faithful, respectful, loving, supportive, flattering. It was all an act, and I knew that when the front door closed, I was in serious danger. Sometimes, I just did what he said. Other times, I tried to fight back or argue. Sometimes, I tried to reason with him, or bargain with him. It's a myth that we have one trauma response that our brains go into every time we are faced with something threatening. Our brains do not 'go offline'. We don't go into some 'autopilot mode'. Very often, there have been lightning quick decisions and analyses made that you haven't realised. That's why so many women and girls cycle through different responses and ways of trying to protect themselves in danger, depending on the situation. There were times when I knew that fighting back would have earned me a fast track to the morgue, but there were other times when I knew that I could appeal to him in some way, and bargain my way out of a situation.

Life was hard enough without having to constantly attempt to predict, and then manage, such a dangerous man. Especially as I was just a child.

The summer moved on, whether I accepted what was happening to me or not. I don't think I ever made a conscious decision to block the spiking out, but I wouldn't think about that assault again until I was twenty-seven years old. There were so many other assaults that I was awake for, that I guess that one got lost somewhere, hidden somewhere, locked away somewhere for another thirteen years until I was sat at my dining table eating some eggs on toast, and it decided to smack me round the face.

Remember when this happened? it screeched at me.

Life had become a blur. It's amazing how much you block out, to just get on with another day. The way some of the most terrifying experiences of your life just become the same as nipping to the offy or making a Pot Noodle.

Summer turned into autumn, and another year at the high school. Balancing high school with this darker side of my life was surprisingly easy. No one was paying attention to me. My teachers had decided I was a write-off. It didn't matter how many A*s I produced, I just wasn't the good little girl they wanted me to be. They had grown annoyed, resentful almost, that I put in zero effort but still achieved so much, so easily. Even my friends had grown weary of me spending all night drunk or high, only to ace a surprise quiz the next day with a hangover. I was irritable, moody, tired and antisocial.

My mum and Mark had a new baby to deal with. My dad had spiralled so far into alcoholism that he had fallen asleep with his leg up against the grill on the gas fire, and cooked through the calf muscle. He woke up and the whole placed smelled like burning pork. He had to have an operation to cut out all the cooked . . . meat.

Stace and Alfie were somehow able to survive these weird years of our lives by either pretending nothing was happening, or because they still had people around them paying attention to their wellbeing.

Life was a dark, council estate, child abuse version of Groundhog Day.

Monday: Go to school. Go to the park. Spark a joint. Drink a bottle of vodka. Go home and lie.

Tuesday: Go to school. Get in some stranger's car. Get knocked out. Go home and hide your injuries.

BAD NEWS HE IS

Wednesday: Go to school. Hang out on the garage roof. Watch the bats fly around. Smoke until you fall asleep. Rub yourself in some conifer trees on the way home to mask the smell.

Thursday: Go to school. Get drunk. Get raped. Go home and question if they love you or not.

Friday: Go to school. Get spiked. Wake up under a dining table in a house you don't know. Throw up. Go home and hide how wasted you are.

Saturday: Get thrown out of the moving car. Get abandoned with no clothes on. Get cold and wet in the pouring rain. Go home. Hide in the outhouse until everyone is asleep. Creep in and hide the fact you are freezing and naked.

Sunday: Get forced to fight another teenage girl whilst a group of men watch and take bets. Not let a single tear run down your face as you hit each other over and over again in the face until the other girl taps out.

Monday, again . . .

'Oi, you. Oi. Hello?'

I felt dizzy.

'Oi!'

I felt my body rocking.

'You all right?'

Pain rushed through my shoulder.

A man stood above me, kicking me.

I started to stir from my deep sleep. The dew on the grass wet my face. What the hell was I doing in this long grass?

'Oh, thank fuck, you're alive then!' He scratched his head.

'Eh?' I managed.

The man with the work boots and the long beard looked down at me. Behind him was a pink sky, broken up by shadowy clouds. He had a rucksack on his back and a flask in one hand.

'Thought I was ringing the pigs about a dead body then, kid,' he chuckled.

'Wha . . . Where . . . What time is it?'

My chest hurt. My back hurt. I was shivering.

He lifted his sleeve to look at his watch, raising one eyebrow at me. His concern returned.

'It's 5:58am. What are you doing out here?'

I clumsily pulled myself off my front, soaking wet from the grass, and stumbled as I tried to get to my feet.

'Uhhh . . .' I looked around me. I was in the centre of a roundabout at the bottom of the estate.

'Are you . . . all right?'

'Uhhh.' I looked at my hands, my legs, my body, felt my face, and smoothed my hair down. No cuts, no blood, no marks, teeth all still there, knickers still on. 'I think so, yeah.'

'You been out here all night? Just . . . face down? On this roundabout?'

Suddenly, I felt embarrassed. Ashamed, maybe.

'Uhhh, I dunno . . .'

I felt around for my house key in the long, cold grass.

'Listen, I gotta go. Be late for work. I bet you've got a search party out there for you, ant yer?'

I bet I haven't, I thought, as I waved goodbye to the kind stranger who kicked me awake.

I was only around 15 minutes from home, and it was only 6am, so I decided it might be a good idea to sneak into the house, and pretend I had been there all night. On reflection, my mum must have known I had been missing all night, but she never said anything to me. I snuck into the silent house and climbed as quietly as I could into my cabin bed, the metal creaking. I snuggled down under my covers.

Mum opened my bedroom door, glared at me, raised her eyebrows, and then stormed off. She was losing her patience with me.

How had I ended up on the roundabout? How long had I been there? Who had I been with?

My eyes grew heavy, and I gave in to another hour of sleep, before grabbing a shower, and getting on with my day like nothing happened.

'You look like shit again,' Hannah had laughed when I limped into school that day.

'Ta very much.' I feigned a laugh, but I was disappointed that my thick makeup and straightened hair hadn't hidden the fact that I had been collapsed on a roundabout all night. Or been dumped there. Or something.

'Where's Molly and Isabelle today? They were supposed to meet me at mine yesterday but they never turned up. Couldn't get hold of either of them.'

Hannah lived on the estate with us, but somehow managed to keep on the periphery of the worst stuff. She knew everyone we knew, but she just hadn't been sucked in like us. Maybe it was her parents, they were always so much stricter than ours. Or maybe it was because she was obsessed with some guy in the military she had been chatting to in secret on MSN for two years, and so whilst we were out on the streets, she was hiding her own dirty secrets in her bedroom, with her parents thinking she was safe and sound, tucked up in bed.

She stopped in her tracks.

'You haven't heard?'

'Heard what?'

'Jess, they got battered yesterday on their way to you!'

My heart skipped a beat. Molly and Isabelle were not capable of defending themselves in a fight. I would be surprised if they had even managed to throw one punch.

135

'What do you mean by battered though? How bad are we talking?'

'Isabelle has got two full black eyes and her mum wants her to go to hospital because she thinks her nose is broken. Molly has a deep gash under one eye and her face is massive.'

'Fuck. But who the hell would batter them two? They're harmless!'

Hannah went silent, turned to me, and put her hand on my arm.

'They were jumped. It was planned . . .' She hesitated, 'It was meant for you.'

'What?' I whispered, as hundreds of kids barged past us in the English corridor to get to break, for a quick smoke, a sausage swirl, the toilets or the football pitch.

'Remember that argument you had with Nina Frankley when she called you a slag, and you gave her a mouthful back? And she said she was gonna get her cousins to knock you out?'

'Yeah, she's all talk though . . . hang on . . . she did this?' I couldn't imagine 4ft 10in Nina doing anything of the sort. She was mouthy and brave, but that was about it.

'No . . .' Hannah shook her head. I knew it!

'Didn't fucking think so, she's nothing. No way she could do that much damage to two people . . .'

Hannah interrupted my rant.

'No, you don't get it. Her fucking cousins did it. About four of them, Molly said. Got out of the car, asked for Jess Taylor, they both said no, but they didn't believe them cos you and Molly have the same hair, so they kicked their heads in at the side of the road. Stood over them and said "That's from Nina!" I think they thought Molly was you . . .'

I just imagined Molly and Isabelle getting knocked around with such ease, with no way of defending themselves, not knowing what to do. I wasn't even there for them. I didn't even know it had happened.

Where the fuck was I yesterday? How did I end up on that roundabout?

I couldn't stop the intrusive visions of my friends being punched and kicked on the pavement.

'Fuck off!' I exclaimed in disbelief and an increasing sense of guilt. My friends were battered for nothing, because of me?

Tears filled my eyes. 'I'm gonna fucking kill that bitch.'

I turned and ran before Hannah could even grab the back of my blazer. Through the corridors. Through the kids. Through the lockers. Past the library. Through the lobby. Past the vending machines. Through the sports hall.

I have only ever seen red twice in my life, and this was the first time. I was absolutely livid with rage. I didn't even know what I was going to do when I found her, and I didn't care. All I could think about was my two innocent friends, in hospital waiting rooms and in their beds at home, covered in injuries that were meant for me.

I locked on to her, stood in the long canteen queue for the pastries.

I shoved through crowds of teenagers in a silent rage.

I walked up to her and pinned her to the canteen wall by her throat. She gasped as she struggled to pull my hand off her neck.

'Think you're hard now, do you? Where are your cousins now?' I growled at her.

A frenzied crowd grew around us as kids of all ages ran to watch another school fight.

I pushed her harder and harder against the wall as she panicked.

'Molly and Isabelle got jumped because of you! Why don't you do your own fucking dirty work? Your cousins are full grown fucking adults! What the fuck is wrong with you?'

I didn't let go of her for a second, and she fought and struggled to push me off her. I put both hands on her shoulders and pushed my head into her forehead, pinning her to the wall.

'Touch my friends again, and you and your cousins can meet some of my friends. You get me?'

She nodded.

I let her go, and didn't even stay to hear anything she had to say. I pushed through the excited crowd of over a hundred kids, and stormed off in utter disgust, in guilt, in horror and in shock. At the injuries of my friends. The danger of the estate. The ease of a hired hit. The power of my own violence. The way my heart felt like it was going to come out of my throat. The way my blood rushed through me, making my hands ache and throb.

'You're going to fuckin pay for that! Watch your fucking back! It will be you next time, you fucking bitch!' she screamed after me.

As I put my middle fingers in the air and walked out of the canteen, I walked right into Miss Rudman, my Deputy Headteacher.

We hated each other.

A tall, thin, blonde woman in her thirties, she looked over her square, black, thick-framed glasses and gritted her teeth. I looked down at her bright red six-inch stilettos and her perfectly pedicured toes. How did she even walk in those things?

'You. Isolation. Now.'

I glared at her. I didn't move. I just held her gaze, trying to calm my breathing.

'Do not test me, Jessica,' she warned, one hand on her hip.

We had a weird relationship in school. She pretended to be a functioning Deputy Headteacher, and I pretended that I hadn't been with her in the pub, dancing on the bar, and throwing up in the flower beds last week. She targeted me every chance she got, probably to exert power over me to ensure I didn't say anything about her drinking sessions with us. Or the time she drunk-cried to us for five hours because her ex had got remarried.

She wasn't the only teacher with a raging drink problem.

I had already rescued Mr Edwards from being run over twice. The first time, I didn't even realise it was him. It was midnight, I had been out drinking, and I noticed a middle-aged man lying face down in the road. Cars were swerving and steering around him, some were beeping at him, but no one was going to help him. He wore a tweed blazer, a white shirt, brown trousers, and some lace up shoes. He certainly didn't look like he was from the estate. I went over to him when the traffic calmed down, and nudged him.

Now it was my turn to find a body on the ground.

'You all right there, mate?'

I tapped his cheek. The stench of booze escaping from his pores was overwhelming. He didn't even stir.

'Listen mate, you're in the road! We gotta get you up!'

Nothing.

I put my ear to his mouth, to see if I could hear breathing. He burped, groaned, and I concluded my medical assessment. He was alive.

'Mate, listen. We gotta get you up. Come on!'

He turned over to look up at me, and I stepped back in shock.

'Mr . . . Edwards?'

My geography teacher winced at me, red in the face, eyes bloodshot, shirt buttons undone, tie loosened, oily hair matted to his head, and a patch of sick on the front lapel of his blazer.

'Oh fuckin great . . . a pupil . . . that's all I fuckin need.' He groaned as he turned over and tried to get himself sitting up. A car slowed down to watch me in the road with my teacher, and then drove off once they got bored of rubber necking.

'I won't say nothing. I just gotta get you out of this road, mate,' I explained, having absolutely no idea how I was actually going to lift him, when I was alone and half-cut myself.

'I don't need your fucking help!' he spat at me.

'Well, you're asleep in the middle of a T junction, so I think you do. Don't be a twat, just let me help you up, sir . . .'

'Don't fuckin call me that! I'm not at fuckin work!' His face flushed red, and I wasn't sure if he was going to punch me or throw up.

I thought about it for a moment, whilst I stood behind him. He leant his back on my legs, and I grabbed a handful of his shirt collar and blazer to stop him from wobbling over to one side.

'Well, what's your name then?'

'Greg.' He moaned, rubbed his eyes, and then added, 'Don't tell me yours. I don't wanna remember it on Monday.'

I chuckled, and tried not to let him hear my amusement.

'Right, Greg. We need to get you to that pavement over there. Do you think you can walk?'

The pavement was only a few metres away, and he was only an inch or so taller than me, but in the state he was in, it may as well have been a mile away, and I couldn't carry him.

'Leave me alone! I can walk!' Suddenly he lost his temper with me, grabbing at my hands and pushing me away. Another car drove around us in the middle of the road, a taxi driver put his window down and asked me if he was okay. I said he was just drunk, and the taxi sped off to its next job.

'You can't fucking walk though can you? Let me help you get out of the road!'

He stumbled to his feet, grabbing on to my clothes, my back, and my shoulders for support. He put all his weight on me, and I struggled to stay upright. I breathed through it, and dragged him to the side of the road. The smell of booze mixed with the smell of stale sweat and the fifteen coffees he had earlier in the day. It made me want to gag.

Still, that incident didn't top the time we were supposed to be going 'orienteering' with one of our teachers, and he hid in a bush and smoked a joint instead. We were supposed to be marked on that assignment, but Mr Lafferty was huddled up in a privet hedge, in his khaki parka, looking like Liam Gallagher, so high that he offered us twos when we found him.

Whatever he was smoking, it was stronger than the stuff I had tried. He was sweaty and incoherent, and so we all decided to just leave him to sleep it off in the hedgerow. No one likes a grass.

I sat in the isolation room, alone. Again.

I kept thinking about Molly and Isabelle.

What if Nina's cousins had weapons? My mind poked at me. They could be dead now.

I shook it off. Don't think about that.

Weapons were still fairly rare back then. These days, kids are carrying around knives like we carried change for the payphone. Only a few of us had anything on us. The only time I had carried a knife was for a few months after some pretty ugly things had happened on the estate, and my entire friend group of girls decided to carry switch blades for protection. A seventeen-year-old girl a street over from me had been slashed twice by her boyfriend. The same guy who had strangled me in the gully a year earlier.

They had had an argument at the summer fayre, and he had told her that if she didn't shut her mouth, he would stab her. She laughed at him, and ignored him. He stormed off, and minutes later, came back with a carving knife. He slashed both her thighs open to the bone, and walked away like it was nothing. She spent seven months learning how to walk again after multiple operations, and he did four measly years in prison.

I kept mine in my sock. I took it everywhere I went. A smooth navy-blue handle hiding a sharp two-inch blade which popped out when I pressed the little black button on the side. I never used it. Hell, I never even came close to using it. We all discussed what we would do if we were attacked, and how to use the knives as effectively as possible. We sat in Maths, and in whispered voices, decided that the best thing we could do was to just stab them into the thigh of the man attacking us, and run for our lives.

'And what if they just nick our blade off us? Then what?' Isabelle had asked, realising that we would probably be arming an attacker with our own knives.

I sighed. I didn't know. That was a risk, I guess. What if the knives were turned on us?

Still, we all concluded that it was better than being unarmed.

I stared out of the isolation room window. I could hear voices echoing down the corridor. Footsteps. Laughter. I lifted up out of my isolation booth to see what it was. Vanessa walked past with her boyfriend, looked into the isolation unit, and smiled at me. I smiled back.

'You okay?' she mouthed.

'Yeah, fine!' I mouthed back, and she ran to catch up with her boyfriend.

We never did speak of that night we spent together last year, but she chatted to me most days. Kaz on the other hand had asked me at least four times whether I fancied going over to hers for another sleepover, which I politely declined. Maybe if Vanessa was going to be there, I had thought.

She hadn't been the last experience for me, not that I ever told a soul about any of them. Just as I often did in my wasted hours in isolation, I let my mind wander.

Not long after the sleepover with Vanessa, I had met a Turkish girl in a hotel whilst I was on a cheap and cheerful little holiday. She didn't speak much English, and I didn't speak much Turkish, but I felt the way she looked at me every time I walked past her for a week. The way she smiled and put her head down. I had noticed her too. Her beautiful, long black hair and dark eyes with the flicked eyeliner. She worked as a cleaner, and sometimes she worked on the reception.

I only knew a few phrases in Turkish.

'*Selam*,' I had smiled at her one morning on my way to the pool.

'*Selam!*' she had giggled back.

Hard to believe it looking back, but it still hadn't occurred to me that I was gay. On the estate, I was surrounded by men who wanted to do stuff to me. I thought it was normal

143

to have empty, boring, meaningless, even painful sex. I had never actually enjoyed it. I thought my purpose was to please them. To keep them calm. To give them what they wanted when they wanted it. If I didn't give them sex, they would cast me aside immediately.

I did wonder why I never came. Why I never felt pleasure. But I just put it to the back of my head. Maybe I was shit in bed, like Jay had told everyone. Maybe there was something wrong with me. I should probably go to the doctor, I guess.

What would I say though? Sex feels like nothingness? Sex feels boring and meaningless? That I just wait for them to come, fake an orgasm, lie to them that they were brilliant in bed, and go home wondering why everyone raved about sex being so good?

I hadn't even considered that my feelings for girls were valid. Or real. Or anything. They were just . . . fantasies, that were best left in my head.

One humid night before we left, I sneaked out of the hotel to explore the bars by myself. The guys on the beach bar had been serving me alcohol all week, and had given me directions to some exciting bars up the road. They told me they would show me a great night out, and I wasn't going to pass up that opportunity.

Plus, I was hoping to see her again on reception, or mopping the floors. I made myself look as pretty as I could (which was no easy task with the worst sunburn I had ever had, skin peeling off my Rudolph-red nose, my dark roots desperately needing bleaching). I skipped, no, floated down to the lobby. My heart sank. No one on reception. I hung around for a little while, hoping to 'bump' into her, but she never came.

It was midnight, and I knew I had to get out of the hotel before someone noticed I was missing. Mum, Mark and the rest of them had gone back to their rooms, and they had been letting me stay up in the beach bar so they would just assume I was there. I checked my reflection in the huge polished mirrors in the lobby, and made my way out into the hot night air.

The directions were perfect, and I quickly found myself on a packed street of open top bars, clubs, and promoter women in bikinis giving out free shots as you walked past, to entice you into their bar. I gladly took as many shots as I could get away with, and then went into one of the bars with a light up dancefloor and a rooftop bar.

Shakira blasted out of the speakers, and I went over to the bar to order a double vodka and orange. I was fifteen but I looked older, and I was never checked for ID. I sipped at my cold drink and watched the men and women jump around, spin, twist and boogie on the dancefloor as the songs changed.

'Wheeeeeyyyyyyy!' I heard a man shout behind me and grab my shoulders. I looked around to see Utku and Mehmet, the bartenders from the hotel beach bar.

I grinned at them both, they looked so sharp in their skinny jeans and slim shirts. Say what you like, but Turkish guys know how to dress. They made the men on the council estate look like Rab C. Nesbitt.

Mehmet was a handsome, tall, thin twenty-three-year-old guy who had recently finished his military service, and had decided to move to the coast where he could live a more liberal life. He liked the tourists, the bars, the drinking, the smoking, the sex. Utku was shorter, athletic, with jet black spiked hair. He was the hotel's tattoo artist, but he sometimes did shifts on the bar for extra cash. They both looked great, and smelled great. Utku had his eye on a woman he fancied from the hotel, but Mehmet gave me vibes that he wasn't interested in women.

Both guys had spent almost every night chatting to me in the bar, and hadn't once made me feel uncomfortable. They taught me about everything from Turkish politics to Turkish food. I had taken their MSN Messenger adds, and they had begged me to come out to the bars before I left.

'You came!' Mehmet hugged me.

'Yeah of course! Told ya I would!' I laughed.

'Can I get you drink?' Utku asked. I looked at my almost-full drink and nodded. Why not? Utku ordered us all another round, and leant against the bar.

'Dance with me!' Before I even had chance to make a decision, Mehmet grabbed my hands and pulled me onto the multi-coloured dancefloor. He was a brilliant dancer, and we spent hours partying, jumping, twirling each other under our arms and doing the macarena. Round after round, more free shots, and hours of dancing eventually meant that we needed to catch our breath.

'So . . .' Mehmet shouted over the music, leaning back into the sofa, 'you like the girl, ah?'

I nearly choked on my drink. What did he just say?

'What?' I laughed at him in shock, attempting to play dumb.

'The girl. You like her. Right?'

I was gobsmacked. How had he noticed that? Had she said something?

'The girl. She is on . . . how you say . . . *resepsiyon* . . . uhhh . . . *masasi* . . . sorry my English . . .'

I laughed at his apology. He could speak incredible English, and here he was apologising to me, who could speak about twenty words of Turkish.

'You laugh?' He grinned and slapped his knee. 'I am right!'

'How did you know that?' I blushed.

'Oh! It is how you say . . . *bariz* . . . in the open!'

Oh god. How embarrassing. This stranger I had been speaking to for a few days could tell I fancied the girl at the hotel. I wonder if my parents had noticed. Oh god. I felt sick.

'Maybe you can talk to her?' He leant into me.

'I don't speak good enough Turkish,' I admitted, omitting the fact that I would have absolutely no idea how to flirt with a girl. Boys were so easy to read, easy to direct, to manipulate – but girls were something else. They were too smart to play like the boys on the estate. For one, girls don't think with their dick, on account of not having one rule their brain.

'You don't need Turkish. Smile. Dance. She will know.' He smiled and looked over my shoulder. 'She is here . . .'

My heart skipped. What? Here? The girl from the hotel?

'Where?' I shook as Mehmet subtly pointed her out on the dancefloor, along with some of the other staff from the hotel. She spun around to the music, her wavy black hair floating on the air around her. Her perfect smile, the way she bent over when she laughed at her colleague's terrible dancing. The golden bangles on her arm. The earrings. The anklet shining in the disco lights.

He laughed as I spiralled (unknowingly) into a gay panic.

'Her name is Afet. She is new this season,' he tried to get through my spinning mind.

'Uhh, yeah. Afet . . . Okay.' I was distracted, watching her laugh, skip, and dance in her minidress.

'*Serefe!*' he proclaimed and put his glass up to mine.

'Cheers!' I laughed back, and clinked our glasses.

'Now go!' he said firmly. I looked at him. He was being serious. He stood up behind me, picked up his drink, and prodded me in the back.

I guess we were going over there together, then.

I took a deep breath, steadied myself on my own huge heels, and prayed I wouldn't slip or trip on my way over to her. The intrusive thoughts as I walked over were out of control. What if I trip down that little step? What if I throw my drink over her as I fall? What if I go flying and knock myself out? What if she laughs at me? What if I fall into her? What if I headbutt her? What if I knock my front teeth out on the multicoloured dancefloor, and I am lying in front of this beautiful girl, toothless, crying, with blood running down my face?

Stop it, I told myself. Be confident. Be cool. Be calm. Be fucking normal, for fuck's sake! Don't think about knocking your own teeth out, that's not sexy. Goddammit.

'*Selam!*' I masked, perfectly. Calm. Cool. Confident.

She smiled at me and put her head down. She carried on dancing with her friends.

Now what?

Mehmet looked at me and rolled his eyes. He took a sip of his drink and gestured to dance.

I held my drink, did an awkward two-step to the music and looked like a wooden prick. At least I hadn't fallen over, though.

After hours of dancing and having fun, I lost the ability to move my body to music. Mehmet was watching me nosedive this opportunity to talk to the girl from the hotel, and was somewhere between bursting into laughter and losing his temper with me.

He grabbed hold of me, danced with me, and whispered in my ear.

'Just relax! You look frightened of the girl!'

Lord. There was only one thing for it. Drink more.

Every drink relaxed me a little more. We danced in a group, and I kept catching her eye. She didn't dance near me, or even gesture towards me though, so eventually, I gave up and just danced with Mehmet, Utku, and the woman Utku had finally managed to pull.

'Need toilet!' I yelled at them around 3:30am, and stumbled off the dancefloor to climb some swanky but sticky glass stairs up to the ladies' bathrooms. I could only just safely get up that deathtrap, and as I came out of the toilet cubicle, I drunkenly decided to take off my shoes to get back down the glass stairs without falling to my inevitable and embarrassing death.

As I bent over to take off my MaryJane platform shoes, I noticed a familiar golden anklet, twinkling under the spotlights.

I followed up her legs, and her little black halter neck dress, to see the girl from the hotel stood in front of me.

'Toilet is free!' I said, pointing at the only toilet that was working in the club.

'Ummm . . . No English . . .' she smiled, confused.

'*Tuvalet?*' I tried, pointing at the free toilet.

I took off my shoes, and noticed she was slightly taller than me.

'No, no, no!' she laughed, needlessly covering her perfect smile as she giggled and shook her head.

'Oh . . .' I mumbled, as I realised she had followed me deliberately. She wasn't here for the toilet.

She looked into my eyes. I knew that look. The same one Vanessa gave me at the sleepover.

'Come!' She took my hand, looked over her shoulder, flashed me her brilliant smile, and pulled me into the tiny cubicle, locking the door behind us.

Her hands were all over me in an instant. She kept talking to me between breathy kisses, but I couldn't understand her, and I didn't care. I ran my fingers through her hair and tasted the rum she had been drinking all night.

I don't know if we were in there for thirty seconds or two hours. All I knew was that I was in heaven, and Afet was there with me.

Heaven was a sticky, tiny, dark toilet cubicle in a cheesy bar in Gumbet.

I sat in the dusty isolation room. The memory of the encounter in the bar toilets faded, and weirdly, I interrogated it no further. Nothing crossed my mind. I can't lie and say that I sat there questioning my sexuality or what it all meant. I didn't think anything.

Ever since Emmy had said it was just experimenting, that's what I had put it down to. Nothing more. Nothing else to think about. Just a silly thing teen girls do when they are experimenting. We all grow out of it. Don't we?

And the rapes . . . the abuse . . . the drugs and the drink . . . the cars . . . the violence around me . . . that was just all part of the road too. Wasn't it? Almost every girl I knew was going through it. It was just part of life on the estate, wasn't it?

We were all living our own wild lives, weren't we?

Emmy was still shagging Ash on his dining table. Kaz was desperate for another sleepover. Lozza had the morning after pill so many times that she was worried she was infertile forever.

Tonie had a black eye from stealing a bag of coke from a guy when he fell asleep. Hannah would nod at me up Fezzi but wouldn't acknowledge me at school.

Rachel was two-timing Danny with his best mate, Billy.

Hannah was still chatting to the dude from the military, and they had agreed to meet up next week.

Molly was spiralling into a deep depression because her dad announced he was living a double life, and had another wife and two secret kids.

Isabelle had shaved her head because the registered sex offender they had placed down her cul-de-sac kept grabbing her hair when she walked to school.

A group of the popular girls at school all got treated for chlamydia because one lad had shagged them all and given them all STDs.

Lorna was pregnant again. So was Sara. And Marie. And Jordan. And Emma.

7

Don't let the hoodie fool you

Summer 2017

The pale, thin, thirteen-year-old girl with the flat, dark hair stared blankly into the camera whilst the thirty-something man in the dirty two-stripe tracksuit raped her. I winced.

The scene switched. Another man walked in. The terrified girl is pinned up against a wall whilst he rapes her too. The scene switched. A fat old guy pushes her face into the dirty bed whilst he rapes her. The scene fades out.

The music played.

The voice of the girl came over the next shot of her crying on the bed after the men have all left her in a crumpled, naked heap.

'You see, I should have seen the signs. I thought I knew what I was doing. I thought I was grown up. I thought I was in control.'

I paused the clip on the huge screen behind me, and turned to stare at the audience of five hundred totally silent social workers.

I gripped the podium in utter disgust. I was shaking.

'Shall we watch one more?' I asked them, facetiously.

Another short silence, and the huge screen kicked back to life.

The blonde fifteen-year-old girl ran for her life, naked from being raped just moments earlier. She ran out of the house, through the fields and out into the darkness. Her breathing was heavy. She sobbed as she ran. But he gained on her. He kept gaining on her. She tripped, and landed face down in the mud.

The music volume increases. Her eyes widen. He sits on top of her. The camera switches to him, as he slams a brick into her head over and over again. Until her screams stop. Until her body stops moving. Until she is still. Until he has done the unthinkable.

As the film ends, her parents identify her body in a morgue and fall to their knees, screaming in agony.

A black screen replaces the imagery.

White text appears.

Stop and think.

When you meet someone online, you don't always know who you are talking to . . .

I gritted my teeth. I gave myself a few seconds to calm, collect my thoughts, and think about what I was going to say next. I turned to look at the audience of professionals from around the UK. A sea of faces, tables, notebooks, lanyards and duty mobile phones.

'Do you know my first thoughts, when I am watching these films?'

A thousand eyes looked up at me on the stage. I straightened my glasses, projected my voice, and made sure to speak into the microphone on the podium. I didn't have any notes to look down at, because I was a chronic ad-lib speaker. There was nothing I could do to prepare for my speeches, and even if I did prepare, I would never even look at the notes in front of me.

I knew what I came to say, and I knew the points I needed to make. I didn't need structure, or prose, or the odd safe-for-work joke about coffee, or presentation cards with neat bullet points on them. I just needed as many professionals as possible to understand that those films should be banned.

'I am going to talk to you about my thoughts, and why I believe these films are one of the worst things that ever happened to our social work, psychological and therapeutic practice with teenage girls. I have around thirty minutes, and then I can take questions from the audience.'

I always knew the professionals that disagreed with me. Even in a room of five hundred people, I had become a master of spotting the shift in body language, the eye contact changing, the lips tightening, the brow lowering, the way the shoulders move when someone doesn't believe something, the way they tip their head back when they are exasperated, the way they fidget when they are uncomfortable, the way they glance over at their colleague in a silent language which says, 'What a load of horse shit' or 'We do that . . . is she talking about us?'

It didn't intimidate me, but I had learned to use it as constant biofeedback. I could monitor which points they accepted and agreed with, and which ones needed more work, or maybe a different angle. I was part lecturer, part influencer.

Huge social change doesn't come from neutrally presenting information and then telling people that they can do what they wish with it. I was at the forefront of presenting some of the most contentious and difficult concepts in my field of work. I was the person brave enough to get up in front of five hundred people and let them ask me increasingly difficult questions whilst I thought on my feet, explained theories, evidence bases, arguments and statistics. I was the person the authorities called in when they needed someone to present a completely different way of thinking and practising.

I was good at it, but it was hard work. And much of it was an act. That's what you have to learn to do, you see – act.

When I stepped on that stage – whether it was a small talk to fifteen people, or a speech to five hundred social workers in a conference venue – I was 'on'. I walked up, and became who I needed to be to command a room, to present new ideas, to influence people to be better, to think critically, and to challenge the status quo. I had learned quickly that I was not my persona. I am much more introverted than the version of me that delivers the speeches, but what good was an introverted, exhausted, private person whilst trying to convince thousands of people to change the way they treat teenage girls? Jung once said that we must never be fooled into thinking we are our persona, and he was of course right, but most people had never seen any other version of me. They must think I wander around my day-to-day life, giving speeches, commanding attention, and debating topics with people.

I cannot tell you how many people have met me over the years and said the words, 'You are nothing like how I imagined you would be! I thought you would be really intimidating and professional all the time!'

Never the words you want to hear when you're six drinks deep in a bar, or you're walking through Sainsbury's with your kids.

I was an excellent public speaker, but I was tired of professionals being fed watered-down, over-simplified bullshit. I was sick of them being given prescriptive instructions.

Processes they had to follow. Their professional judgement was often ignored in favour of risk averse practice, and their critical thinking had all but packed up and fucked off.

The way I saw it: They had brains. Let's use them. Let's challenge them. Let's wake them back up and light a fire under them. These are capable humans.

I became the force that could move a room of experienced and smart people from totally disagreeing with me – tutting, shaking their heads – to realising that they had never looked at the issue from my perspective, they had never seen my evidence base before, and maybe, I was right after all.

I had been forced to become that powerful and engaging public speaker over the years for three main reasons.

The first was that I was a woman. The second was that I was in my twenties. The third was that I was a Stokie. Three of those together causes three main reactions.

The first is that my ideas are not listened to, and people assume I am talking out of my arse. The second is that people become annoyed that someone half their age is telling them how to do their job. The third is that people question my background and my qualifications because I don't 'sound like an academic' or 'look like an academic'.

Sometimes I wondered if I would be taken more seriously if I turned up in tweed and a monocle, smoking a pipe and dragging around a chaise longue for effect. Maybe people would take me more seriously if I went off on wordy, meandering tangents that sounded intelligent but meant fuck all.

I had lost count of how many times a psychologist, teacher, social worker, CEO or academic had put their hand up during my speeches and confident as anything, asked, 'How old are you?'

Tiring. Rude.

And don't even get me started on how many times I was mistaken for the cleaner, or the admin, or the students, or a stranger who shouldn't even be allowed in the venue. One time, I was told to take my seat because 'Jessica was about to start speaking'.

'No, thank you,' I had smiled to the irritated young man.

And I had smiled at him again, whilst I asked everyone to take their seats, take out their notepads and laptops, and began my lecture.

He had sunk into his chair.

But this wasn't an audience of young undergraduate students, this was an audience of experienced and qualified social workers. A mixed bunch. They always were. Some of them would be exceptional. Some of them shouldn't be working with anything with a pulse.

But most of them were passionate, caring, exhausted, under-resourced, traumatised and overworked. They were holding thirty or forty cases of child abuse each. They were doing their best. Their days consisted of some of the worst abuse imaginable. They were woken up in the night to rush to A&E because a newborn baby boy had been thrown at a wall by his own dad, who just lost a game on his Xbox. They were frantically searching for missing children. Begging services to provide therapy to the five-stone teenage girl who hadn't eaten since her uncle raped her. Desperately trying to keep families together. Saddened when they realise that the only option is to place children into foster care.

They were distressed. They were disillusioned. They were drinking. They were sleep deprived. They felt immense guilt at dropping their own kids off at childminders at 6am and not picking them up until 7pm every day. They survived on junk food and gin.

And I was stood in front of them, telling them that the films they had been showing to teenage girls for the last seven years should be banned. You can probably see why I had a reputation like Marmite.

There were just as many social workers aggressively nodding along to every word I said, as if their head might actually fall off their neck in agreement and validation of their own concerns about the films, as there were social workers who wished I would just shut up and go home.

I understood my audience. I empathised. But we all had a responsibility to protect these teenage girls from harm and abuse – and that included those films. It was non-negotiable for me. The films needed to end. Ideally, we needed to borrow the DeLorean, get it up to 88 miles per hour and go back to the moment someone thought it was a good idea to make a film about a teenage girl being repeatedly raped in order to show it to thousands of other teenage girls to 'make them see the risks they were putting themselves at'.

I wish you could see my face as I just wrote that sentence. My eyes just rolled harder than the time I was caught doing it live on camera on BBC's *The Big Questions*. Not my finest moment, but my face never lies.

A Black woman in her late forties put her hand up, and a runner passed her a microphone. She stood up and smoothed her long patchwork skirt down with one hand. I smiled at her reassuringly. I knew how nervous people could get when asking questions of a speaker.

'Thank you for your talk today. We have been showing these films to teenage girls for years. I think many of my colleagues here today will agree that we were told that by showing these . . . hard-hitting . . . films to the girls, they would understand the . . . risks . . . they were taking . . . and then they would be less likely to be sexually abused . . . Are you saying that these films have no value in preventing sexual violence?'

I loved this question. Great question. I told her so.

She smiled and sat down. Five or six more hands went up. I looked around the room, they were engaged and ready. I began.

'Great question, thank you for starting us off. Do the films have any value in preventing sexual violence? In my view, the answer to that is no.'

A sea of faces displayed a range of responses. Some smiling. Some nodding. Some glancing at their work bestie. Some shaking their head. Some staring at their feet.

'Let me explain my answer here. Showing those films to girls will never stop the perpetrators. The abusers. The rapists. The only prevention possible in sexual abuse of teenage girls, is to stop the perpetrators and to protect the girls. This is because the only people responsible for sexual violence – are the sex offenders themselves.' I scanned the room. Most people were with me so far.

'Girls who are being groomed, abused, controlled and raped by grown adult male sex offenders should not be expected to watch traumatic, graphic films and then take that learning to protect themselves.' I was clear, calm, firm.

'When a girl sits and watches these films in assembly, in her classroom or with her social worker, will that prevent her abuser from controlling and manipulating her? No. Will it stop the power he already has over her? No. Will it stop him from wanting to harm her? No. It will not prevent any sexual violence. But it makes us feel like we are doing something useful, doesn't it? Like we have intervened? Like we have done something to write on the case notes?'

Some people winced. It was a spiky point to make. It was the elephant in the room. They didn't like it, but they didn't disagree, either. I decided to continue whilst I watched the runner take the mic to the far end of the room.

'Oftentimes, the films are used in response to resourcing issues – busy teams with high caseloads show the films because they simply do not have the time or staff to implement complex and nuanced preventative and protective work. Again, in these examples, it does nothing to actually prevent the sexual violence towards the girls, but everyone can feel as though they have done something practical. Of course, this does mean that people can say things like "But we showed her the film! Why didn't she see the signs?" which is ultimately just another way to victim blame . . .'

A middle-aged white guy in chinos and a light blue shirt at the back of the room stood up as he was handed the mic.

The poor runner was getting her steps in today.

'Lovely to meet you, Jessica. I think we have exchanged emails before, and I follow you on social media. I just wondered if you could be clear about whether you feel the films are being shown deliberately, out of malice or whatever, or whether this is an example of a resourcing issue rather than victim blaming? Isn't it just a case that it is easier and quicker to use the films, pile a few hundred kids into a sports hall, get them to watch the film and then we can all say we showed them the film? Job done?'

Men did this sometimes.

They would rephrase something I just said, not to take the conversation any further, but to publicly show that they understood what I was saying. I didn't mind too much. It was a waste of time for everyone else whilst these men peacocked about the fact that they had done the absolute bare minimum of simply listening to what I was saying. Some women crossed their arms and rolled their eyes whilst he mirrored my own point back, and then asked me whether

I agreed with him – but at least he wasn't asking me how old I was.

I thanked him for his 'question', and he sat down, proud of himself. Oblivious to the number of us that had just been humouring him for his few seconds with the mic.

The mic was passed to a younger white woman, her hair scraped up into a messy ginger bun. She was wearing a stripy navy and white blazer and dark navy skinny trousers. She cleared her throat and tapped the mic before speaking.

'So, you say these films are harming girls. You showed us the films, and I must say, looking at them with fresh eyes, and hearing you speak today, I hadn't really considered what we were doing. Some of those scenes made me want to be sick. I have sat here with my team today, and we all feel thoroughly uncomfortable. We have a residential care home for teenage girls, and on all of their care plans, we are told that we need to show them the films, make them do the sessions and the exercises, and teach them about their own risk-taking behaviours which "led" to them being raped and abused. I don't even know what my question is any more . . . sorry . . . I just . . . what are we supposed to do? If we don't use these films any more? How do we get them to see what they've done . . . uhh . . . what has been done to them?'

I felt for her. This kind of stream of confused and competing ideas was common in my sessions. People needed time to process what I was saying, but sometimes, they jumped to wanting solutions before they had even realised how embedded the victim blaming was.

She sat down awkwardly, looked around, and passed the mic to the runner. One of her colleagues patted her on the arm to reassure her. She looked upset.

'Thank you for that. I just want to say that you won't be alone in this room. The way you are feeling is common.

You will be surrounded today by professionals who feel the same way as you. Let's be honest – most of you in this room have made girls watch those films. I know without asking you that some of you have watched those girls have panic attacks in front of you. Some of you have even made girls watch those films over and . . .'

She stood back up. The runner took the mic off someone else and rushed it back to her. Her voice wobbled and cracked.

'I have personally made girls watch those films. I . . . have done that. Last year, a girl was referred to us who had been trafficked all over Birmingham . . . and . . . she was . . . described as difficult . . . and putting herself at risk. I was told to make her watch the films over and over again until she "understood what she had done".' She paused, she welled up. She gulped.

I smiled at her as reassuringly as I could. 'I understand.'

'But, but . . . she hadn't done anything wrong. She had been trafficked. She had been drugged. She had been driven all over the city. She had been given drugs and alcohol by men for years. She thought it was normal. She had been raped hundreds of times. She had miscarriage after miscarriage. She was cutting herself. She tried to kill herself four times . . . And everyone was blaming her. She was seen as the problem!' she continued.

I felt sick. My head spun. She carried on talking, but I couldn't hear her any more. Her voice was this empty, echoey blah blah blah, just bouncing around my head.

Shit. I had triggered.

Fuck. Stay calm. Fuck. Do not go back there. Do not go back there, Jess.

Stay in the present. Stay here. I gripped the podium so hard that my fingertips went white.

I breathed. I started my grounding ritual whilst trying to maintain some connection to the conversation, to the room I was in, to the year I was in.

I rubbed my ear. I played with my earring. I tucked my hair behind my ear. I rubbed my ear. I played with my earring. I untucked my hair, and then tucked it again.

I felt myself coming back. I took a sip of my cold drink on the podium. I tried to remember what she had been saying, but she was still in full flow. To my relief, it was easy to pick back up with her, as she was still telling the same story.

How long had I been out for? A few seconds? A few minutes? Who knows?

Focus, Jess.

'And . . . we showed her that film eleven times. Eleven . . . She begged me not to keep showing it to her, and I just kept telling her . . . that she needed to . . . do the work to process her own . . . risk taking . . .'

Her colleagues were looking up at her. Some were horrified at her confessions. Some were looking at her with love and concern, and one of them was crying.

I decided to intervene as she continued to spill out this traumatic realisation that she had harmed a girl she was trying to help.

'What is your name?' I asked gently, still practising my grounding technique to pull me back.

'Me? Uhh . . . Marie . . .' She hesistated.

'Marie, I just wanted to take a few moments to thank you so much for being so honest, and so reflective today. I can tell this has hurt you. I can hear it in your voice, I can see it in your eyes. I can see the way your team are looking up to you. They should be very proud to have such an honest team leader . . .'

Marie looked down and around at her table, as if she had forgotten there was anyone else in the room other than me and her. She looked up and around the room. The gravity of what she had just said hit her. She quickly sat down, her hand shaking as she took a sip from her water bottle. Her team shuffled and moved around her to check she was okay.

I let her rest.

'What has just been discussed is common practice. Teenage girls who have been groomed, abused, drugged, controlled, threatened, manipulated and raped are often the ones positioned as the problem. The perpetrators very rarely see the inside of a police station, and our conviction rates in the UK are less than 2 per cent in sexual offences. We know our justice system is broken, and we don't understand how to stop sex offenders, so we hyperfocus on the victims.' I began to relax back into teaching, and my act took over again. Phew.

'If we can focus on the victims, and make them change something about themselves, we never have to address the massive systemic issue of child abuse and sexual violence towards girls and women. If we can convince each other that showing these films to teenage girls will prevent sexual violence, we can feel as though we are useful and valued. No one wants to feel helpless and hopeless at work – I know you all want to feel that you are doing something positive to protect children – but this isn't it.'

I looked around the room; I had every single person's attention.

'Listen to my words. This isn't it. This isn't right. These films perpetuate victim blaming. It places responsibility on the girls you work with to protect themselves, when you can't even protect them from these rapists yourselves!'

The mic was passed to an Indian woman in her fifties. She wore a sharp suit. I recognised her from somewhere.

'Jessica, thank you for such a challenging session today. I think I agree with all of the points you are making, but several of my leadership team and I need to know what we are supposed to use instead. Are you making some more ethical films? What do we use with these vulnerable girls?'

She seemed robust enough, so I pushed back.

'Why do you need a film at all?'

She hesitated.

'Sorry, what do you mean?' she clarified.

'I will certainly not be seeking to make more of these films, but I wondered if you could explain why you feel there is a need for the films at all?'

'Oh, I see.' She relaxed again. 'Well, the staff use them to explain the sexual violence to the young girls we work with, and then to talk to them about consent, and risk taking, spotting the signs of abuse, reporting to the police and so on . . .'

This response was alarmingly common. Professionals with an abundance of skill had become over-reliant on these toxic films, and were using them instead of real conversations.

'Interesting . . . so, could your staff not just talk to the girls about those topics? Why do they need the films?'

She was stumped. It was as if no one had ever actually discussed the use of these resources, despite estimates showing over one million children had been shown them across five to seven years.

'Do you show films of domestic abuse to children who are being subjected to domestic abuse at home? Films of Daddy beating Mummy up, perhaps?'

'No . . .'

'Do you show children films of child neglect? Films of starving children, with no clean clothes, being locked in confined spaces for days at a time?'

'Well . . . no, obviously not . . .'

'So why would we use that tactic with sexual violence? Why are we so set on showing these girls scenes of child rape? Are these films even ethical? What about the child actress who has been forced to film simulated rape for days on end?'

She pondered. She fidgeted with her lanyard.

'I had never really questioned why we don't use the films in other areas of our work. I guess in those areas, our staff just build the relationships with the children, and explain everything to them in an age-appropriate and sensitive way. It doesn't make sense that we put on a DVD and get them to watch these films in our sexual abuse practice, but not in our other areas of safeguarding. I mean . . . come to think of it, we don't use it in familial abuse either. We don't show little children films of Mum and Dad sexually abusing them in the bath, do we?'

I smiled. She gets it. And not only her, but she had hundreds of people nodding along with her.

'You're absolutely right. We don't. So, what we need to step back and ask ourselves, is why we thought this was acceptable practice with teenage girls in the first place. Why have we done this to them, and why did we think it would help them?'

Suddenly, the host for my session appeared in my peripheral vision and I realised it was time for me to wrap up my talk.

'I would just like to say thank you for listening to me today, and thank you for engaging with these ideas. If you have used these films, you cannot undo what has already been done, but you can move forward, from today, without them. No other children need to see scenes of child rape in order to be supported by your services. I understand that for some of you, this will have been a particularly challenging session, and I encourage you to seek some support, talk to your supervisors and the colleagues you trust, and potentially host a reflection session tomorrow in your team meetings, to discuss how you all feel about changing your practice from now on . . .'

The host walked towards me, holding her notes. I gave way to her on the podium, and stood to her left.

'I would like to add, before you all go to lunch, that it has been a fascinating and thought-provoking morning with Jessica, and it has given me a lot to think about. I think we all owe her a round of applause, don't you?'

Oh god. No matter how many times this had happened, I never got used to it. What do you even do whilst five hundred people stand there and clap at you?

I cannot tell you how many times I had clapped along. Clapping. Myself. For no reason. If you ever see a video of me doing the rounds, looking dazed, clapping myself after my own speech, you now know it's because I panic from embarrassment, and don't know what else to do.

It goes on for way too long, and I just stand there, blushing, feeling totally silly, and waiting for them all to go and get their sixth coffee of the day.

Eventually it ended, and I then had the inevitable string of professionals queue up to talk to me privately. It happened at every event. Some people would never dream of standing up to ask me a question, but they would make sure to wait for me after my speech to grab five minutes with me. I met hundreds of intelligent, fascinating and inquisitive people that way.

However, that day was different.

A silver-haired man in a smart suit made a beeline for me. Determined. Quick. Forceful. He pushed past a woman, briefly apologising, and carried on towards me. I pretended I hadn't noticed him, and started to pack up my things. I could feel his energy before he had even got near me. I took a deep breath in and out, and put my game face back on.

'Hello. I just wanted to come over and tell you about something I am working on at the moment. To prevent sexual violence towards children as young as three. I don't agree with anything you said in that talk, and I am surprised by how many of my colleagues were taken in by what you were saying . . .'

Oh lord above. Here we go, I thought.

Here it comes. The monologue.

'I am head of development over at Abuse Support Foundation. I have been there for the past seventeen years, and I manage a team of around thirty staff, all working with sex offenders and those who have the potential to offend against children. I also sit on the equalities board, and the development board for the organisation. As you probably know, I am the sole author of the programme of work we are developing for children as young as three years old,' he listed at me.

Also, I did not know this man from Adam. 'As I probably know?' Who was this dude?

My blank expression did not stop him in his flow at all, and he merely continued listing position after position, board after board. He was like a shit Strippergram who mansplained his entire CV to me instead of doing the strip-tease. Monologue-a-gram. Monologue Man.

I didn't even care what his name was any more.

I dub thee Monologue Man.

I zoned back in, and unsurprisingly, he was still going. Living up to his name.

'And so I am just testing my programme now, and I know you won't agree, but I do think young children can keep themselves safe from sexual predators. Small children need to know that it is not okay to go into the bathroom with their parents. Their parents could be abusers themselves. They need to know that their parents could abuse them in the bath, for example, and we need to be teaching these children how to protect themselves . . .'

Wait. What?

'Sorry, did you just say that children need to know that they shouldn't go into a bathroom with their own parents?'

'Yes.'

'How will they be potty trained?'

'I knew you wouldn't agree. This is why I think your talk today is misguided, and misrepresents preventative work. The world isn't all sunshine and flowers you know. These abusers exist, and the only way we can stop the abuse is by getting these children to protect themselves!'

'You're right about one thing. I don't agree with you at all. Who are you again?'

Oh god. That was a mistake.

'My name is Eric. I am head of development over at Abuse Support Foundation. I have been there for the past seventeen years, and I manage a team of around thirty staff, all working with sex offenders and those who have the potential to offend against children. I also sit on the equalities board, and the development board for the organisation. As you now know, I am the sole author of the programme of work we are developing for children as young as . . .'

What the fuck was he doing now? He was like a broken AI chatbot.

'And you are . . . What? Just a mum or something?'

A mum or something?

What a misogynistic little prick.

He stared at me, waiting for me to launch into a huge defensive answer about my experience and my PhD. And reader, I very nearly bit. I was so close to falling into his little trap.

But then a spark hit me. He couldn't answer my questions so instead he reduced me to the lowest thing he could think of: a mum. Wow. I just learned an incredible amount about Monologue Man.

I performatively laughed at him. I wasn't going to let him get the best of me.

'Darling, I'm the keynote speaker,' I stated as I left him stood in his place.

What an idiot, I thought to myself, as I got comfortable on the train. I had treated myself to a first-class ticket home, and waited for the service. I still thought it was absolutely brilliant that I could be served food, drinks and snacks in the first-class carriage of a train. To be honest, I still haven't got bored of that.

It was five hours home on the train, and the kids would be ready for bed by the time I got there. Just like the social workers I was teaching, childminders and afterschool club was saving my ass Monday to Friday. I was working full time, getting home, feeding the kids, getting them bathed and ready for bed, washing their uniforms and then settling down to do a few hours on my PhD every night.

It was heavy, but it was a million miles from my life only a few years earlier, and I was grateful for every opportunity I had worked for.

After the speech, I had changed into a tracksuit and oversized hoodie for the train, hoping I could pull my hood up and get some sleep once I became tired of reading and writing. I pulled out my dark green notebook with the gold paisley patterns, and my favourite uniball pen.

Freewriting was, and still is, my favourite writing technique. I am doing it right now, to write this book for you to read. I started freewriting when I was twenty-five years old, having never heard of it before. I usually have to freewrite by hand, as for some reason, it is much more effective that way.

For those of you who don't know what this technique is, it is a brilliant method for overcoming self-judgement, procrastination and writer's block. All you have to do is write. Anything. A stream of your consciousness. No edits. No deleting. No going back. No changing anything you have written. You just write and write and write, even if it is a load of waffly bollocks. You just keep going.

What it does is clear your mind of all the other things you are thinking of, by letting them flow out. Rather than repressing them, let them out, get them down on the paper, and keep writing until your writing and thinking becomes clear and linear again. Get your ideas out as they hit you, in an unstructured and organic way. Time yourself for 20 minutes, and do not stop. Just write what you think. It helps with everything from journaling to reflexive practice in science.

I'll show you what I mean, ready?

Okay, so this paragraph is going to show what freewriting is.

God, I never thought I would be writing about this in the fucking memoir. How boring has my life got? Ah well, maybe someone will take something from it. It changed my life. I went from staring at a page for two days in my undergraduate degree to being able to write ten thousand words per day using this technique. I mean, not immediately, obviously. It takes time. The first time I did it, I think I wrote waffle. Actually, that makes me think, I need to go and dig out all my old journals and my old PhD notebook to have a flick back through my old stuff. I love doing that. I bloody loved those moleskin journals, do they still exist? I think they were from Rymans. Was it Paperchase? Paperchase stopped selling my wife's favourite biros recently, and she has gone on about it for months. I wish they would bring them back just so I didn't have to hear the story about Paperchase stopping selling her favourite biros again. I had better stop really. I dread having to say this out loud for the audiobook. The fucking producer is going to be sat there thinking, 'Who the fuck gave this idiot a multi-book deal?'

Okay. Enough of that. I am going to leave it there, unedited, and see if I get that past the editor. If you're reading this, woohoo!

Anyway, so I was sat on the train, cuddled up in my huge black hoodie, headphones in, freewriting as usual. I had a sharer bag of cheese and onion crisps next to me because that's the law, and I was in my own little world when I felt a tap on my shoulder.

I looked up at the man in the navy suit trying to get my attention.

I pulled my Beats headphones down and took my hood down.

'You all right?' I asked, confused.

He seemed annoyed with me.

'This is first class,' he stated, as if I didn't know. He crossed his arms and raised both eyebrows.

'Yeah, I know . . .'

'Well, standard coaches are that way.' He pointed through the doors and down the train.

'Yeah . . . I know . . .' I paused my music on my phone.

He tapped one foot in annoyance. He cleared his throat.

'Some of us pay to be in first class, you know. It isn't for . . . everyone . . .' The man lowered his voice whilst he told me off like some stupid teenage girl. Some things never changed.

I sat up straight, closed my notebook, placed my pen on the table and looked him in the eye.

'I paid to be here,' I tried to say it politely, but I accidentally gritted my teeth instead.

'What? You?' he sneered, still stood over me.

'Yes, me.'

'Well, we will see about that, won't we? They will throw you off at the next station if you don't have a ticket, you know!' He stormed off down the carriage, and I slumped back into my seat.

I looked around the first-class carriage. Was anyone going to intervene in this ridiculous confrontation, or was I going to be left to deal with this alone? Was anyone going to ask if I was okay?

Several people in business suits, both men and women, put their heads down, looked at their laptops, or tried to pretend they weren't fascinated by the unfolding drama.

It was frankly amazing how something as simple as a hoodie could cause me to go from standing on a stage giving a speech about my research one minute, to being talked to like I was back on the estate the next.

Had I paid for my ticket? Pfft. Paid?

No, I had been practically robbed for that ticket. It was cheaper to fly to Benidorm, get fucked up all weekend, and fly back than it was to get a first-class train ticket from Stoke to Glasgow.

As I settled back down, the annoying man came storming back into the end of the carriage with a train attendant closely following him.

For fuck's sake, I rolled my eyes. Not this again.

I decided to pretend I hadn't seen or heard them, turned my back slightly to the aisle, turned my headphones up, and carried on with my writing.

'Excuse me. Excuse me. Excuse me,' the brown-haired man in the train uniform tapped on my table to get my attention. I toyed with completely ignoring them both, and sending them into some testosterone rage meltdown, but I thought I had better engage if I didn't want to be thrown off the train five hours from home.

I pulled my headphones down around my neck again, and looked up at them both.

'This man here has reported that you don't have a ticket, could I see your ticket please?'

'Did he really? And how would he know if I had a ticket?' I challenged the attendant.

'Well, um . . . he said that you do not have a first-class ticket, and that you should be seated in the standard coach. We have lots of available seats down there, so if you would like to move . . .'

'I won't be moving. I have paid for this ticket, and this man is harassing me.'

'I am not!' the original man in the suit exclaimed, genuinely offended by the mere suggestion that he was harassing a young woman on a train.

'Could I please see your ticket?'

'On what grounds?' I tested.

'On the grounds that I have asked to see it, and you must prove you have a ticket.' The attendant was getting impatient, but I was getting less and less amicable.

'But I have already shown my ticket to your colleague who checked all of our tickets only 20 minutes ago. Could either of you explain what makes you believe I belong in standard class and not here, on my seat, in first class?'

I smiled at them both. Go on, I thought, I dare you.

They both hesitated.

Tell the truth, I thought. Go on. Do it.

'Anything?' I prodded, both of them suddenly lost for words.

'You . . . er . . . your . . .'

I raised one eyebrow at them both, enjoying the sudden twist in power dynamic.

'Because . . . it couldn't possibly be . . . what I'm wearing. Could it, guys?' I smiled at them both.

Neither of them wanted to admit it, but that was exactly what it was. A hoodie was like an invisibility cloak. No, that's not right. That's not right at all. A hoodie was like wearing a fucking neon sign saying 'SCUMBAG'.

Just like the time that woman had told her kids to stay away from me in the Co-op when I had gone to get my own kids some Calpol, because they had chickenpox. One of her little children smiled at me and I smiled back. The woman nearly broke her poor kid's wrist the way she snatched her away from me and said, 'Get away from that person' like I was going to sell her kid a squirt of the Calpol I'd just bought.

And like the time my wife and I went to an art gallery and the attendants showed everyone around except us. I had already bought four large pieces of art from that gallery, but because I turned up in an adidas tracksuit, I was completely ignored. Needless to say, I bought nothing more from them.

'Is it the hoodie?' I asked them both.

176

Come on, I thought impatiently, you were so brave beforehand. This is so much more boring now you have both disappeared up your arses.

The train attendant refused to answer me, but I could see the other guy just desperate to tell me what a lowlife piece of shit I was for sitting in the first-class carriage with him. It was right on the tip of his tongue.

Go on Gordon. Or Roger. Or Eric From Earlier. Monologue Man.

Do it. Let all your pent-up misogyny and classism out. Say it with your chest.

But like the anti-climaxes only men can truly deliver, they said fuck all. Just like I should have done, in that gully all those years ago.

I lost my temper.

'Here's my first-class ticket,' I hissed, shoving my ticket at the attendant. 'Now if you wouldn't mind fucking off, I have a speech to write for tomorrow, a dataset to analyse, about two hundred unread emails to sift through, and an invoice to submit, on account of me owning my own business which affords me the luxury of sitting in this lovely first-class carriage with bellends like that guy.'

They both stared at me, horrified.

'Don't let the hoodie fool you, lads. A chav can grow up to buy her own first-class tickets, ya know.'

I put my back to them both, pulled my hoodie and my headphones back up, turned up the Missy Elliott album, and muttered to myself like Muttley from *Wacky Races*.

Something about never judging a book by its cover. Or a CEO by her hoodie.

You wait till I finish this PhD, I wrote in my notebook. Then I'll be Doctor Jessica Taylor. Still in my oversized tracksuits. I'll piss the entire world off, then!

8

You can't survive this one

Winter 2006

I stood staring at my completely empty bedroom. Even my shock echoed around it.

Mum had once let me decorate my room with my own doodles, graffiti, poems, song lyrics and artwork. Every wall was covered with black marker pen. Every time a friend came over, I drew around their hand on my wall, and they signed the middle of their handprint. One side of my tiny boxroom was dedicated to song lyrics. Around the single window that overlooked the street, I had written sayings and phrases that inspired me.

It sounds so artsy and lovely, doesn't it?

Honestly, it looked fucking terrible. It looked a lot better in my head. I had virtually no artistic talent, and my handwriting was illegible.

I'm surprised the council didn't fine us.

I just stood there.

Where were my clothes? My furniture? My bed? Where were all my possessions, my memories, my toiletries, my junk?

Mum stood behind me, thoroughly pleased with herself, and yet absolutely fizzing with rage.

'Yep! It's all gone, Jess!' She smiled at me, the anger glinting in her eye, her teeth clenched into a painful smile.

'Wh . . . what do you mean? Where is all my stuff?'

'Got rid of it.' She was joyous. Triumphant. She crossed her arms and leant against the door frame.

'Sorry, what?' I clapped my hand over my mouth. She had done her fair share of shit to me over the years, but to sell every single thing I owned in two days was pretty far-fetched.

'It's gone. All of it.' She was loving this.

'Are you being serious, Mum?'

'Do I look like I'm joking to you?' She glared at me.

No, she didn't, I thought.

All that was left was my old mattress on the floor in the corner of the room. My covers had been ripped off and slat up the corner. I didn't really have much to begin with. There was the old cream wood and canvas set of shelves that were falling apart. And I had a bed frame. And I had a mirror. But that was pretty much it.

I didn't have my CD collection any more because she took a key to them all and destroyed them, and then played dumb when I asked her how every single one had deep cuts through its centre. And I didn't have my violin any more, because she sold that too.

'There's a black bin bag of your clothes downstairs, you can take those, and you can go and live with your dad. I've had enough,' she spat at me, pointing back down the stairs to the bin bags.

'I don't get it, what have I done?' I panicked.

'You like staying with your dad so much, maybe you should go and live with him! He can deal with you!'

I was lost. I had only been at my dad's for two days over Christmas. Mum was hard enough to cope with, but

Dad was a nightmare to live with. They both had their own issues. Whilst Mum was volatile and duplicitous, Dad was a selfish alcoholic who had lost touch with reality. He had set the kitchen on fire twice recently, and both times I had found him asleep on the sofa whilst the fire licked up the grill, up the wall and on to the ceiling tiles.

We would all be dead if I hadn't woken up to the smell of burning. Twice.

Mum and I had a complicated relationship. She blamed me for many things in her own life, and the resentment was palpable. Even as a teenager, I could feel that she was in some sort of competition with me. I desperately wanted her to love me, but she would do and say increasingly unforgivable things to me as the years went by. Once she left Dad, much of her distress was projected on to me. She would scream at me that I looked just like my dad, and just like his mum, the Taylor side of the family. She would tell me that her and my sister looked like her and her mum, the Jackson side.

'You'll always be a Taylor!' she would spit at me. 'You look just like them!'

I guess she was right. As the eldest of seven siblings, I am the shortest, and I am the odd one out. One of my sisters has at least a foot of height on me. All of my siblings are giants compared to me. When we take family photos, I look like I am kneeling in a pair of fucking shoes for a laugh. When we all stood together, I looked like I was adopted, and I spent many years hoping I was.

Only the Ancestry DNA kit that my wife bought me for my thirty-first birthday could truly kick that sliver of hope from me, and trust me when I say, it did.

It was also the day I learned that my mum had lied to me about my heritage my entire life. Do you know what it feels like to look at your DNA profile, and to think that the day had finally come where you could learn much more about your Indian and Romany Gypsy ancestors, to learn you don't have any?

Well, I do.

'But . . . How am I going to get to school? Dad lives miles away!'

'Not my problem,' she shrugged. I followed her through the house, searching for the right thing to say to get her to see sense.

At times like those, I couldn't help but think of my baby book. Pages and pages of diligent, detailed and beautiful handwritten stories and notes about my first years. Mum had spent hours, even days, recording everything from my first feed to my first day at school. At the front, she had glued a huge painting of green splodges I had done at nursery. A few pages in, there was an entire lock of my hair from my first haircut. There were photos of me covered in chocolate spread, some of me playing on a little plastic firetruck, and one of me sat on a donkey at Blackpool beach.

The book was bursting at the spine. Mum had added more and more pages as the years had gone on. She had added more paper, and slotted additional photos and school awards inside.

I flicked through the cream book with the flowers on the cover sometimes, wondering what had gone wrong. It just seemed that the older I got, the more she resented me. I had gone from her pride and joy to being a constant irritation.

I had spent years watching as my sister and brother had been treated to lavish birthday parties, joint presents, school trips, new trainers, and games consoles, but I was being charged to live in my own home.

'But I pay you board to live here . . .' I tried.

As soon as I had landed my first part-time job, Mum had demanded I pay board. I was only fourteen, and she was already receiving benefits and tax credits for me and my siblings, but she seemed annoyed that I had found a part-time job in the little restaurant in town. It was keeping me out of (some) trouble, I had my own cash, and I was able to buy myself my first ever branded piece of clothing – a zip through adidas hoodie.

I paid her £30 a week, and to this day, I cannot tell you what for. As a mother of a fifteen-year-old now, I have absolutely no inclination to charge him £30 to live at home, either. Arguably, I appear to be paying *him* pocket money every week to live in *my* house, so, you know that they say, 'the cycle stops with you' folks!

'Well, pay it to your dad,' she shouted from the kitchen as I sifted through the black bags. There wasn't much left, and it was hard to determine what had gone, and what was still in there.

I stormed into the kitchen, starting to lose my temper.

'Is this really because I went over to Dad's? You know I only went over there to let you calm down after you hit me in the face!'

'Bollocks. You fucking went over there because you can drink and smoke there, so you can fucking stay there!' Her face flushed, and her blue eyes widened. She tensed her jaw.

'I went over there to prevent another argument! You hit me, again! You are always starting on me!'

She stared at me, the stare she always gave me before she slapped me, or before she exploded. She was a good deal taller than me, not just because I was a child, but because as I have said, I somehow drew the literal short straw. My siblings are all tall, blonde, and slim – and I look like their dumpy brunette second cousin twice removed.

Mum towered over me in these arguments, and I was constantly frightened of her losing control. Her teeth were gritted again.

'You do nothing for anyone else but yourself! You're selfish, and you have a fucking attitude problem!'

I really didn't enjoy arguing with her, but that one really pissed me off.

I snapped back.

'I can't believe you just said that to me. I missed weeks of fucking school caring for Alfie when you were in and out of hospital with Stacey. Every single day, I got up, did his nappy, fed him, dressed him, cared for him. I watched *The Fimbles* so many times I could fucking lip sync the episodes. He made me watch Crazy Frog until I lost my mind. I even did the weekly shop on foot, with the pram. I had school ringing me every day asking where I was. I had to pretend to be you on the fucking phone! I had to look after him like my own baby for weeks! People stared at me in the street wondering how a fourteen-year-old had an 18-month-old screaming baby!'

She gasped at my audacity.

'How dare you throw that in my face? Your own sister could have died! She was in intensive care for god's sake!'

On the morning of her twelfth birthday, Mum had sent me in to Stacey to get her up for school. I was sick of her skiving off, so I shook her awake. As she turned over with a groan I jumped back in horror.

'Muuuuuuuuuuuuuuuuuuuuum!' I called out, staring at my little sister's swollen, purple face. The huge black eye. Her forehead swollen into her hairline. I couldn't wait any longer. I ran into Mum.

'There's something wrong with Stacey. Her face. Her face is . . . We need an ambulance!'

Mum leapt out of bed and flew into her room, to be met with the same shocking sight, and a completely oblivious twelve-year-old daughter, looking at us both like we had lost our minds. She touched her face with her hands and shrieked.

The ambulance screeched down our street and before I knew it, I was a full-time parent to my baby brother. Stacey was in theatre for eight hours whilst they drained the fluid from her brain, eye socket, and sinus cavities. Doctors argued over what it could be. Was it meningitis? Cancer? Tumour? Infection? No one knew.

Stacey spent weeks in hospital recovering from the surgery, got herself a shiny new scar from her tear duct, up into her eyebrow and into her forehead where they had fitted a drain, and suffered temporary amnesia as a result of the emergency surgery.

When I finally got to visit her when she was out of intensive care, I couldn't help but wind her up. The nurse was doing her observations, and I took my opportunity for a bit of fun.

'Stacey, can you remember the name of our dog?'

'We don't have a dog,' she mumbled back, cuddled up in her hospital bed, surrounded by helium balloons, new toys and teddies.

'We do. Don't you remember him?'

The nurse glanced at me, concerned. I smiled at her and shrugged.

Must be the memory loss, I mouthed at the nurse, shaking my head.

'Jess, we don't have a dog . . .' Stacey stared at me through one eye. I tried to keep a straight face.

'He's seven. He is white with black spots. Don't tell me you've forgot our dog . . .'

Suddenly, the nurse stared through me, behind me, and I whipped my head around to see Mum staring at me. She was half seething, half stifling a giggle.

'We don't have a dog, Wendy. She's just being a shitbag to her little sister,' Mum had reassured the worried nurse.

The nurse scowled at me and stormed off.

That was the only time I got to see Stacey. Her recovery was difficult, and the metal drain had to stay in longer than expected. Mum and Mark took turns sleeping at the hospital, and I stayed home to care for my brother. Nothing annoyed me more than being told I never did anything for others, when I got myself into mountains of trouble for missing weeks of school, and got behind on my GCSE coursework in the process. I couldn't tell my school the real reason I hadn't turned up for weeks, so I was punished for truanting.

'I'm not throwing it in your face, I am telling you that I have done loads for this family, and I still do. I'm not perfect, but I'm not harming anyone! I am still the one who can get Alfie to sleep every night because he won't settle with anyone else!'

Mum leant on the worktop.

'Just like you to hold a fuckin grudge, innit?'

'I'm not holding a grudge! I don't get why I'm being kicked out.'

But Mum had made her mind up. She was past caring, and accused me of not caring about her, and not loving her. Not this again. For years, since the divorce, I'd had to listen to her and Dad complaining about each other. And Mum was the worst. All I had to do was say something remotely nice about Dad, and she wouldn't speak to me for days.

'Remember last year when you asked what we'd done at Dad's house, and I told you he'd taken us to the fayre in Stoke, and you kicked off and told me to go and live with him cos I loved him more than you? Just because I said we had fun at a fuckin fayre?'

'Oh fuck off, I did not say that! You're a liar, Jessica!'

I rolled my eyes again. If I had a penny for every time my mum had done something, and then claimed I was a liar when I confronted her about it, I would be able to start my own civilisation on Mars. Away from everyone.

'I'm not lying, and you know it. You do it all the time, that's why whenever I see Dad now, I just tell you we have done nothing. It's not worth the aggro you give me if I say anything about him!'

'Shut up, now!' she growled at me from across the kitchen.

'No! You never take responsibility for anything!' I snapped back.

'Quit while you're ahead, Jess,' she threatened me through gritted teeth.

I didn't care. I was so sick of being scapegoated and gaslit.

'The only fucking time you want to talk about Dad is if he's done something stupid, if his drinking is out of control, or if he's let me down. Then you're right there. Loving the drama. Loving the failure. You make out you care about us when Dad lets us down, but you're more than happy to ship us off there whenever you want us out the way. You were more than happy to leave us there when Dad wasn't even in. You left us there again when Dad was so drunk he couldn't even talk. You took me back there even when I walked the six miles home to get a fuckin yoghurt because I was so hungry! I don't care about you? You don't care about us!'

Silence fell between us. We were both out of breath, and red in the face.

'I dunno how you fuckin dare speak to me like that!' She slammed something down into the kitchen sink and water sloshed down the side of the worktop and on to the lino.

I stared at her. I never wanted such a volatile relationship with my mum. I loved her immensely. But no matter how much I loved her, I knew this was never going to work. Mum had always told me that it was normal to have a really toxic relationship with your parents growing up, but I was beginning to think she was just replicating her own relationship with her mother, with me. My friends didn't have arguments like this with their mums.

I was exhausted by her. I could feel myself welling up.

'Do you know what? Fuck it, fine. I will go and live with Dad.'

She didn't even look back at me, even as my voice cracked.

'I don't care what you fucking do, do what you want, you always do anyway!'

I watched her furiously scrub a coffee mug, but she still didn't look at me.

'Whatever!' I breathed.

I slung my school bag over my shoulder, and reached behind the cupboard for my GCSE coursework folder. I picked up the thin, fragile black bags stretching in my fingers, and headed for the front door. As I turned to close it, Stacey appeared next to me.

'Are you really moving out?' she whispered.

Fuck. She had heard everything. I sighed.

'She's got rid of all my stuff, Stace. I can't stay here with her, she's a nightmare. She's not like this with you lot . . .'

'She doesn't mean it. You'll come back, won't you?' she said, holding back tears.

'I dunno, babe. I dunno. But you come to Dad's every week, and I'll be there, so I'll see you at least every weekend anyway. And you can text me. You've got that new phone, and you got my number. Just remember to text me. Okay?'

'Yeah. Okay . . .'

She looked sullen, and I wished I had the energy to explain everything to her, but I just didn't. This was the first time in months she had been concerned about me. Usually, she was Mum's golden child, and would side with Mum even if she told her the sky was pink and clouds were cotton candy.

I closed the door gently, holding eye contact with my little sister until the moment came when the door ended our gaze.

I blew a huge breath out, picked up the worryingly light bags, and walked down the street to the house I knew Jase would be at. I had tried to leave him once already, and it had ended in disaster. The last straw had come when he had spent all week accusing me of cheating on him with Kalen. I had told him a thousand times that Kalen was my friend, but Jase could never let go of it.

He had threatened him twice, but Kalen had stood his ground, which had made the situation even worse. Jase was now almost nineteen, and me and Kalen were still in school, doing our GCSEs. We had been dating for years, and I swung from being convinced I was in love with him, to being frightened to death of him.

One cold Wednesday night, he had turned up at my house at 11:30pm and thrown rocks at my window to get my attention. I hung out of my bedroom window and asked him what he wanted. He told me he needed to talk to me, urgently. I told him it would have to wait, because my mum would kill me if she realised I was sneaking out of the house again.

Instead of driving away, he came to the front door, bold as brass, and asked my mum if he could speak with me.

I knew it was going to be bad. There was no other reason why he would be this persistent.

As her voice rang up the stairs, telling me that Jase was at the door, I dragged a big T-shirt on over my knickers and ran down to the door.

'Ten minutes!' she instructed me.

'Yep, no worries, Kimberley! Really appreciate it, thank you so much. Didn't mean to trouble you.' He smiled sickeningly sweetly at my mum. His fake smile faded, and his eyes changed to rage as his gaze moved to me.

Uh-oh, my mind went. This wasn't good.

He waited for her to leave.

'Get in the car,' he ordered.

'What? I can't. I don't have clothes on. Mum said ten minutes . . .'

'I said, get in the car,' he repeated.

'I can't! She'll kill me!'

'I don't give a fuck, get in the fucking car. Now.'

I looked back. Mum had her back to the front door, watching *Never Mind the Buzzcocks* and having a glass of white wine. I panicked. If I left, Mum would lose her shit with me. If I didn't go and get in the car, Jase would lose his shit with me.

Who was more dangerous?

My mind played out both scenarios. Jase was definitely more dangerous. I got in the car.

He got in and slammed his door. He didn't speak. I hated it when he did that. I sat there, stewing in my own fear. His breathing got heavier. His eyes glazed over. He stared at the road.

'Have you been cheating on me?' he blurted into the silence.

'What? No! I am always with you!' I was so tired of being accused of cheating on him when he had already cheated on me seven times (that I knew of).

'No you're not. What about when you're at school? That fuckin Kalen. He's all over you. I'm sick of it. You're not going to school tomorrow if that fuckin wanker is gonna be there!'

Not this again.

'Kalen has been my friend for years. He's got a girlfriend. He's looked after me. He's not interested in me like that. He's never so much as held my hand. He is not all over me at all! You really need to stop this . . .'

'Give me your phone!' he demanded.

'It's . . . upstairs, in my bed . . .'

'So? Go get it then!'

'But if I go back in there, Mum will expect me to be going bed for school . . . I have mock exams tomorrow . . .'

He turned away from me, and stared into the distance. I tried to read what he was thinking, but I was coming up empty handed. I didn't know if he was going to apologise and calm down, or stab me in the throat.

Suddenly, he turned the car on, dropped it into first gear and slammed his foot to the floor.

'Whoa! What are you doing?' I shrieked.

He ignored me, and just climbed up the gears, and up the speed. Houses whizzed by us. His dark eyes focused on the road. His jaw was clenched. His knuckles were white. I was in deep trouble now.

'Please Jase, my mum is gonna kill me! Please take me home! Please, I'm begging you!'

But he didn't even look at me. He increased his speed more and more, until we were weaving in and out of parked cars, and hitting speed humps at 70 mph. The body kit scratched and cracked as it hit the road. The suspension knocked and banged. I had no seat belt on, and frantically searched for it behind me whilst being slammed from side to side in the passenger seat.

'Where are you going? I haven't done anything, I swear to ya!'

'You're a fuckin lying little bitch!'

'I swear to you, I'm not lying! Please calm down, you're gonna kill us both!'

'Good!' he screamed, and turned to me, foaming at the sides of his mouth. His eyes were dead. He looked like he had been possessed. The tendons in his neck stuck out. He had a weird smirk across his lips. A vein appeared down his forehead.

I felt like I was in a horror movie.

He drove higher and higher up into the hills above Biddulph, through the black winding single track roads. I was sure he was going to murder me and dump me up there. I didn't cry, I just froze like I always did. I accepted my fate. I knew I wasn't in control. There was nothing I could do. Just another time to be beaten up and abused. Just stay still until it ends. Until it is all over. Until they get what they want. Until they are satisfied and walk away.

But suddenly, something inside me rose up. An instinct? An urge? A deep, unconscious need to survive?

I yanked at the door handle, and the door swung open.

'What the fuck are you doing, you crazy bitch?' He laughed at me.

'I wanna get out!'

'Oh, you do, do you?' He laughed again, slowing his car down on the pitch-black country roads.

This was not going to end well for me.

He pressed the button on my seat belt, it loosened then whipped back into place behind me.

'Go on then!' He goaded me, pointing at the open car door, 'I dare you!'

Everything went through my head. Do I just throw myself out? What speed was he doing? I glanced at his speedo – 40 mph. Would I survive that? Would he reverse over me and kill me? Would he get out of his car and kill me with his bare hands?

So many risks to assess in just a few short seconds.

'Get out then, bitch!'

His car had slowed down more, as he was distracted and losing momentum – 30 mph. Would I survive that? Could I throw myself now? What if I went under the tyres? What if I got stuck between the car and the door? What if I hit my head? Fuck. What do I do?

Suddenly, my mind was made up for me.

He braked the car suddenly, and launched himself at me, shoving me out of the car door and onto the cold, wet road. I hit the floor hard, and rolled over into the grass verge. The pain seared through my back and my neck. I quickly pulled my legs under me in case he went to reverse over them.

He braked next to me.

'There you go, Jess! Is that what you fucking wanted? Look what you made me do!'

I rushed to try to gather myself and stood up, barefoot on the gravel in the road. It was freezing. The wind sliced through me up there, on the moors high above the town. I had no idea what he was going to do to me next. Do I run for it? Do I try to calm him down? Offer him sex? Get back in the car? Find a house, and run to that? Get someone to call 999 for me? Hope the people in the house don't do something even worse to me?

What do I do?

But again, he made the decision for me.

'See you later, stupid slag!' he sang at me, slamming the door on me, putting the car back into first gear and pulling off into the darkness. Within seconds, the red glow of his brake lights was gone, and I was stood totally alone, in nothing but a T-shirt, barefoot, on a pitch-black country road a mile from my house.

I ended it with him as soon as I got home. I text him and told him I never wanted to see him again for as long as I lived.

Mum had predictably screamed at me the moment I turned back up, over an hour later. I had lied and said that he drove round the corner to sit in a carpark so we could talk. She seemed to believe me, but I had noticed her staring at how cold and blotchy my skin looked after a mile walk in the biting weather.

Maybe she was beyond caring, but she didn't ask how I had ended up so freezing. Maybe if she had seen the soles of my feet, it would have given it away.

Jase hadn't even bothered to text me back, and I realised that I was relieved. That break up lasted for nearly four months. It was bliss. I worked hard on my GCSEs, saw my friends, went to the gym, learned how to run long distance, wrote poetry, and found myself again. I lay on the grass in the park at the centre of the council estate, watching a meteor shower with my friends, and talking about the universe.

Underneath it all, I was still the same soul.

'What do you reckon we are here for?' a girl from the estate asked me, as she passed me the joint.

I had known her for about two hours, and now I was lying on the ground with her discussing the meaning of life.

A group of lads we both knew were flipping the swings just across from us.

I exhaled, and thought about my answer.

'To learn something? To make a difference? Fuck knows. My family are dead religious but I don't think I believe in anything. Maybe there is no meaning. We are born. We live. We die. Maybe the lesson we need to learn is that we are not fuckin important enough to have a meaning of life. Maybe we are so fuckin self-obsessed, we assume there must be a deeper meaning, when there is none . . .'

Silence fell.

'Fuck me, you're a right buzzkill you are,' she laughed, choking on the smoke.

I giggled. Was it the resin, or was the sky alive? Why did it look like the stars were breathing? Why could my eyes perceive movement?

'Soz,' I laughed, 'I just . . . don't you think we're just a mess? Aliens probably fly past us and lock their fuckin spaceship doors. Earth is the Stoke of the Universe . . .'

We both burst out laughing, rolling around in the grass.

'Chavs of the Universe!' she yelled triumphantly into the night air.

Everything changed the day I got home from school to find him standing in my house holding a huge bouquet of flowers.

'Look who's here to see you!' my mum beamed at me.

My blood ran cold when I saw him. He looked at me with those dead, glazed over eyes. That smirk came back. My heart pounded in my chest.

'Wha . . . what are you doin' here?'

'Fuckin hell Jess, that's not very good manners, is it?' my mum scolded me.

He looked at me, a look that said, 'Yeah Jess, where are your manners?'

'Jase came to us to apologise to us all for your terrible break up. He was just explaining how heartbroken he was that you cheated on him . . .'

'I didn't cheat on him!' I protested.

'Jessica! Let me finish!' she said, putting her hand sympathetically on his shoulder. 'He came to apologise to us. And he explained that he made a lot of mistakes when he was upset. And to ask for another chance with you. He even went to your nana and grandad, didn't you mate?'

He did what?

'I did, Kimberley. I just love Jess so much. I just want her to love me the way I love her. I just need one more chance!'

Mum looked at me like she was literally melting. Like I was in the crescendo of a romcom. Like the handsome prince had just proposed to me in the Disney film. Like the glass slipper had just slipped perfectly on to my tiny little foot. How could she not see the game he was playing here?

This was not a Disney happy ending, this was a fucking nightmare.

'Absolutely not. I don't want to get back with you. End of story.' I stared at the evil little smirk on his face, remembering the mile-long walk back to my house in nothing but a T-shirt.

I still hadn't told my mum that he had pushed me out of his car. Or that he had abused me repeatedly – although of course, I was nowhere near ready to realise or admit that bit yet. I hadn't even told her that he had cheated on me umpteen times. Or that he had beaten me up. Or that he was absolutely obsessed with threatening Kalen.

'Jessica!' my mum shouted. 'At least hear him out! You're being ridiculous!'

I glared at them both. Jase looked back at me, and I watched him make himself cry for effect. He let one tear drop down his face, and then strategically turned to my mum.

'This is what I mean, Kimberley. She just doesn't love me any more . . .' He dramatically put the bouquet of flowers on the dining table next to me, like he was laying them on a casket. My casket. I was truly trapped, and somehow, I was talked into giving him another chance.

I called his phone.

'Hello?' he mumbled.

'Hey. Are you around? My fuckin mum has kicked me out, and I need get over to me dad's . . .'

'What? Why has she done that then?' he laughed.

'Search me. Could ya just pick me up please?'

'Yeah, stay where you are, I'll come and get ya. Let's get your dad to get the beers in . . .'

'Uhh, I don't think we should be encouraging him to drink. He fell through a roof at work last month and broke three ribs, remember?'

He breathed out, getting annoyed.

'Well, if I don't get beers out of it, I'm not driving you there. Your choice.'

I sighed.

'Look, I will get you some beers in if you take me over there. That okay?'

'You're the best baby!' he said in a weird, babyish voice.

Moving in with Dad was everything I thought it was going to be. I got sucked into the drinking culture with him and his friends within days. I was sinking a bottle of wine a day at some points. I was rarely getting up early enough to get the bus to school, which now took almost 45 minutes.

My friends drifted away from me, and got used to me never being around. I fell behind on my coursework and my revision for my GCSEs, and I looked like shit. I did everything I could to keep up with schoolwork, but it was getting harder and harder. I had to get a second job to pay for the bus fare to school every day, and so I was going to school all day, and then working every night and all day on weekends. One job was in an Indian restaurant, and the other was in a family pub that served food. I was a waitress in both, and it was hard, challenging work, but I was being paid fairly well for a teenage girl, cash in hand.

I was just about keeping my head above water when my dad suddenly had an epiphany.

Stood in the kitchen, in his dark grey dressing gown, Dad asked me how much I earned a week. I told him the truth, some weeks around £100, other weeks up to £180.

'Fuckin hell, you are doing all right there then!' he said.

I mistakenly thought he was proud of me.

'Thanks, Dad!' I had smiled at him, whilst pouring the last dregs of the orange squash into a plastic cup I had found.

The atmosphere changed.

'So, why are you only giving me £40 a week to live here?' he asked.

I was confused. He was many things, but I didn't expect this.

'Umm, cos that's what you asked me for . . . And you told me I had to buy my own food, and pay my own bus fare. So, I did all that. And you said you needed £40 a week towards the bills . . .'

'Right, but you are earning way more than that. What are you doing with all that extra money?'

'I buy myself a week of food. I pay bus fare to school and back. I look after myself. Go out. Stuff like that . . .'

He put his hand on his hip and raised his eyebrows at me before shaking his head.

'No. No. That's not fair. I am just scraping by. I think you should be giving me more than £40, Jess.'

Before the drinking and the divorce, Dad had worked for the council for seventeen years. He was a landscaper, and helped build some of the most wonderful family parks in Cheshire. He had started as an apprentice as a teenager, and been there ever since. He was a well-loved member of the team, and had won many awards for his work. When he had started turning up to work drunk and out of control, his managers and colleagues had supported him, offered him some time off work, and told him they would always be there for him. Instead of taking the offer, he told them to shove the job up their arse and stormed out.

He wasn't paying the bills. The phone and TV had stopped working. He had maxed out four credit cards. He was doing casual work every now and then, renovating houses and plastering.

'Well, uh, how much do you need?'

He paused. He thought about it. Without even looking at me, he told me that £120 a week would do it. Everything I had, and some weeks, more than I had. How was I supposed to pay that? How was I supposed to get to school?

He still didn't look up. He stared at his phone screen. He wiped down the side in the kitchen. He put the kettle on. Anything but look at me. As if a little voice had just whispered in my ear, I suddenly realised what was going on. He wanted the money to drink. He knew it was extra cash he could be using, and he wanted it for himself. I was gutted.

'Dad, if you are going to charge me £120 a week to live here, plus pay for all my own food, and my bus fare, and everything else, I will either . . .' I searched my brain for solutions. 'Well, I will either have to find somewhere else to live, or I would have to stop going to school every day and get a job.'

I hated how much he perked up at the idea of me quitting school and getting a job.

'Well, you don't have long left at school anyway do you? It's only a few months and then you have GCSEs.'

I thought about it. I guess he was right.

Most of my coursework was finished and handed in. I had already secured good grades on those pieces, so now all I had to do was smash the exams. I needed to revise though, and there wasn't much chance of that at Dad's. The house was a regular meeting place for when the pubs closed. I often woke up to strangers wearily making themselves a coffee, holding their head, fumbling around the small galley kitchen, looking for where the mugs were, then the spoons, then the milk.

And frankly, I could do without listening to people having drunk sex all night in the spare rooms of the house whilst my GCSEs loomed. I sighed. Grown-up life was getting harder and harder, and I was only sixteen years old.

'He probably just wants to drink the extra cash!' Jase had laughed down the phone. 'For that price, you could get your own fuckin house. There are some little terraced houses going down bottom of Tunstall for £300 a month. Be cheaper to move in there. We could move in together! I can use my wages, you can use yours. Why don't we just get our own place?'

Before I knew it, the idea had taken hold, and I was determined to get out of my dad's house. But out of the frying pan and into the fire, I moved from living with my unpredictable alcoholic Dad, to living with my unpredictable, violent boyfriend just three streets away. And whilst this may be hard to believe, it somehow got much, much worse for me.

The place was a thin terraced house squeezed between two others, packed into a street with hundreds more. My first house – 106 Nash Peake Street. It faced hundreds more terraced houses, and backed onto a huge derelict factory which had become home to a sea of rats.

The front door opened straight into the first reception room, which I had put a metal second-hand dining table in. I rarely used it, and often just ate on my knee in the living room. I'm not sure why I got it. I think I thought it would make it look like a real house, if it had a dining table. The room linked through a narrow doorway into the tiny living room. I didn't have money for a proper sofa, so I managed to get two musty old blue draylon single armchairs for £50, a wooden coffee table for £10, and a small second-hand TV for £20. That was all that was in there.

If you walked through further, it took you to a cramped, old, dirty galley kitchen with a rat infestation. I used to lie awake at night and listen to them crawling through the wall space and the floorboards. I often came downstairs after hardly any sleep, to the kitchen cupboards open, and food spilled all over the worktops or the floor.

Past the kitchen was the only bathroom in the house. Needless to say, I would be far too scared to go to the toilet in the night when the rats were running around my kitchen – and so I would stay upstairs with the doors shut, not daring to drink any fluids before bed or during the night. There were two bedrooms upstairs, but no landing. There were two doors facing each other at the top of a steep, broken staircase off the living room. One bedroom was empty, and I had dumped my binbags and other junk in there. The other was my bedroom. All I had was a second-hand double bedframe and mattress, a double wardrobe I had picked up for £20, a cheap second-hand wooden dressing table, and a small mirror from Matalan.

The rent was £320 a month, and whilst Jase had suggested we pooled our wages together, he had retracted that offer as soon as we had moved in. He guarded his own money with his life, and I ended up spending every penny I had trying to keep us afloat. It was a steep learning curve.

I felt like I was having endless confusing conversations with companies who were demanding money from me. I knew about gas and electric, but paying money for water? I was baffled. I had only been there a couple of months, and already I was in debt for using water. To drink. To wash.

But it didn't stop there. I had to learn about council tax, and then I had to find the money for that, too. And then there was the day the men in suits came to the door.

'We are just here today for a chat about your TV licence. Have you got a TV in the property, miss?'

'Yeah, why?' I replied, unsure of what they wanted.

'According to our records, there is no TV licence for this address.' He looked at me sternly.

Now I had absolutely no idea what he was talking about.

'So?' I shrugged, 'I don't need a licence or whatever, I don't have the money for whatever it is you're selling . . .'

Now he was confused.

'Sorry? This is about your TV licence . . .'

I shook my head.

'Look, I'm not interested mate!' I started to close the door when he put his foot in the way, and glared at me. The door bounced off his foot and I scowled at him.

'I don't think you are understanding me, miss. You have to have a TV licence. I'm not here to sell you cable TV, it's a licence to use your TV.' The big bald guy raised his voice through the gap made by his steel toe-capped boot. His colleague with the clipboard stared at me.

'What? Why the fuck do I need a licence to watch TV?' I laughed at the ridiculousness of it. Did I have to take TV lessons to get my TV licence?

'It's the law, miss.'

'That's not a reason,' I snapped back, disinterested.

The other guy stepped forward and tried to explain the concept of the TV licence to me. Something about the money going to the BBC. You have to pay a fee to them because they provide the broadcasting on behalf of the government. I don't remember the rest of it. It sounded like a scam to me.

'Well, I will just stop watching the BBC then. I've got ITV. And Channel 4. BBC is only good for *EastEnders* anyway . . .'

They started to get agitated with me. Both became restless.

'It doesn't work like that. You have to pay it regardless of which channels you watch. Look, you are wasting our time now.'

'Well, I just won't watch TV then. I am hardly ever at home anyway.'

One of the men looked like he wanted to reach into my house and throttle me, and the other one looked like he was losing the will to live, but I just couldn't understand what they were saying.

'Why should I have to pay for a licence I don't need?'

'Everyone pays for a TV licence, otherwise you can be fined up to £10,000, or put in prison!' the bald guy explained, exasperated.

'What? Ten grand? Prison? For watching TV? How much is this fucking licence?'

'It's £135.50 per year . . .'

I couldn't believe my ears.

'Per year? I have to pay it every year? This is ridiculous. I don't have £135. I can't afford that!'

They rolled their eyes and shifted on their feet. We all stared at each other. I was tired. I was poor. I was trapped. And I was sixteen fucking years old.

'Then you will be fined,' one of the men eventually sighed.

'Well, tell them that they can fine me all they like. Do they struggle with basic maths? If I don't have £135 for the licence, I'm not going to have the ten grand for the fine, am I? Whose stupid idea was it to fine people with no fuckin money?'

'Look love, we don't make the rules, we just enforce the law,' the bald guy snapped.

'Then you should get another job. Is this really what you wanted to do when you grew up? Fuckin hell . . .' I rolled my eyes, arms crossed.

The bald guy was truly sick of talking to me, but the guy behind him put his head down and tried to hide his laughter. Looking back, I am sure this was one of their more amusing visits.

Incidents like this were common whilst I was figuring it all out, and I quickly realised that I didn't have enough money to live on. I was neglecting my exam revision, and instead, working more and more hours. One day, when I was extremely hungry, and with no money left in the bank, I found my old cheque book in one of the black bags. I stared at it.

Cheques take a week to clear. I would be paid by then. Maybe I could buy something with a cheque? I wandered around the streets of Tunstall, looking for a takeaway or a supermarket that took cheques. Finally, I found a small Chinese takeaway on the corner of a junction near the dodgy underpass. I went in and nervously ordered some chicken chow mein, some chips, a portion of the chicken soup, and some cans of Tango. I wrote out the cheque and passed it to them. They took it without even hesitating, and I waited for my fresh, hot food. The first I had eaten in days.

I couldn't believe it worked.

Back in 2006, cheques were still used everywhere. Asda. Argos. Takeaways. Finding that chequebook saved my life. And also caused me to overspend. Seriously. Consciously. I just stopped caring.

The cheques were bouncing left, right and centre. I was getting bank charges, fines, and threatening letters. I threw them all in the bin, and assumed they would shut up and leave me alone eventually. At sixteen years old, and with no one to guide me, I had absolutely no idea how much trouble I was getting myself into, and how hard it was going to be to get back out of it. To this day, I still do not understand how I was issued a chequebook at sixteen years old, but I guess the bank found out the hard way what happens when you give a child in poverty an endless source of money.

The gravity of what I had done only truly hit me when late one night, in the middle of my GCSE exams, a gang of Chinese guys with weapons turned up at my door, one guy was waving a knife, and another guy was holding a fan of the rejected cheques I had used to buy food when I had nothing to eat. I hid in the dark, hyperventilating under the peeling, damp wooden windowsill, whilst the Takeaway Mafia tried to kick the front door in.

'We know you're in there! Give us the fuckin money!'

People peeked out of the windows, but didn't dare come outside. The men had driven down the street and left the cars diagonally across the lanes, so no one could get in, or out.

I cried to myself. Jase was nowhere to be found, yet again. I was alone, and it was only a matter of time until the old door buckled under the pressure of the kicks. Or until they figured out that the back gate was broken, and the back door was made of single pane glass.

I heard a loud voice in the dark.

'Oi, you bunch of cunts, what are you doing?' Scally yelled, lunging at the guys kicking my front door. A scuffle ensued, but not even the Takeaway Mafia were a match for a guy who had taken six pills.

'Yeah, what the fuck are you doing? She's just a fucking kid in there! Fucking wankers! Fuck is wrong with you? You want to fucking die tonight, do yer?' Fox came out of the doorway next, eyes wide from whatever he was on, skin flushed, fists clenched like he was ready to take them all on barehanded.

All I could hear was mayhem outside. Shouting, banging, running, throwing, slamming. I didn't dare watch, or give away my position in the dark.

I didn't move from my hiding spot until I was absolutely sure they were all gone, and all that was left was Scally and Fox shouting through my letterbox. How they had survived that fight, and convinced a gang of men to get in their cars and leave, I guess I will never know.

'Jess! They're gone, little duck! Are you okay in there?' Scally's voice rang out through my house and up the stairs to where I was hiding. I sighed, and crept back down the stairs to let them in.

They were a real weird couple of guys, but I couldn't deny how much they had tried to look after me since I moved in next door to them. Scally was a lizard-looking guy in his early forties, no taller than 5ft 6in, very thin, tiny eyes, tiny mouth, completely bald, scaly skin, and for some reason, he always wore a formal shirt with a pair of baggy blue jeans. Fox was stocky, even shorter than Scally, with messy bleached blond hair and a terrifying look in one eye, even when he was happy. He looked kind of like a washed up, coked up, bloated version of Eminem from the 'Stan' video.

They were running some sort of drug den next door, and were heavily into raves, pills, coke, dealing, and selling. The bass pumped every day, all day, all night. It was a small price to pay for having a couple of friends who would throw themselves into a fight for you. Every time I went round there, there were people high as fuck, bouncing off the walls, or people on the worst come down of their lives, huddled up on the sofa, feeling like they were dying.

I had never taken any Class As, and that house was enough to put me off for life.

I once watched a woman they called 'Legs' swallow a handful of ecstasy like she was eating a pack of Smarties. A 6ft 5in, skeletal white woman with a shaved head and a nose ring, she thought nothing of emptying a worryingly large plastic bag of pills into her hand and knocking them back with a bit of lemonade.

I remember sitting there, watching the clock, just waiting for her to die right in front of me, but she didn't seem anything other than a bit higher than usual. She was chatty, friendly, a little bit strange at times, but nothing more. It made me question how on earth she had become so tolerant of those pills, especially considering she had taken enough to fuel an entire house party.

One of the worst decisions I ever made was to move into that house with Jase. He had complete control over me, and because I had stopped going to school, and then finished my GCSEs, I had no one checking in on me either. I had become an expert at masking the abuse, lying for him, hiding my injuries, and conjuring up stories about why I was late, or why I was distracted, or why I didn't have enough money for the bus to work.

You become a weaver of fiction when you are being abused like that. Stories layered on stories, not about the abuse, but about this alternate reality you have created to cover up the abuse. The stories I told to explain why I had no clothes, after Jase had demanded that I didn't go to work because he wanted sex, and then tipped all of my clothes and shoes into the bath and doused them all with bleach until they were all faded into a horrible tie-dye mish-mash. The story I told to explain how my third phone got snapped in half. The stories I told to explain how my only photo album from when I was a child got ripped up and thrown out of my bedroom window, out into the rain, whilst I frantically ran around the street in my pyjamas chasing pictures of myself as a baby.

I said I had no clothes because I accidentally donated them all when I had mixed up some bags. I had no shoes because my neighbour's imaginary puppy chewed through them when I was dog sitting. I dropped my phone again when I was drunk in the pub. A huge gust of wind from the bad weather knocked my photo album off the windowsill of my bedroom and out into the street.

But some things, you cannot lie about. Like screaming for your life, desperate for your neighbours to hear you through the paper-thin walls, and maybe call 999, or come and kick the door down.

It had only been a few weeks since he held a knife to my throat and ordered me to scrub the oven. And it had only been a few days since he had thrown a large glass vase at me, which had then smashed all over the floor. He had thrown me into the shards of glass, and dragged me through them, screaming at me to clean them up, pushing my legs and arms into the bloodied shards as they pierced and sliced the skin on my hands and knees.

It had only been a few hours since he had ordered me to buy him eight more cans of Carlsberg, and I had walked to Bargain Booze to pick them up for him, like a sixteen-year-old live-in slave.

'You never give me sex any more,' he complained, sipping at the can.

I remained quiet. This was not a safe conversation, and I could feel the anger rising in him.

'I could go out tonight and fuck any girl I wanted. Every time I am in the pub, I've got women fucking begging me for it, but I always come home to you. I could go down Cobridge and get a prozzie. They'd give me whatever I wanted. Sometimes I think that's what you want me to do!'

I tried to stay calm, stay small, stay non-threatening. Do I reply? Do I speak yet?

'Don't fucking ignore me!'

Okay, I had better speak.

'Sorry. I wasn't ignoring you. I just . . . didn't know what to say . . .' I put my head down. I really didn't want another argument. They were getting out of control. After the knife to the throat the other week, I was beginning to realise that I was frequently only moments from death.

'Well are you gonna give it to me or not? Or do I have to go out and find some other bird to give me what I want?'

I really didn't want to. He had been drinking and smoking for hours. He was disgusting. He was violent. Years had passed and I still felt nothing when I had sex. I was still faking orgasms to get him to leave me alone. I was still lying to him, telling him he was amazing in bed. He was right when he said that I never gave him sex any more, because I was avoiding it. There's only so many times you can vary your fake moaning noises. Only so many times you can lie there, whilst they thrust over and over again, and you look at the ceiling thinking, 'I'm sure that crack is getting longer, I'm sure it used to stop near the light fitting . . . since when did it stretch over to near the window? Maybe the house is moving. But it's a terraced block. Surely that would mean they are all moving though? Can a whole street move?'

He leant over to me as I was sat on my bed, and started touching my face. The smell of cigarettes and beer as he spoke made me feel nauseous. I desperately did not want to give him head. Anything but that. He grabbed my hand and put it down his boxers, and I instantly pulled my hand away.

He glared at me with those dead eyes again. A look that said, 'Do what you're told, and no one gets hurt.'

I gulped. I decided to be brave.

'No. I don't want to . . .'

I didn't even finish the sentence and he had already launched himself at me. I was slammed back into the bed as he got on top of me and fought with me to get in between my legs.

'Please. Please don't. Don't do this, please stop . . .' I begged him whilst still trying to wriggle and writhe my way out from underneath him. He was determined, but so was I. For once. I tried to fight back.

'Shut the fuck up!' he screamed in my face.

'Fuck you! Get off me!' I screamed back.

He urgently, suddenly, got a massive amount of strength from his rage, and managed to pin me completely to the bed by my shoulders and neck. At first, I thought he was just going to get it over with, but then he seemed to reach for something. One arm was pinning me to the bed, and the other arm was doing something else. I tried to look up to see, but I couldn't move my head. I could hear him scratching around for something, and the terror in me was rising. What was he looking for?

The scratching around stopped. He stopped. I didn't even dare breathe out, and then I froze when I saw the glint of the silver metal in his hand. It was a long, sharp pair of scissors. Every fibre of my body wanted to fight, and run, but I knew if I did that, I would have probably been butchered with those scissors. I stayed very still, and very quiet. My wriggling stopped. Even my blinking stopped.

He smirked at me. He stared at me. He looked down at my body.

He got on top of me, and put both hands either side of my shoulders. With one hand, he put the sharp end of the scissors just next to my neck, under my ear lobe.

'Now, stay fucking still,' he seethed at me, and then smiled sweetly.

I nodded.

Every time his body pushed against mine, the sharp end of the scissors scratched my neck, to remind me to stay still. He had all his weight on them, and even when they were beginning to dig and stab into the side of my ear and my neck, I still stayed perfectly still until he finished.

As he stood up to get off me, I stayed frozen. The only thing that moved was the single tear rolling down the side of my face, and my rib cage, heaving up and down from trying to hold in the sobs.

'What are you fucking crying for? Eh?'

I didn't reply. I just curled my legs up to my chest, and turned over in my bed. I lay on my side with my back towards him, staring at the damp, mouldy wall next to me.

'I said, what are you fuckin crying for?' He raised his voice, becoming more and more irate. I couldn't even see him, but I could picture the look in his eye. I braced myself.

'Answer me!' He roared at the top of his lungs as he grabbed hold of the metal bed frame and flipped it over in one smooth movement. I was thrown face first into the wall, and crashed to the floor. The mattress had slipped, and the metal bed frame was hovering just a few inches above my head. I was stuck. My legs and torso were trapped underneath the mattress, which was underneath the upside-down chrome bed frame.

As I tried to drag myself free, he did the unthinkable. He did one of the most terrifying things he could have possibly done to me in that moment.

He stepped on the bed frame. He took a step. Then another. The weight of the bed frame, the mattress, and then all 17 stone of him was just too much for my legs and my back. I screamed out in pain. But he didn't stop. He kept climbing up towards my head, stamping each step down, harder and harder until the bed frame was no longer hovering over my head at all. He was stood on it, and it was balancing on the side of my skull.

I can tell you now, I have never felt pain like that before, and never since. He stood on the metal frame as it piled into the side of my head, and I begged to die. In that moment, the pressure and the pain in my skull as he silently put more and more weight on it was one of the most immense and overwhelming forms of pain I could ever imagine. I was absolutely sure my skull was going to crack open like a fucking easter egg at any second.

I screamed in agony, I screamed like I was being slowly tortured to death. I banged with one free hand on the wall, desperate for the neighbours on the other side to hear my cries for help.

I screamed and screamed and screamed, with everything I had.

'Help me! Call the police! Help! Someone help me!' I screamed as loud as I could.

'Shut the fuck up!' He hushed me, stamping one more time on the bed frame.

And it was at that moment, I gave up. I decided to lie there, and die. I couldn't stand any more pain. I couldn't stand any more abuse. Any more neglect. Any more loneliness. Any more drugs or drink. I couldn't keep trying to survive.

I knew I was seconds from death, and I stopped fighting. I stopped screaming. I stopped moving. I just fell silent, and closed my bloodshot eyes for a moment. It was time to go, I told myself. This is it. Just let it happen. You can't survive this one. You did your best. No one is coming. At least death would be safer than this.

I let my face nuzzle into the scratchy, smelly carpet, and I looked over at the tatty little cardboard red box of my things, which contained the tiny, grey, dirty little stuffed puppy I was given on the day I was born. It had been with me for my whole sixteen years of life. And I knew it was in there whilst I gave up, and waited for the inevitable. It would be right next to me in my final moments.

Maybe it was my stillness, maybe it was my acceptance, maybe he thought I was dead, or maybe it was simply that he thought I had learned my lesson – but he suddenly stopped what he was doing, got off the bed frame, and walked away without saying another word. It was as if he been commanded by God, or remote controlled by aliens. He didn't make a single sound. He just got off me, walked down the stairs, and walked out of the house.

I heard the door slam, and I lay there, wondering if I was dead. I hoped I was, but I was quickly disappointed to realise that I was, in fact, very much alive – and in a mind-blowing amount of pain.

I'm sad to say, that life simply went on for me. The pain in my skull lasted a week or so, but I had to push through it to revise for my GCSEs. I took paracetamol and ibuprofen, and hoped for the best. The exams themselves were much easier than the way I was treated by my teachers and my classmates.

I didn't have any school uniform because Jase had destroyed it all, so I turned up to all fifteen exams in jeans and a T-shirt, which caused uproar. The way the teachers reacted, you would think I had turned up dressed as a giant chicken. Can a child really take their GCSEs in jeans? Would their brain work? Who knows?

I was exhausted. I was having to get buses every day to each exam, and some days, I just hung around the school grounds whilst everyone else went home to rest or get some lunch. It was too far to go back and forth between exams.

In the maths exam, I took one look at my paper and stood up, stormed over to my maths teacher and whispered to him.

'Why have you put me in for this paper?'

I waved the express paper in his face.

'Because you are good enough to take the express version. You have been in the express set for maths for three years, Jessica. You need to try it. Just do your best.'

I scowled at him.

'This isn't your life, sir. It's mine. I told you to put me in for the standard paper like everyone else, I can already get an A in that, why make it harder for me and put me on this fucking thing?'

In my year, there were the normal sets for subjects that ran from Set 1 (the top sets) to Set 5 (the bottom sets). There was also an express set, which was for a small number of children deemed to be above the other sets. To my horror, as a kid who hated maths, I was placed in the express set for three years, and begged to be dropped down to Set 1 for the entirety of those three years. I was the thickest kid in the group, and I dreamed of being dropped down to the normal set. However, three years of moaning at Mr Bishop had achieved absolutely nothing.

'To stretch your potential. You really need to sit down, or you can get disqualified. The invigilators might think you are asking me for answers before we start.'

I looked around as the kids in my year piled into the old sports hall. The invigilator was indeed watching me with suspicion. The girl in the jeans, kicking off at her maths teacher over in the corner. I reluctantly accepted my fate, and opened the paper when instructed. I stared at the first algebra question and thought about egging Mr Bishop later.

The morning of the GCSE results was confusing. No one text me to say good luck. No one invited me to the after parties. No one in my family even remembered that it was GCSE results day. It breaks my heart to admit this, but I concluded that my family must have been planning a surprise party for me.

I got on the bus, having been up all night at work, and cuddled up against the window for a nap on the way back to my school grounds for the final time. As the hours passed, and with still no contact from my parents, I was becoming more and more sure that they were planning a surprise for me.

I walked into the hall where excited and nervous teenagers I had known my whole life were wandering around, opening their envelopes, being congratulated and hugged by teachers, or being supported and comforted by friends. All of my teachers were there.

I had been a straight A student for years, and I expected nothing less than thirteen A grades that day. I walked up to the table alone, and was handed my brown A4 envelope, filled with GCSE certificates. Someone had written my results in pencil on the front.

I felt the shame rise up in me. Not a single A grade. My face felt hot, my skin prickled, my heart dropped into my stomach and I felt like vomiting. Teenagers chattered around me, and teachers rushed to them to see how they had done, and how they were feeling. I stood, dizzy and alone on the wooden floor. Surrounded, and yet isolated.

I looked once more at the front of the envelope. A sea of B grades. I cringed when I saw I had been awarded a C in maths, my lowest ever grade. I was disgusted at myself. I was so embarrassed. Ashamed.

So ashamed, that I didn't open my tatty brown GCSE results envelope until I was twenty-five years old.

I walked out of the hall and tried to rationalise. Thirteen GCSEs, all passed, eleven of them at B or B+, two of them at a C. Why was I so embarrassed by that? I couldn't understand it, but I was mortified. The only thing that was lifting me up was the false belief I had created, that I was definitely going to walk into a big surprise party around the corner at Mum's house.

The kids from the posh estate were getting jaw dropping gifts for their GCSE results day. Huge house parties. Trips to Alton Towers. Holidays to Zante. Cindy's parents bought her a Mini Cooper. Gemma's dad promised her £100 for every A–C grade she got, so he had rewarded her with over a grand in cash. Amy's parents bought her a fucking house. A house. An actual real live bricks and mortar house.

It reminded me of the way prom was, too. The glitz. The glamour. The stretch limos. The dresses. The hair. The nails.

The Tiffany's necklaces. The designer handbags. The hired Cadillac. It was a wonderous night. That's what I heard, anyway. I didn't get to go. Firstly, because I couldn't afford it, and secondly, because Jase wouldn't let me. Whenever anyone asked me why I wasn't going, I told them I wasn't interested in paying £60 to have dinner with twenty-five teachers who had taken part in a sweepstake that I was going to fail my GCSEs.

I walked through the gully and back on to the estate, turned right and walked up to Mum's house. Where I used to live, only a few months earlier. The cars were in. That means they were all home. I knew it!

I practised being surprised.

'Oh my god! Thank you so much! This is so kind of you!'

'No way! I can't believe you did all this!'

I walked up the drive, between the old Toyota and Mark's white van, heart beating fast, imagining the balloons and the cards and the hugs.

I stepped through the front door and into the dining room to see Mum in the kitchen. She turned around.

'What are you doing here?' she asked plainly.

I was confused. Where was the party? The balloons? The hugs?

'Today is GCSE results day ... I went to pick 'em up, and I thought ...' I looked around the rooms. There was nothing. No one. The house was empty.

'What? I didn't know it was today,' she mumbled, making herself a cup of tea.

'Ya did, I told ya loads of times ...' I bit my lip, trying not to cry. I held my brown envelope at my side, hating it even more than before.

She poured the milk into the brew. 'Well, the world doesn't revolve around you, ya know.'

I looked at the floor. I looked at my dirty trainers. I didn't want to be there any more.

'I got good grades, anyway . . .' I mumbled quietly to her, not even believing my own words.

'Good,' she muttered. She looked up at me briefly as she walked past me, and went to sit on the sofa in the living room.

That was it, then. Cindy got a Mini Cooper, and I got that.

9

Are we out of the woods yet?

Winter 2017

Social media sure does make people brave.

I've said it many times, it's where the middle class, the registered professionals, and the cowards go to start fights because they don't actually want to go toe to toe with you.

I didn't really know how it was happening, but my public profile, my blogs and my articles were everywhere. Whilst I was drunk from half a bottle of port, I had banged out a clumsy, ranty blog about the way people always derailed my work to ask 'what about the men?' And it was read over three million times. I had a small, but quickly growing social media following, and whilst it meant I could share my ideas and my work around the world, it also meant I was attracting a lot of abuse.

I have been sent so much abuse online that I could keep the police busy for the rest of humanity. The world would literally explode before every incident of abuse, violence, threats and hate against me had been investigated.

Another day, another dickhead.

I woke up and resumed my terrible habit of checking Twitter first thing in a morning. Every day I did it, and every day I regretted it. It was the same routine every morning. Twitter. Emails. Facebook. WhatsApp. LinkedIn. Instagram.

A day rarely went by when I wasn't confronted with a disgusting message, nasty comment or long, incoherent raging email from a stranger on the internet. That day was no different. The night before, I had been on Radio 4, discussing the way the female victims of Hollywood producer Harvey Weinstein were being blamed and accused of lying in the media. I had been doing a lot of radio interviews recently, and I had even done two television interviews about my work.

I was always so proud to be able to share my ideas, but it also caused a wave of abuse and trolling every time I did it.

I opened my Twitter inbox to a message from a man called Daniel.

'Your body is hot, but your face fucking ruined it for me.'

He included three printed out photos of me giving a presentation about my PhD. In the photos, I am wearing a navy-blue dress and flat shoes. I am smiling, stood next to a display about my psychological theory of victim blaming of women and girls. Except, I was not smiling, because he had cut my face out of them all. I frowned. What a prick.

And then I noticed something that made me feel physically sick for the rest of the day: he had ejaculated on the pictures. It was gross. Absolutely disgusting.

'At least he spared me the picture of his actual dick though,' I mumbled to myself.

Being in the public eye as a woman means that I've seen more dicks than a fucking urology doctor. Except, hopefully, urology doctors don't wake up to non-consensual dick pics in their Facebook inbox. I've got my fingers crossed for you all, if you are reading this. Although it has just dawned on me that I bet female doctors often deal with men sexually harassing them, and sending them pictures of their dicks, come to think of it. In fact, wasn't there an NHS report which found that female nurses and doctors were most likely to be sexually assaulted and harassed at work by their own male patients?

I had been using social media to share my studies, my theories, and the free resources I had been building for women and girls subjected to sexual violence and abuse. I rarely self-disclosed – and this had been grating on me. It had especially been grating on me, since I knew the anonymous person sending the emails about me had mentioned my own personal experiences as a reason for why I was problematic.

There was a strong culture in psychology, and in academia, that you should never disclose your own experiences. Especially not to a client, or a patient. To begin with, I had simply accepted this as 'professional practice', and had not interrogated it any further. However, as my understanding of trauma and abuse had deepened, and I had worked with more and more women and girls, this concept of hiding ourselves from the women we helped had begun to perplex me. Irritate me. Nag at me.

I understood why we couldn't sit in a room, cry, project and self-disclose to a traumatised woman or girl we were supposed to be helping – but what I couldn't understand was the smoke and mirrors. What I couldn't understand was the false dichotomy we had created of 'us' and 'them'.

Almost every single professional I had ever met in psychology, social work, therapy, mental health and helping professions was there because they had a personal connection to the work. Some were there because they had been abused in childhood. Some were there because they had never got justice for what happened to them. Others were in their roles because they were in care as a child, and wanted to support other children.

Just as a heart surgeon is passionate about what they do because their dad had a heart condition and died when they were twelve, a psychologist is passionate about what they do because they had some connection to psychological suffering. Except, the first is seen as heroic, and the second is seen as attention seeking, or worse, as a 'wounded healer'. Gah. I hate that phrase so much.

Why did we hide who we truly were? Why did we have to be perfect? Why did we have to pretend we were flawless professionals? Why did we have to stop ourselves from crying with our clients, whilst they sobbed in front of us, recounting the worst moments of their lives? Why did we have to remain neutral? Why did we expect to build honest, meaningful, human connections with people, when we couldn't even communicate with them on an equal platform?

Think about it. Think about the last conversation you had with a therapist, a psychologist, or a professional. It wasn't natural communication, was it? It wasn't a conversation where you shared a story, then they shared a story, then you both shared a story, then you asked a question, then they answered it, then they asked a question and you answered it. It wasn't equal, was it?

It's more likely that you experienced the hyper-professional version of therapeutic conversation, where you disclose in great detail for 40 minutes, whilst they nod, hmm, aah, I see, go on, and the worst of them all, 'How did that make you feel?'

All the while, they won't even tell you their fucking surname or where they live, or whether they have any kids in case . . . well, I don't know! In case you are everything they claim you are not: dangerous, manipulative, vindictive, violent, obsessive, I guess.

As I have written about in my other books, it is alarmingly common for mental health professionals working with women and girls with bogus diagnoses of 'borderline personality disorder' to be told to never tell them anything about themselves, for fear the 'borderline patient' will store up all those snippets of information and then use them against them.

I had to get up out of bed, stop thinking about the disgusting cum-covered headless pictures of myself, and get ready for work.

That day, I had been invited to give a speech. Not just any speech though. I had been asked to chair a parliamentary debate session on the responses to male violence against women and girls. I was absolutely overwhelmed by the invitation, and even ignored the fact that they hadn't paid me a single penny, but charged the delegates £350 a ticket. It was a sell-out event, and for the first time ever, I had actually written a speech.

I had also invited Laura. I guess I wanted to show her what I was capable of. She had been quieter with me since the emails to her started, and I felt that she was becoming suspicious of my talent and skill. I knew that I could show her exactly why I deserved to be on my PhD programme, if she would just watch me give a speech and chair an academic debate at such a prestigious event.

I titled my speech, 'Are we out of the woods yet?'

I looked at the room full of senior professionals, CEOs, journalists and academics. I knew I had to do a good job. A woman I vaguely recognised made a beeline for Laura and went to sit next to her. I completed my usual housekeeping comments, and my official welcome to all speakers, and then began my opening speech.

'The day I was asked to chair this event, a song came on my iPod by Lily Allen. The lyrics go "we've never had it so good, we're out of the woods, and if you can't detect the sarcasm, you've misunderstood". They made me laugh, and they inspired this speech.'

I looked around the room, several people laughed and shook their head, but most people were staring at me. They probably weren't used to a young woman chairing an event like this, much less a young woman who opened the event quoting Lily Allen. Still, I had faith in myself, and I knew I could capture them by the end of my speech.

'It made me think about whether we are really out of the woods, and it made me think about the growing narrative that women and girls are already equal. It made me think of the people who say "Why do we need a violence against women and girls strategy at all?" Mark my words, these narratives are becoming more and more powerful. We are being told that our work is an unneeded movement.'

They were listening intently now. The room was silent. They watched me as I challenged them all to take a breath, step back, and examine the barriers and the hurdles that lay ahead of us all. Every now and then, I glanced over at Laura, to see how it was landing, but she was almost silently whispering to the woman who had gone to sit next to her.

'We are told that women can work now, does that not make us equal? Women can wear what they like – as much or as little as they want, does that not make us equal? We are told that women can choose when and where they have sex, who they have sex with, and can simply say "no" if they are not interested. Does that not make us equal?'

I can hear them breathing, shuffling, thinking.

'You can get drunk. You can party all night. You can be sexually liberated. You can marry who you want, when you want, then divorce them when it isn't working. Does that not make us equal? And when the bad things happen, you can report, you can seek help, you can get justice, you can be vindicated . . . all without stigma, apparently!'

A woman chuckled and shook her head. There would always be at least one person in the room who was on my wavelength from the beginning. She looked at me and nodded.

'But what about the gender pay gap? Lack of promotion? Sexism in the workplace? Questions about whether she is going to have a baby? Sexual harassment? And if you work hard, and you make it to the top, someone will say you slept your way there, gave some blowjobs along the way, shagged the guy on your promotion panel . . .'

A few winced at my language. It never fails to amaze me that these people can sit around all day talking about violence, murder and rape, but can't stand it when I swear in a speech.

'And they can say that we can wear what we want, but it won't leave you free from judgement. If something happens to you, what you are wearing becomes one of the first things that will be questioned. In fact, it might even become the single factor that destroys your case against your rapist. Why did you wear that? Was it to draw attention to yourself? What did you expect was going to happen? Why did you try to look sexy? Why are we still asking these questions?'

I thought of the time I had supported a sixteen-year-old girl to give evidence against the twenty-two-year-old man who had raped and beaten her up. I remember my heart sinking as she walked into the courthouse wearing a low cut, sleeveless, almost transparent vest top. It wasn't that

I cared what she wore, hell, she could have turned up in her pyjamas for all I cared, but I took one look at her and knew how the judges were going to react. Just last week, as I was writing this book, I was working on a case where the police officers told me that they knew the CPS were going to drop the rape charges against an extremely dangerous man as soon as the teenage victim turned up to do the video interview in a crop top and hot pants.

The system isn't changing. Progress is a myth. I know that now, and I knew that back in 2017 when I was making this speech.

'They say to us, you are equal now. You can have sex with who you want, you even have to give your consent, and the man has to listen to you. Yes means yes, and no means no. But I just don't accept this to be true. If it was, none of us would even be here today, sat in a conference room in London, discussing our responses to the increasing violence against women and girls in our communities. Most of us in this room would be instantly, and happily, made redundant if women were protected from sexual violence. Hundreds of thousands of women and girls are subjected to rape and abuse every year in this country alone, and those figures are going nowhere.'

The mix of the leaders in the room started to show itself. Those in leadership in the criminal justice system were uncomfortable, but those working with victims knew that I was speaking the cold, hard truth. Something, in a highly politicised and incestuous system, that is actually quite rare. Ironic really, for something supposed to be based on finding the truth through testing evidence.

I moved on.

'Consent education might be the "next big thing", but it won't work . . .'

It was like taking shots at everyone in the room, one by one. It was Feminist Tin Can Alley.

I wasn't doing it on purpose, but in order to break down our failing systems no stone could be left unturned. There had been far too much reliance on the belief that you could simply teach 'consent' and it would end sexual violence, which completely ignores the most obvious facet of sex offending: they don't give a fuck if you say no.

'Teaching "yes means yes" and "no means no" sounds simple enough,' I continued, 'but that ignores the fact that the media pushes powerful and endless narratives of token resistance. Now, some of you may never have heard that term before, but token resistance is the concept that women and girls say no, when they really mean yes. They play hard to get. They act coy. They make it difficult for men, so they don't appear easy. And you might be thinking, "what on earth does that have to do with consent?"'

I looked around the room, and indeed, there were many confused-looking faces. But I was about to clarify it for them.

'I want you to think about the last chick flick or romcom you watched. The film where the guy meets the girl. The love story,' I smiled, and waited for them. Some of them smirked, nodded, glanced at their colleagues.

'Now listen to me carefully – almost all romantic comedies are stories of token resistance. The main character is always a woman, doing all right for herself, a good job in a city, going off to college, or working on a project she cares about – and then she is distracted by a male main character. But she always begins by telling him that she isn't interested in him . . .'

They watched me intently. It was as if I could hear their collective thoughts.

'And then you watch, as the next 90 minutes is a story of him winning her over. Following her. Throwing rocks at her window to wake her up. Serenading her at the park. Turning up at her workplace with flowers. Challenging her ex-boyfriend. Deliberately bumping into her. Sending her love letters. Getting a job at the place where she works. Flying out to where she is on holiday with her friends. Proposing to her at her nan's funeral . . .'

The room chuckled and shook their heads. Colleagues looked at each other. One woman pointed at her friend and mouthed 'You love those films!' They knew what I was talking about. They had all seen films like that, and they were beginning to realise just how common token resistance narratives were.

'So basically, you watched 90 minutes of sexual harassment and stalking.'

And with my punchline delivered, the whole room fell about with laughter. I smirked. I loved that bit. I let them chatter and gently poke fun at each other. Some people moaned that I had ruined their favourite films for them.

I started speaking again, and they settled.

'You see, we are being groomed. From birth. When I first started talking about token resistance, many of you had never even heard of it, and yet, I give you an example, and you all know exactly what I am talking about. What is the benefit of teaching millions of women and girls, men and boys, that no really doesn't mean no, it means maybe, it means try again later, it means try harder?'

I looked over at Laura, who was watching me carefully. She had been working in sexual violence research for years, and I think it is fair to say, had become one of those academics who was clearly excellent at what she did, but was cut off from the reality of sexual violence all around us. Her connection to sexual violence and abuse had been reduced to running statistical tests on datasets in her office overlooking the campus, in her seventy-grand-a-year job.

'We are being told we can be equal members of society, but when we participate and take up space, we are told we are bitches, mouthy, bossy, aggressive, demanding, arrogant, self-obsessed and out for ourselves. We are told to love ourselves by companies that want us to buy their fucking moisturiser, and then when we actually do love ourselves, we are told we are narcissists!'

Some people laughed, and some people grimaced at the swear words again. Frankly, I was bored of the prudes. Imagine being so offended by mere words.

'And you can go out and party if you like. You can drink alcohol. You can get a bit wavy. Get smashed, if you like. But let's not pretend that you won't be blamed when you are sexually assaulted or raped. Research is still telling us that alcohol is one of the other factors that will very quickly be used to blame you for whatever was done to you whilst you were under the influence . . .'

A very senior investigator for the police told me that attacking the character of a woman who was drunk when she was raped was 'like shooting fish in a barrel'.

'And we still have that really strange dichotomy where the more drunk the woman is, the more responsibility she has in a rape committed against her, and the more drunk the man is, the less responsibility he has in the rape he committed.'

A crowd of faces nodded with me. I could feel that my points were landing.

'We know our criminal justice system is broken. We have a 2 per cent conviction rate of sexual offences. Less than 15 per cent of women report sexual violence to the police, and of teenage girls, it is less than 5 per cent. Every year, the police record hundreds of thousands of sexual offences – and yet, there are probably ten to twenty times more that we don't ever hear about. What would happen, if every woman reported every instance of male violence she had ever been subjected to?'

I paused, to let them think. I had realised over the years that many professionals had never actually considered how common male violence is. They become narrowminded, and they start to only consider the violent rapes and the horrific child abuse. They forget about all the times they were wolf-whistled on their way to school. Or the way their driving instructor touched their leg. Or the gymnastics instructor who told them they had gorgeous legs. It all gets shoved down somewhere. They don't realise how much they have lived through themselves.

And that is where the 'them' and 'us' dichotomy thrives: in the belief that some women are just more prone to being abused and assaulted, and others are protected from the same violence.

'What would happen, if today I asked you all to sit and take ten minutes, to write down every single time you were wolf-whistled, stalked, followed home from school, had your skirt lifted up, had your bra strap pinged, were shouted at by some greasy builders on some scaffolding, yelled at by some men in a white van on your way to school, touched up by a bouncer, grabbed in a crowd, hit on by your teacher, hit, smacked, choked, shoved, pushed, kicked, spat at, thrown across a room? Forced to have sex when you didn't want it. Forced to do stuff you didn't want to do. What about how many times you were told they would leave you if you didn't give them what they wanted? Woke up to them having sex with you in the middle of the night, whilst they assured you that you came on to them in your sleep. How many times have you laid there and let them have sex with you whilst you just waited for it to be over, so they would leave you alone and stop being mardy?'

I paused again. I let it sink in. I let it soak in.

'I will tell you what would happen if I asked you to recount those things. You would all have a list as long as your fucking arm.'

Some women stared blankly, clearly recounting time after time after time. Grope after grope. Fear. Coercion. Abuse. Assault. Rape.

'So, on the surface, it might look like we are "out of the woods" but then you and I know that isn't true. We are so deep in the woods, that we can't even see the daylight any more. Sometimes we are not even sure which direction it is to get out of the woods. We think we know the way out of the woods, but then realise there are huge fallen trees blocking our way out . . .'

I was adlibbing again. But I liked my woods metaphor. It was working.

'And I need you to realise that there are many who don't ever want us to find our way out of the woods at all.'

I looked around the room. How I wished they would all realise that as we become tied up with bureaucracy and politics, we lose touch with reality. We buy tickets at £350 a pop to listen to someone else say the same shit as someone else said last week at the other conference. I was a firm believer that we needed to stop patting each other on the back, telling each other we were making progress, and instead, start being honest about the state of the world for women and girls.

'We are making mistakes. I know this is hard to hear. But our policies, procedures, service design, processes, interventions and risk assessments are all pointing in the wrong direction. They all hyperfocus on the personality, the behaviours and the characteristics of the woman or girl. They all force her to change something about herself. They force her to take responsibility for male violence, and protect herself better . . .'

This is where I tended to lose people. Once they realised that I was advocating that we rip up the playbook and start again, their defences usually went up.

'I have written some things down here that I have seen in the last few months in real practice in this country. We are telling women "don't get raped", "look out for abusers", "spot the signs", "take rape self-defence classes", "wear anti-rape knickers", "walk home with your house keys sticking out of your fingers", "ring us when you get home", "check your backseat before driving off", "don't walk home", "check the taxi is registered before you get in", "do not take any risks", "never accept a friend request from a stranger", "never meet a date in a private place", "never send nudes to your partner in case two years later, they decide to put it on Facebook", "don't wear your hair in a ponytail", "don't walk around with your headphones in" . . .'

I slowed down for them.

'Don't move, breathe, blink or fucking speak a word – because you might just get raped!'

A few women laughed, muttered under their breath and nodded to me.

'And so, to you all, my question is this: Have we given up on changing society? Have we decided that the only thing we can do, is make women's lives smaller and smaller, until they have no life at all? What are we going to discuss here today that could change the world for women and girls, without having to ask them to change themselves?'

The other speakers shifted nervously, and looked up at me from the panel. A couple of them were carefully striking out parts of their own presentation notes.

'Are we out of the woods yet? Are we fuck!'

I looked around the room as they burst into applause. I breathed out. I had done it.

The day was perfect. I hosted as well as I could. I kept the speakers on time. I managed a fascinating and interactive Q&A panel. The speakers did a great job. The delegates left, and many of them stayed behind to chat to me, ask for my card, or congratulate me on my speech.

Laura waited behind, and we walked back to the train station together.

'How did you find today?' I asked her nervously.

'Yes, it was very interesting. Lots of influential contacts there, too. People seemed to love what you had to say. The people on my table were talking about your work, too . . .'

'Ah, that's good to hear. I'm glad everyone had such a useful day . . .'

It went quiet between us.

'I really appreciate you taking the time out to come along, Laura. Thank you for coming. I know you haven't always understood what I do outside of my PhD, but I am so glad you have been able to see the kind of influence I can have to encourage leaders and professionals to think bigger, and to think more critically. Lots of these professionals become institutionalised, and they lack critical thinking – I love being able to shake them up a bit!'

'Hmm. Yes. About that actually . . .'

I looked at her. I knew she had been off with me. I watched the traffic of people and vehicles charge through London, at a pace only known to the city. A place that used to intimidate me. A place that was alien to me. A city I had only ever heard of on the TV, that I had only set foot in for the first time at twenty-four years old, had become a place I frequented. It had a tense energy. An urgent energy.

And yet we were stood still outside Waterloo station.

'I know you are probably expecting this, but we have had more complaints about you. They are getting more serious . . .'

People pushed past me, but I was stuck in that moment.

'In what way?' I asked her.

'The concerns they are raising, the action they want us to take . . . the allegations being made . . .' She gave a sympathetic smile and tucked her thick brown hair behind her ear.

'Allegations? What on earth?' I laughed and pushed my glasses back up my nose.

She changed.

'I don't find this funny. I am surprised you are laughing, to be quite honest with you . . .'

I looked at her. We were clearly in very different positions. She couldn't understand why I was laughing at the complaints, and I couldn't understand why she was taking them seriously.

'Look, it's an anonymous troll, who won't even reveal who they are, Laura. If their complaints are so serious, tell them to submit them formally to the university. If there was any substance to these complaints, I'm pretty sure you would have already referred them for investigation anyway, so I don't really see the point in entertaining these emails any further.'

She frowned.

'People are talking about your . . . professionalism,' she picked over her words slowly.

'In what way?' I asked again.

'The way you talk. The way you are. The way you say things. I think a lot of people find you challenging, confrontational . . . and aggressive.'

'Oooh. Original! Have they included "bossy"?' I smirked, but she wasn't amused.

Silence fell between us.

'Oh come on,' I prodded, 'you must realise what is happening here. A bunch of emails from someone who won't formally complain, who makes petty personal comments about me, who criticises where I'm from, makes comments about me being a teen mum – this is personal, and I think you already know that.'

Oof, that was brave of me.

'Are you suggesting this is targeted, and personal?' she pressed me.

'No, I am not suggesting it, I am telling you directly. You're just refusing to accept it,' I quipped back.

'It seems that you have many people who "target you".' I didn't like the tone of that sentence.

'What is that supposed to mean?' I said, raising my eyebrow.

'Nothing. I am just thinking about all the instances that you tell me of, where you have been targeted online. Why do you think that is?'

I knew that question wasn't genuine, but I decided to answer her.

'Because I am saying things that make people uncomfortable, and I am making changes that people do not want. Because I am young. Because I am a woman. And probably, because I am working class.'

Those were not the answers she wanted to hear, and she sighed.

'Do you talk online about the times you are targeted and trolled?'

'Sometimes. If I did it all the time, it would be all I ever posted. Just this morning a dude sent me photos of myself with my head cut out of them, that he had wanked off over. The other day, a guy sent me a message telling me to kill myself. Most days I get called fat, ugly, bitch, cunt, slut . . . everything really. Some of them are just one-off messages, and some of them are obsessed with me, and will post ten times a day for months . . .'

Her face went through disgust, shock, horror, annoyance and impatience in the space of my sentences.

'Hmm. One of the complaints references something about you alleging a man is harassing you . . . and that you should not allege harassment unless there is a conviction.'

Hang on? What?

'That's not how the law works,' I muttered. 'What a ridiculous comment to make. So, I can't say I am being harassed unless I have reported them, been to court, and they have been found guilty? What a load of shit! Hang on . . . is the person emailing you a man?'

'I'm afraid they have asked to remain anonymous . . .'

I became annoyed at the level of loyalty to the email sender.

'But what if they are harassing or stalking me, then it would be a crime, and I could report it to the police . . .'

'I don't think this is the case,' she dismissed.

'I don't think that is your decision to make,' I responded firmly.

Silence again. Laura checked her watch.

'Look, I have to get going, I have a train to catch in 10 minutes, and the platform is quite a walk away from here.' We said brief and awkward goodbyes, and I watched her walk away.

My mind kicked into detective mode.

Clues. Clues. Clues.

Breadcrumbs. Everywhere.

Laura is weirdly defensive of the person sending the emails, so she must know them or have some connection to them, I thought to myself as I walked to check the train times.

The sender has a motive for defending a man who has been harassing me on the internet, too. They seem to have a stake in discrediting my work . . . I stared at the train times, but I wasn't taking the information in. I shook my head, and forced myself to concentrate. Platform 10A. Focus.

As I walked to the train, I mused on the fact that the sender of the emails seemed to understand the structure of academia, and knew to email my professor directly rather than using the university complaints form. They also seem to be utilising my background against me.

Hmm, I thought, staring out of the train window.

Who are you?

And why are you doing this to me?

I took to social media, and started a new page in my notebook. Everyone left a trace, and people were mighty brave on Twitter, so I started there.

Within an hour, I had a list of possible senders, and a list of motives. All the evidence kept coming back to one person.

10

How did those stitches come out?

Winter 2007

We sat on the old wooden bench overlooking the vast graveyard in a tense silence. The wind blew, and I wrapped my coat around me tighter.

'Pregnant?' she echoed back to me.

'I know,' I mumbled.

'But he nearly killed you,' she whispered, staring out at the hundreds of wonky, frosty headstones.

'I know,' I mumbled again, watching the tiny cars in the distance speed down the A500.

'But you said . . . After the last time . . .'

I couldn't even muster up another 'I know'. I had already had one miscarriage because of him pushing me down the stairs, and after that, I had sworn I would never ever get pregnant again. It wasn't as if I wasn't protected either. I was taking the pill every day, well, when I remembered to take it. And I barely had sex with him.

Especially since the incident with the scissors. I shuddered.

'When are you leaving?' she started again, as her long blonde hair flew around her in the cold wind.

'Next week,' I admitted, suddenly realising this would probably be the last time we saw one another.

I had bumped into Gray and Jodie whilst drunk. We were all around the same age, only Jase was older than us three. Him and Gray had hit it off, and started chatting at a local pub, which left me and Jodie to get to know each other. How she had ended up with Gray was beyond me. He was a short, chavvy, funny sixteen-year-old lad with piercings in one ear. He wasn't unattractive, but there wasn't much going on upstairs. Gray lived with his mum and six siblings, in a council house up the road.

Jodie on the other hand was a petite, well-dressed, pretty sixteen-year-old girl with long natural blonde hair. She lived in a detached house on the other side of town with her mum, her dad, and her little sister. She did well at school, her parents were protective of her, and they were less than impressed that she was dating some kid from the estate.

The first time we kissed, it had come as a shock to both of us. The guys had gone to the shop, and we had been smoking weed all afternoon and chatting. The stoned conversation had moved on to us taking turns recounting stupid trends and fads from when we were kids. We were on the floor in the living room, trying to remember how to do the crab. We were way too high to be trying anything so ambitious, and had ended up in a heap on the floor.

We were laughing, gasping for air, and suddenly, we stopped. Our eyes met each other. It went still. And then she leant up and kissed me. We stayed on the carpet, our kisses becoming more and more urgent, until we were interrupted by the sound of the front door opening, and the guys coming in, laughing and arguing about which one of them would win in a fight.

We had sprung apart, breathless and terrified, but they hadn't even noticed. As they walked right by us and into the kitchen, we burst into laughter, and they assumed we were both stoned, and giggling at nothing.

It had happened many times since. We had found umpteen ways to convince Gray and Jase to become best friends, so we could spend more time together. She had become an oasis in my extremely violent and terrifying life.

'I'll miss you,' she said eventually.

'I'll miss you, too.' My mind wandered, and I imagined finding ways to sneak out to see her, but I knew Jase would never let me out of his sight.

She wrapped her arms around me, and put her head on my shoulder.

'I think you'll make an amazing mum,' she whispered into my hair. I would miss this. Whatever this was. I wished it could be something else, but I was pregnant. I was having to leave and go back to my old council estate. A smart girl like her, with her loving family, with all the opportunities in the world – she didn't need to be mixed up with a kid like me.

'I don't have any other choice,' I whispered back, stroking her soft hair with my cold fingers. She sat back up, but shuffled up to me. I put my arm around her.

'What is your mum going to say?'

'I've already told her, she wasn't best pleased,' I muttered, rolling my eyes at the way she had reacted.

'Because you're so young?'

'No,' I laughed, 'because she is pregnant, and she probably doesn't want the limelight taken off her pregnancy and new baby!'

'Your mum is pregnant?' Jodie gasped.

'Yep. We have the same due date.'

'What?' She burst out laughing. 'You do not! Are you taking the piss?' She tickled my ribs, making me laugh and squirm.

'No . . . No . . . Honest . . . We are both due the same week,' I chuckled. What was my life?

'She will become a grandma, the same day she has her own new baby?' she cried.

'I guess so!'

'My mum would fucking slaughter me if I got pregnant with Gray . . . '

I curled my fingers around hers. Her long, manicured nails looked so much prettier than my own, bitten down to nothing.

'What did Jase say when you told him?' she asked quietly.

'He just wants a boy. He has already decided it's a boy. I'm not sure how he would react if I had a girl . . .'

She glanced at me. We both knew.

Jodie asked where we would live, and when she checked that I had friends there, back on the same road on my old estate, to look out for me, I lied and said I did. I didn't want her worrying about me, when she could be getting on with her life.

I kissed her one final time, knowing I would spend months pining for her. I walked back to the house trying not to cry. I couldn't risk Jase noticing anything was wrong, and he thought I had walked to the shops.

We didn't have enough money to pay the rest of the contract, so the only thing for it, was a good old moonlight flit.

The house back on the estate was an old council house that had been bought by one of the rich families from the new estate. They had started buying up our council homes, and renting them back to us at higher prices, of course. It wasn't great, but it was a damn sight better than the rat-infested hell hole I had just come from.

I needed somewhere safe to build a home for the new baby, after all.

Everything about that pregnancy was hell. My body wanted out from the moment I conceived. I had weird pains that lasted months. Red, vicious stretchmarks ripped up my stomach, across my boobs, up my arms, down my legs and made my teenage body unrecognisable. My back hurt. My feet swelled. I was tired, and I was miserable.

Jase was busy with his own life: working, socialising, drinking, shagging. He had quickly bored of the fact I was pregnant, and became resentful that I wasn't giving him sex. I had long realised I was in deep trouble with him, but every girl I knew around me was living the same life as me.

Bianca and Jack had recently had a baby too, and their relationship was one long Jeremy Kyle episode of screaming, cheating, drinking, slamming doors and much worse. She rang me one night when she had locked herself in the bathroom. I could hear him threatening her through the door, kicking the bottom of it and demanding that she let him in. He always got like that on whisky, she said, but I knew it was the coke. It didn't help that he had recently discovered steroids, too, and was frequently smashing the house up in roid rage.

When we saw each other in the street, or at a christening, we all pretended we were grown-ups, living calm, happy, healthy lives. Our boyfriends put their arms around us, and smiled to our friends and families. We kept our boyfriend's secret for them, because the alternative was admitting that we were absolutely terrified of them, convincing others of the truth, and then finding a way to safely escape.

The only thing that cheered me up in those lonely months of pregnancy was food. Pies. Cakes. Sweets. Chocolate. Crisps. Pizza. Chinese food. Chippy tea.

I used to walk to the pie shop in town to buy myself a pie, but buy two, so I could eat one on the way home from the pie shop, and then one later. I convinced myself that I could even buy a third pie, as a treat for walking all that way . . . to the pie shop. My eating was spiralling out of control, but I had nothing else to lean on. Food was the only thing that filled the gaping holes in my life.

Even the women at the Co-op had noticed. Although I don't know how you wouldn't. There's only so many times you can lie about why you are buying a birthday cake twice a week. Who the fuck knows that many people, and why would I be the one buying everyone's birthday cakes? The truth was, I was just going home to eat an entire birthday cake with a spoon, cuddled up on the sofa watching trash TV.

In the nine months I was pregnant, I went from a size 8 to a size 22. I kept telling myself that the 'baby weight' would drop off me once I had it, but let me tell you something, cakes and pies is not baby weight. As a result, I have struggled with eating issues ever since. It is one of the only topics I will not lecture on, teach about, talk about or research. It's just too close, and too painful for me to recount the origins of my toxic relationship with comfort eating.

Mum spent the entire pregnancy in competition with me. When her baby kicked for the first time, it was a miracle moment. When my baby kicked for the first time, she told me it was probably wind, and I needed to stop attention seeking.

I couldn't afford the vast haul of baby items, accessories and equipment I needed to bring a baby into the world, but Mum took great pleasure in showing me her brand-new Mamas and Papas pram, her matching suite of nursery furniture and her beautiful baby clothes. She bought a baby activity mat and bouncer that looked like an infant version of Alton Towers, and I found an old metal and cloth baby bouncer for £5 outside a charity shop.

When I had become upset about the fact that I couldn't afford the babygrows I would need for a newborn, she had told me that I was overreacting, whilst holding a basket full of brand-new clothes, little boots, blankets, bottles and bibs.

On the day I had my twenty-week scan, I was in no doubt of the sex of my baby. I was having a boy. I knew at eleven weeks. I could feel it in my bones. I could feel it in my body.

'Do you want to know the sex?' the sonographer said wearily, like they had already asked that question fifty times that day alone.

'Yes, please,' Jase answered for me from the chair at the side of the room.

'Okay . . . one moment . . .'

The black and white screen came to life, and I watched as the sonographer pushed and tilted and rolled the probe over my swollen stomach. She was silent as she worked, but I could already make out a head, a body, hands, little feet, and long kicking legs.

I was fascinated. I couldn't believe how clear it was. And how small it was, especially considering the massive weight gain, and a bump that resembled a fucking planet.

'It looks . . . like you . . . are having . . . a . . . little boy,' the sonographer told us, still not looking at me.

'Yes!' Jase exclaimed, jumping up and punching the air. He had gotten what he wanted. I had heard what I already knew. A boy. I was going to have a son.

'I'm going to get him a Stoke kit!'

'You . . . don't support Stoke . . .' I had said in the car, gently, so as not to anger him.

'So?' he snapped back. 'My son lives in Stoke, he is going to support Stoke!'

'But . . . you don't like football. You've never played football. I've never even seen you watch a match. Can you name a single person in the Stoke line up?'

'Can you?' he sneered.

'No . . .'

'So what you asking me for then, if you don't even know yourself?'

'Well, I am not the one wanting to dress him in a football kit of a team I don't support . . .'

'He's going to be a Stokie bloke like his dad. He's not supporting Vale, that's for fucking sure. I hate Vale!'

'You don't know the first thing about Port Vale either!'

'Robbie Williams supports Vale, so I hate Vale.'

'That's a stupid reason. I love Robbie. He's the only thing good that's come out of here.'

'I know you love him. That's one of the reasons I fuckin hate him so much. Prick. His music is shit as well.'

Silence.

'He will be born here. He will live here. He will die here. He will be a proper Stokie. My little mate! I'm going to have a son!'

That moment took me to another level of realisation. Not only was this man violent, abusive, jealous, deceitful and disgusting, but he was about to become a father to a real live human, who he was going to mould into a version of himself. What had I done?

It wasn't that I wanted a daughter over a son, or a son over a daughter. The pregnancy had forced me to consider how I would feel about either of those possibilities, and neither of them filled me with much joy. If I had a daughter, she could grow up in the same violent, hate-filled, sexualised world I was living in, with a rapist as a father. If I had a son, he could grow up in the same violent, hate-filled sexualised world I was living in, and become exactly like his father.

The way I saw it, sat there on my second-hand sofa, was that it was lose-lose for the baby coming into this household. The only buffer this baby had between themselves and their destined life of utter shit was me.

I passed the lonely days and the long summer nights watching re-runs of *Charmed* on Channel 4, surrounded by snacks.

I had been captured by anything magical since I was small. I was absolutely convinced that there was more out there. When I had seen *Matilda*, I had spent months trying to move things with my mind. She was so small, and so smart. So smart, that she could use the power of her mind to spin Uno cards around in the air, and fire carrots at her horrible big brother. She even destroyed the monstrous Miss Trunchbull with the power of her mind.

I knew what the moral of the story was. I knew what the deeper meaning was, but still, maybe there was such a thing as telekinesis? I had stared for so long at glasses of water that I had gone cross-eyed. I had never really given up hope, though. I figured that one day, I would release my inner power, and I would be able to use the other 90 per cent of my brain that the newspapers always said we didn't use. Or something like that.

And there I was at seventeen years old, heavily pregnant, eating something that resembled the chocolate cake from *Matilda* – and looking something like the chubby little boy – and watching four beautiful, smart sisters discover that they were descendants of a long line of witches. That series kept me alive during months of the usual pregnancy stuff: back ache, sleepless nights, fatigue, sickness, swelling and the feeling that it will never end; and the not so usual stuff: the abuse, the attacks, the verbal abuse, the drunken boyfriend, the cheating, the lies, the isolation.

The sisters were named Piper, Paige, Phoebe and Prue. I had watched every episode of every series, and was just getting more and more enthralled in the story of their lives. Piper was in a relationship with a man that perplexed me. The thirty-something floppy-haired blond dude was nice to her. Like, really nice to her. He spoke to her without shouting or swearing. He supported her dreams and ambitions. He was there for her when she needed him. He cared about her sisters and her friends. He took responsibility when he made a mistake, and he apologised if he needed to. He even stuck up for her and protected her when she was being harmed by someone. I mean, obviously, sometimes that was a shapeshifting demon in a top hat from another dimension, but same difference.

It wasn't as if it was portrayed as one of those sickeningly perfect relationships – it was hard for them. She was a witch. He was a whitelighter. She lived in Halliwell Manor, in San Francisco. He was an elder in The Heavens, with the Council of Elders. As you can imagine, they were pretty busy. They had to juggle their marriage, their magic, their parenting, their family life, and saving the world at least once a week.

They still argued. They disagreed. They got frustrated or irritated with each other sometimes. But he never shoved her. Or hit her. He never called her a fat bitch. He never told her he was going to fuck her friends. He definitely never beat her up, or forced her to have sex with him. And he shared all the parenting when they had a baby, too.

He was such a good guy. And if I was going to have a son, I wanted him to be a good guy, like Piper's husband, Oliver. And so, I named my baby Oliver.

It was a record heatwave the day I reached the forty-second week of my pregnancy, and I was ready to drag him out myself. He was more than comfy in there, and was not remotely interested in coming out. I had spent weeks begging nurses, midwives, doctors and hospital receptionists to help me get this massive baby out, but they seemed as relaxed about it as he did.

Jase had me painting the fence and sweeping the patio, because he had complained I had been getting fat and lazy. He had obviously missed the part when the doctor told me I had a disorder of the pelvis which meant that I could hear my bones grinding together every time I tried to move, walk, or even put my own knickers on.

I had ended up almost completely disabled, and for the last eight weeks, had been on crutches to move around the house. Whenever anyone asked how my pregnancy was going, I told them that the baby was trying to kill me from the inside. Piece by piece.

I learned that people did not want to hear that response.

I also learned that other women seemed to look healthier and happier during pregnancy than ever before, whilst I looked like I was turning into a huge, sweaty, spotty, moody blob. I couldn't believe the diversity of how women carried their babies when I was at my antenatal appointments. There were women in there who looked like they had shoved a basketball up their T-shirt to pretend they were pregnant for a laugh. They sprung out of their seats for their appointments, their bump was at the front of their body, their skin glowed, their hair was thick and luscious.

I, on the other hand, had a bump that seemed to go around my sides and my back. My arse had its own timezone. My ankles had disappeared, and my feet were so swollen that they looked like blocks of corned beef with toes on the end.

I could press my fingers into my legs and feet and watch as the dents stayed there for a minute or more, like a memory foam mattress. My boobs were so swollen that I could have rested my chin(s) on them. Oh yes, reader, I was the not-so-proud owner of a double, no, triple chin, that joined my neck somewhere. A 'check', if you will.

My hair had gone through multiple phases of falling out in handfuls, and growing in patches, which had left me with the shittest mullet I have ever seen in my life, and I was having skin breakouts like a fucking teenager. Oh wait, I was a teenager. Maybe it was just a puberty breakout then. Awkward.

On top of everything else, I had developed a craving for chewing the foam they use to make kids swimming aids (which thankfully, I never gave in to), and salt and vinegar crisps suddenly smelled of metal. Salt and vinegar crisps tasted like blood for nine fucking months. It was heartbreaking.

The sun beat down on my skin, and the sweat poured from me. Next door had their paddling pool out, and all I wanted to do was rip the fence panel out and jump in. It wasn't helping that with every stroke of the paintbrush, all I could think about was the scene from *The Karate Kid*, and I was losing the will to live. The baby had slowed down, and I was sick to death of the advice I was being given from everyone I walked past on the council estate.

'Still not had that baby yet?' they would frown, shaking their head in disbelief.

'Have you tried a vindaloo yet?' my neighbour asked over the fence every few days.

'What about a good, hard shag?' Jase's dad had suggested over dinner, whilst I tried not to throw up in my mouth.

Eventually, the hospital relented and induced my labour. I was absolutely insistent that I wasn't going to use pain relief, because I was frightened of drugs and medication of any kind. Everyone in my family was sensitive to gas and air. Most of us are allergic or sensitive to opiate based medicines, and I was worried that they would push me to have an epidural.

The woman in the room next door to me was screaming at the top of her lungs, but I could hear the midwives stood outside my room gossiping about her. They laughed as she screamed through her contractions, called her a drama queen and an attention seeker. One of them whispered loudly that they wished she would shut the fuck up and get over herself.

I decided that I didn't like the midwives on the ward.

One of them popped her head around my door and smiled at me.

'Don't you worry about her next door, duck. I know she's loud and it might be frightening you, but she is only a few centimetres, and she's just . . . a bit . . . dramatic! You're further along than her, and you're in here lovely and quiet!'

I smiled a fake smile at her through my contraction, and she rushed off. I didn't want to get on the wrong side of her. Note to self: do not scream in pain.

'How long is this gonna take?' Jase groaned, rising into a stretch.

'I don't know . . .' I murmured, breathing through the pains.

'Well, are you going to like, push, yet?' he asked.

'I don't know. I don't think so. She said I am about 4cm dilated the last time she checked. I don't know how long it takes to get to 10cm. I don't really know how it will work . . .'

'Well, I'm tired. I've got no phone signal. I haven't had a fag in ages. I am going to go outside for a bit. I'll see you in a bit,' he mumbled, looking down at his phone.

Just before we had left to come to the hospital, I had been packing the last of my hospital bag when he had come to sit next to me.

Agitated, pale, anxious, he had tapped on the table a few times, checked his phone repeatedly, and then said he needed to tell me something.

'I've been cheating on you. For months. With Jordan. She's pregnant,' he spat out.

I fucking knew it. He had been denying it for months, but I had sensed it. But Jordan? And she's pregnant?

I didn't say a single word to him. I had nothing to say. Inside, I raged at him. I slapped him around his smug fucking face. I told him to get fucked, go and have a baby with her then, and leave me and my baby alone. But I just continued packing my hospital bag, and double checking I had everything I would need.

He sighed.

'I feel so much better now I have got that off my chest, babe. It's been bothering me for ages. Phew. Glad I did that.'

The fucking audacity of this guy. I raised my eyebrows in secret, with my back to him, and folded a tiny white baby grow.

'Now we can just focus on being a family, and having our baby, and . . .'

Now I was pissed off.

'Didn't you just say she was pregnant?'

'Well, yes . . .'

'So?'

'Oh, don't worry about that. I have told her she has to have an abortion. I will take her myself on Monday. She probably doesn't want to keep it anyway.' He said those words like it was nothing. Like shagging her for months, and then demanding she has an abortion was just as simple as ordering a pint at the bar.

I hated him, but I still had no other way to get to the maternity ward to give birth to my baby, so I reluctantly got into his car, and we drove there in silence.

I knew he would have been going outside to call her, but I knew I had to focus on the labour. He was useless when he was in the room, so I decided I would probably be better off doing it alone anyway.

As the evening turned into the small hours of the morning, the contractions became more and more unbearable. I bit down on a towel. I breathed through it. I used visualisation to get through the peaks of the pain. I pictured myself lying in a field of lavender. The smell. The purples and greens. The sky above me. The wind on my skin.

As the slippery, bloodied, slimy body of my baby was lumped on to my bare chest, Jase walked into the room. He pretended to the midwives that he had only been gone for a few minutes to call his dad, but they had all been in the room with me for hours, and knew full well he had been missing.

In the weeks before the birth, I had several nightmares about what the baby would look like. In one, I gave birth to a little boy with a mop of dark hair, and small dark eyes like his dad. I woke up drenched in sweat. In another, I gave birth to a four-year-old boy in dungarees, and he came out of me, asked me if I was okay, asked me what was for dinner, and then sparked up a cigarette. He leant on a wall and chatted to me about the birth like he was a builder giving me a quote.

I looked at the tiny, squishy face of the baby on my chest. He was calm and quiet. I stared into his big blue eyes, and stroked his wispy blond hair. He stared at me. The whole room may as well have been silent. It was as if there was no one else there. We stared at each other. I couldn't stop. He barely blinked.

I felt like I had known him my entire life. Like I knew him. Like he was familiar. What a peculiar feeling. It wasn't how I thought I would feel. The warm sun streamed through the blinds as I realised I had been in labour all night. The rays of sunlight fell on us both.

Suddenly, I had a deep sense of responsibility.

Shit, I thought, as tears rolled down my face.

I had just brought this tiny, defenceless human into abuse. I had brought a baby into a relationship where I couldn't even keep myself safe. A few hours ago, it was just me being abused and mistreated. Now, it was me and this baby. I didn't feel guilt. I didn't feel blame. I didn't feel resentment. I didn't even feel fear.

Instead, I was consumed with a feeling of power, and duty. I knew what I had to do. I had to escape.

But that was easier said than done.

'Are you being picked up, me duck?' the nurse on the postnatal ward asked me, for the fourth time.

'Yeah, yeah,' I lied again, 'I'm just waiting for them to get here, they've been stuck in traffic.'

She smiled and walked over to check on another new mum on the ward.

Who was them? Who was they? Who knows. No one was coming for me.

I had been calling Jase for hours. The last time I had heard from him, he had told me he was meeting his friends for a pint to 'wet the baby's head'. Originally, he had told me he would only drink a lemonade. Then it was a shandy. Then he told me he was going to have just one drink, and assured me he would then drive over to the hospital ward to pick us both up.

My baby was sleeping soundly, swaddled up, with his little blue hat on his head. I had managed to have a bath, which was frankly disgusting. I don't know why the nurses sold it to you like it would be relaxing. A bath in your own blood whilst you wince in pain, and the room spins from the exhaustion? The bath looked like the scene from *The Shining*. I was just desperate to go home to my own bathroom and my own bed. I just needed to rest.

Postnatal wards are not a place to rest after you have given birth. In a room with seven other women, everything you can think of can happen. Babies screaming, women crying, flapping bed curtains, the sound of vomiting, women arguing with their partners, talking loudly on the phone, asking the nurses for help, pacing back and forth between the beds whilst rocking their babies.

The wait was getting embarrassing. The nurses had noticed something was wrong, and when he finally turned up over six hours late, I tried my best to assess how drunk he was. As we got into the car, I became suspicious of where he had been. If he had been drinking for six hours with his friends, he would have been sideways somewhere, and there would have been no chance he could have driven the 10 miles to the hospital without wrapping his car around a lamppost.

I was relieved he was sober, but I was seething that he had obviously abandoned us both at the hospital whilst he had gone to meet (and probably shag) Jordan. He took the speedbumps far too fast, and I panicked as I watched Oliver's tiny head bump against the baby seat. He was so much more fragile outside my body. At least when I was pregnant, I had complete control of his physical safety. Now, it just seemed that everything and anything could hurt him.

The first few weeks of my life as a new mum were some of the worst of my life. They were also the weeks that I was faced with the depths of Jase's hatred towards me. I was struggling to cope with multiple injuries from the birth, being extremely sleep deprived, and adjusting to being a new mum – but he couldn't give a fuck.

Every time Oliver cried in the night, he would tip a jug of cold water over my face to shock me awake. I almost sobbed with the injustice of the fact that he would wake up to the noise of crying, and instead of picking his baby up, he would get up, walk to the bathroom, fill a jug with cold water, bring it back, and throw it at me to wake me up. Most of my night feeds were spent freezing cold, sniffing back tears, and wringing wet through.

He would switch into Dad of the Year mode when his family or friends turned up to visit, and would even do a nappy in front of them, but the second the front door closed, he would scowl at me, stand up and walk away. He went out and got a tattoo to commemorate the birth of his first son, but wouldn't even feed him.

Two days after I had given birth, I was cuddled up on the sofa when he started to lose his temper with me.

'Well Bazza told me that his missus shagged him the day after she gave birth and it was fine. One of the lads at work said he fucked his girlfriend when she was still in the postnatal ward. So don't fucking make excuses!'

I didn't believe him for a moment. I knew Bazza's missus, and there is absolutely no way that happened. And having been on a postnatal ward, there was no way some imaginary guy at work had had sex with his girlfriend on a busy ward filled with women, partners, families, babies and nurses.

'Well, everyone is different. I had forty-odd stitches. I'm in agony. I'm still finishing off those painkillers. I can't even go to the toilet without crying . . .'

'You're exaggerating!' he snapped, stood above me.

'I promise you, I'm not exaggerating, but I just can't do it,' I tried to calm him down. Oliver was asleep in my arms. I didn't want any trouble.

'So when are you going to be able to give it to me, then?'

'I don't know. The midwife said the stitches might take a few weeks,' I answered carefully, feeling the tension rise.

'Are you fucking seeing someone else?'

'What? I had a baby two days ago. I haven't even left the house!'

'So? There has to be a reason why you are lying about not being able to have sex with me. Let me check your phone. Where is it?'

'It's on the worktop,' I sighed.

He scrolled through it, faster and faster, getting more and more irate. He was finding nothing to support his wild theory. He slammed my phone down on the old folding dining table.

'Stop fucking lying, and just give me what I want. You know I will just walk out of this house and go and get it from some other girl,' he growled at me.

I knew what was coming. I slowly put Oliver down in his Moses basket, and tucked him in so he was safe. I couldn't keep myself safe, but I could keep him safe. I stood up, and walked away from the Moses basket, to make sure whatever was about to happen to me, would happen away from Oliver.

Jase dragged me to the ground, and I felt the carpet burn my skin.

'Please don't do this. Please, I don't think I can. I don't think I can . . .'

I don't remember the scream I let out, and I don't remember how long it went on for. I will never forget the pain of the stitches ripping open. I will never forget the look of disgust on his face as I limped to the bathroom to run myself a bath, covered in fresh blood.

'Sort yourself out! Fuckin gross, you are. And then don't even think of sleeping in my bed tonight. You can sleep in the spare room. And take that fuckin baby with you!'

I don't know how I kept it together over the days and weeks that followed. Every day felt worse than the last. I had to keep up appearances to everyone else, and I was lying at every turn to hide what my life was really like. I was being beaten, abused, controlled and threatened almost every day – and I would pretend to my friends and family that my life was like wedded bliss.

The only person who knew I was full of shit was my health visitor.

'How did those stitches come out?' She watched me like a hawk.

'Umm, I don't know . . .' I lied, ashamed.

'I think you do know.' The woman with the white short hair looked me dead in the eye, and willed me to speak the truth.

'I think they just fell out . . .'

'Did someone do this to you?'

'No.'

She stared at me, and gave me a look that said, 'I can't force you to tell me, but we both know how those stitches got ripped'.

'You know you're going to need more treatment for that. Don't you?'

I nodded. I did not know that. At all.

'There is a possibility that your body will heal it naturally, but there is a possibility you will need an operation one day. I am going to write up your notes, get you some medication to prevent any infections, and some more painkillers. You must be in agony, duck.' She looked like she wanted to hug me.

'Thank you,' I gulped, trying not to cry. It was so alien to have someone care for me. I was so desperate to tell her the truth, but he would have killed me. And I was scared she would call social services and remove my baby.

I was living a double life. I was trapped, tired, injured, desperate and scared. I was pouring everything I had into being a good mum, and making sure my baby was perfectly looked after and cared for. I walked every day. I took him to baby groups. I talked to him, sang to him, and told him stories. I followed all the guidance. I did everything I could to give him the best possible start. People who knew me then, wouldn't have known that I was recovering from my stitches being ripped out a couple of days after giving birth. They wouldn't have known that I was being drenched awake every time I slept through the little cries. They wouldn't have known that I spent those small hours, seventeen years old, holding my tiny baby, and dreaming of release, of escape, of something more.

11

All the baggage you carry

Spring 2018

'I don't get it, why won't they let me in? I'm telling ya now, this is dodgy as fuck. Something up with this,' Rachel panicked.

I nodded. Something was most definitely up with this.

'You are entitled to have someone with you for a meeting like this. I am the PhD student rep. I should be there. Why the fuck won't they let me in?'

'I don't know mate. I just don't know . . .'

But I did know. The only reason someone would call a meeting about the anonymous complaints about me, and then refuse to let me be accompanied, is because there was something underhand going on. No witnesses means no evidence. No evidence means no consequences. Maybe these academics weren't so different from the people on my council estate after all.

Or maybe humans replicate the same shady behaviour at every level of society, whilst we only associate it with poverty and deprivation. Maybe we have been stupid to believe that people in the higher social classes, and in these professional positions, were any different from the thugs I used to walk past in the gully, hoping not to get strangled, groped, or wolf-whistled.

'I don't think you should go today. Reschedule or something. Tell them you are ill.'

Rachel was one of my best friends, and I adored her. We had met on the first day of our PhD, and we had hit it off right away. Only thirteen people secured a place on our PhD programme that year, and as I listened to each of them introduce themselves, their specialism, their background and their interests, I realised I was the poorest person there. My hands were clamming up. My heart pounded.

Please don't make me introduce myself sounding like this, with this Stokie accent.

Everyone had introduced themselves, and only two of us were left. She went first, and I snapped to attention.

'Hey everyone, I'm Rach. Uhh. Rachel. Did my degree in psychology. Masters degree in neuropsychology. My PhD will be specialising in the neuropsychological basis of hallucinations using fMRI comparison studies.' She introduced herself confidently, loudly, and in a wonderful working class cockney accent. Small, with short dark red layered hair and small, round glasses, with tattoos up one leg. She was smart, assertive, and I liked her instantly.

It was my turn.

'Hey. My name is Jess. My PhD is in forensic psychology, and I will be specialising in the psychology of victim blaming women and girls subjected to sexual violence. I own a research and consultancy company.' I smiled at everyone, but hoped Rachel had noticed me too. I looked over at her, and found that she was grinning at me.

As we went to the break, we found each other, and the conversation was easy. We chatted like we had known each other for years. She had been with the same guy since her undergraduate year, and they recently bought a house together near Birmingham. She grew up in London with her sister and parents. She wanted to be a neuroscientist. She had two cats, she was a brilliant gardener, a bit of a hippy, and, importantly, loved old school hip-hop as much as I did. I had never met another person who knew as much as I did about hip-hop history, and it was so exciting to be able to talk in such depth with someone who understood my passion for music.

'Wanna skip the rest of this induction day and get some lunch together, then?' she laughed.

'Oh, 100 per cent!' We were going to be great friends. I could feel it.

Two years later, and we were sat on a bench on the same campus, trying to figure out what the fuck was happening to me.

'I better go, the meeting is in ten minutes,' I sighed and raised my eyebrows at her. She tucked her hair behind her ears and straightened her glasses. I pulled my rucksack on my back.

'Something ain't right. I don't like it. Record it. Put ya phone on record, and record it for me. I wanna know what's going on!'

We hugged, and I promised her that I would try to secretly record the meeting.

'Don't take any shit, you hear me?' She looked into my eyes, as if she was trying to hypnotise me to do what she said. God, I loved her.

I walked into the room and was instantly taken aback. Who were all these people?

Three women sat in front of me. I had walked into the lion's den, and I could feel it. This had been pre-planned. They had met before my meeting, and they had already discussed whatever was about to happen to me. The secret words of their prior agreements and approaches still hung in the air.

The room was tiny, and there was only just room for all four of us. A large window looked out over the campus. Whilst the tension in the room was obvious to me, I decided to act like I hadn't noticed.

'Afternoon, everyone!' I breezed in, making them all instantly uncomfortable in their seats.

They tried their best to mask, and offered polite welcomes and small talk for a few moments whilst I settled into my seat and got my notebook out. I made sure my phone was recording in my bag, and steeled myself for whatever ambush I had just walked into.

I smiled at them. Show your hand then, I thought.

Laura started, shakily.

'Um Jessica, I have invited Melinda today, and Rosie. They are clinical psychologists and lead on our programme of teaching. They are just here to offer us some advice about the complaints, as they are both experienced in dealing with issues of this nature. I did feel that we would benefit from having them here, so we can find the most effective way of responding to the complaints being submitted about you.'

Well, that is a blatant lie, I thought to myself, whilst deliberately holding eye contact with Melinda and Rosie. Two complete strangers. Both similar looking. Both in their forties, petite, blonde, smartly dressed, wearing glasses. Both holding a handful of paperwork, slightly tilted away from me, again. Both suddenly brought into this situation, without any forewarning. Or were they?

I wasn't allowed to bring Rachel, but Laura had managed to round up not one, but two clinical psychologists with busy schedules and hundreds of students to attend this meeting?

Playing dumb isn't the same as being dumb, friends.

What I had realised during the PhD was that when people already think you are thick, and they already believe they have the upper hand over you, they don't watch you as closely. They don't notice when you play up to their beliefs. They don't notice that you can see right through them.

And so, as much as I hated being regarded as some thick council estate nobody, it came in useful when I realised that I was in situations where I was already being looked down upon, or regarded as unaware. It meant I could pretend I didn't understand things, to force them to explain it again, or repeat something they had just said. It meant I could watch their body language and eye contact. It meant I could ask questions that I already knew the right answer to, to see how they answered me. All the while, I assume they thought my brain was some vacuous, distracted, disadvantaged lump of mush, only concerned with tattoos, drinking, and Gala bingo.

I mean. You can't knock tattoos. I am covered in them. Or drinking. Done my fair share of that. Not a fan of the bingo myself, but each to their own.

And that was the double-edged sword of code-switching. I could hold a room full of academics whilst I presented my theories and findings – and people would regard me as intelligent, astute, capable, powerful, and influential. But I could also sit back, stay quiet, play the role, people-watch, read between the lines, play dumb when I needed to, and let them believe I was too thick to realise what they were really doing.

There was a reason there were two clinical psychologists in this meeting, and it was nothing to do with their pretend experience in dealing with complaints.

'As you know, Jessica, we have now had multiple complaints submitted about you, your work, your social media and your behaviour,' she started again, much braver than usual. Clearly emboldened by her colleagues being with her, I thought. This was going to be interesting.

'And as you know,' I interrupted, 'I am frequently targeted online. I have a large social media following, and a tendency to annoy some people with my critiques and comments about systemic failures. These complaints are malicious, and if the person doesn't wish to follow a complaints procedure, we should be ignoring them.'

Laura glanced at Melinda. Melinda gave a subtle look back. It was a 'this is what I was telling you about' look. It was a 'I told you she would say that' look.

She ignored my comment, and continued.

'As a recap of the complaints, which I think would be helpful for Melinda and Rosie, there have now been nine emails submitted to me directly. Many of them focus on the campaign you have been running to put an end to the use of the films used with children which you claim traumatise them. However, some of the other emails state that you overestimate your own knowledge, that you are unprofessional, aggressive, argumentative, opinionated and self-promotional,' she read out from the pages in her hands, without looking at me.

'It reads like a list of words misogynists use about women,' I sneered. 'Do you really expect me to take that seriously?'

'Yes, we do,' Laura said firmly, looking me in the eye.

'Well then, can I ask you something? In the years we have worked together, have we ever argued?'

'No . . .'

'Have I ever been difficult to work with? Argumentative? Overestimated my knowledge? Been aggressive to you or anyone else? Been unprofessional whilst lecturing, researching or studying?'

She looked down at the printed emails again.

'I don't think that is relevant,' she replied.

'I think it is. And do you want to know why? Because I think this person is a stranger. I don't think this person has ever met with me, talked to me, worked with me or otherwise. I think they are someone from social media who has a problem with me, and has chosen to target me via you. You on the other hand, have known me and worked closely with me for two years, and prior to this we have had a good working relationship. You have offered me lecturing work, research contracts, and I have presented with you at conferences and symposiums. Why does this person have so much influence over you?'

'They wish to remain anonymous,' she reminded me.

'Oh yes, I think you've made that abundantly clear. But that is not what I asked,' I snapped back.

Melinda stared at me. She didn't like me, and it radiated from her. I could see her words burning in her mouth.

Come on then, I thought. Say your piece.

'You believe the person sending the emails is targeting you, and you think they are in a position of influence?' Melinda probed.

'The person sending the emails is clearly targeting me, and the person is either in a position of influence,' my mind connected some dots somewhere, 'or it is a friend of Laura's . . .'

I realised I hadn't thought to check the connections between the names on my list, and Laura. I made a mental note to do some more digging when I got home. Laura looked uncomfortable.

'And why do you believe that?' she pushed a little further.

'Because there are no other possible reasons as to why such petty and personal emails would be taken this seriously. If I was receiving emails like this about one of my undergraduate students, I would quickly conclude that the person was malicious, and ignore the emails. If they continued to send them, I would probably reply to tell them that their behaviour amounts to harassment, and if they carried on, I would report them, to protect my student. At no point during the last few weeks has anyone talked about the impact on me, or how to protect me from this person. The emails have been taken seriously from the beginning, despite the fact the person refuses to follow our complaints procedure.' I set out my arguments logically and clearly.

'So, you think Laura has something to do with this?' Melinda twisted.

I knew she had added that bit herself, but I couldn't lie. I was growing more and more suspicious of her motive in pursuit of these ridiculous complaints.

'Possibly. At the very least, she is protecting and prioritising the sender. There will be a reason for that,' I looked directly at Laura as I said it, and she tried to hold my gaze, but eventually looked away. I knew I was right. So, it was someone she needed to protect. Interesting.

Laura took over from Melinda, and Rosie remained silent.

'There have been some concerns raised . . . about . . . your mental health, Jessica,' Laura started.

Whoa. Curveball. Alarm bells went off in my head. My mental health? Who by? On what grounds?

'Sorry?' I managed.

'The person sending the emails has raised with us, that there are two interviews of you on the internet where you disclose the fact that you grew up in poverty, lived on a council estate, that you were raped, and had a baby from that rape.' She looked at me as if that was the worst thing in the world.

'Right?' I asked, irritated.

'Well, they are very detailed . . .' Melinda said gently.

'And?'

They all became uncomfortable. Was I supposed to be ashamed of the interviews I did? Was I supposed to apologise, tell them I would have them removed, tell them I regret them? Was I supposed to be shocked that someone dug them up from years ago? I wasn't sure how they wanted me to respond.

'Well, it just seems that you are still very traumatised by what happened to you, and we are not sure it is healthy for you to be carrying that into your profession as a psychologist . . .' Rosie piped up.

'Sorry, what evidence do you have that I am still "very traumatised"? A few weeks ago, when you didn't know these things about me, I was being given so many opportunities, I couldn't even keep up with the emails. Now you have read some interviews about my life on the estate, I am "very traumatised"?'

'It just seems that, if you had moved on from it all, you wouldn't feel the need to give interviews like that, would you?' Melinda tried.

'Please tell me you don't work with victims of abuse and trauma,' I laughed at Melinda, obnoxiously.

Laura stared at me, clearly shocked by my response.

'You don't actually believe that when someone has "moved on" from trauma and abuse, it means they never speak about it again?' I prodded Melinda, ignoring the outrage I was causing.

She swerved my questions.

'The complaints about you raise the fact that you may not be suitable to be a psychologist, especially with your background, and all the . . . baggage . . . you are carrying. Let me ask you something, have you ever had therapy?'

'How is this relevant to my PhD?'

'Answer her question, please,' Laura directed.

I thought about my answer. If I said yes, she could claim I was unstable. If I said no, she could claim I was in denial.

'Yes, I accessed therapy years ago, and it was a very important part of my journey. I also have monthly clinical supervision due to my work with victims and witnesses, which is considered best practice,' I explained, knowing every word I used would be scrutinised.

'So you're still having therapy, then?'

'No,' I said slowly, 'I pay for clinical supervision, which is suggested as best practice for anyone who works directly with clients, like I have done. I started having it when I was working in a sexual assault and rape centre, and I have had the same supervisor for five years now. I pay for two hours per month, and we work through my projects, clients I was seeing at the time, how I was feeling in general, how to manage any difficult issues at work, and anything else I needed to discuss in my session. Everyone I worked with had it, it was mandatory,' I explained.

'Sounds like therapy to me,' Melinda quipped, and looked at the others.

'Then you mustn't understand it,' I snapped back.

'I just think it is important that people . . . like you . . . get the right help they need . . .'

'People. Like. Me?' I repeated back to her, wondering if she could hear herself.

'Have you ever had a psychological assessment, Jessica?' Rosie chipped in.

'I think I might be having one right now,' I said, scowling at all three of them.

My comment cut the conversation dead. They knew what they were doing. I knew what they were doing, and now, they knew that I knew.

I had been mentally noting down every little red flag in my head. The description of me as aggressive, opinionated, and overestimating my knowledge. The fact that they kept pushing me about feeling targeted. The way Melinda tried to belittle me for saying that the person sending the emails was clearly a person of influence, or was connected to Laura. Then the comments about my life. The comments about my mental health, about disclosure, about baggage, about psychological assessments.

They were formulating me, right in front of me.

The reason they didn't want Rachel there, another smart psychology PhD, is because she would have sniffed it out too. And then I would have had a witness to this surprise psychological interrogation.

The realisation dawned on me. They thought I was unstable. They thought I was mentally ill. They were siding with the sender, because they agreed that I was not suitable to become a psychologist. They were ignoring my skill, my knowledge, my academic abilities, and were now looking at me through this dirtied lens. I wasn't 'Jess, our high-flying PhD scholar' any more, I was 'Jess, that woman from the council estate on our PhD programme who kept a baby from rape'.

My face flushed, hot and red, and my eyes welled up with tears.

Do not fucking cry in front of these vultures, I screamed inside my mind. Do not give them what they want, Jessica. They will smell weakness and pick over your corpse. Do not cry. Breathe. Breathe, for fuck's sake.

But it was too late. I was already crying.

They all looked at me in silence. It had only taken them forty-five minutes, and I had become what they claimed I was: emotionally unstable, and traumatised by my past.

Who are you? my mind screamed. Stop fucking crying

and defend yourself! They cannot do this, and you know it! Don't you dare give up now!

Everything I had ever lived through spun through my mind like a kaleidoscope. The estate. My old houses. The poverty. The bailiffs. The suffering. The miscarriages. Years of abuse. The violence. The drugs. The drink. The rapes. The disappointments. The pain. The anger.

And then I thought about how I had got myself to this stuffy little office in the first place.

The long nights studying. The exhaustion. The self-discipline. The sacrifices I had made. The early mornings getting the kids ready, and the late nights writing assignments. The determination. The commitment to learning and reading. The thousands of disclosures. The women and girls I had helped over the years. The meetings. The case notes. The helplines. The focus groups. The training. The dreams. The ambitions. The tenacity. The fucking obsession with giving my kids the life I never had.

'You know what?' I stood up, and angrily started packing my notebook back into my rucksack. 'If this is how you want to do this, let's do it.'

They all looked up at me.

'Whoever you are protecting might not want to make this formal, but I do. Let's do this properly, and let's find out what's really going on here. I am going to submit a formal complaint.'

The women exchanged glances, but said nothing.

As I walked towards the door to leave, Melinda just couldn't help herself. She had to have the last word.

'It's all a bit . . . rich isn't it? Fantastical? A convenient conspiracy theory, that you are being targeted by an anonymous person, someone connected to Laura, who has something against you because of your background?'

I stopped in my steps.

'A conspiracy theory?'

'Yes.'

'We'll see,' I warned them, and walked out of the office, down the dusty corridor, out into the daylight, and back to the multi-storey carpark.

My sobs filled the stale air of my car. My safe space. The place I could let it all out. Tears streamed. My chest heaved. My hands shook. I knew I was walking into an ambush, that much was obvious, but I was not prepared to be psychologically scrutinised by two women I had never met, and a woman I had looked up to for years.

I needed to read those emails.

I wracked my brains. How could I get access to them?

And then I was struck with an idea. If the emails named me, I could use the data protection policy to request any written data held about me, which included all emails. Inbox. Sent box. Deleted box.

Game on.

12

How long is a piece of string?

Spring 2009

'Would you like to place a bet today?' I asked in my best telephone voice.

'Uhh. Yeah.'

'Do you have your account number there?'

'Yeah, 432985 . . .' he read out.

'One moment whilst I just access your account.'

'No worries love,' he mumbled.

'Could you confirm your surname for me?'

'Adams.'

'And your first name?'

'Mark.'

'And the first line of your address and postcode?'

The guy on the phone exploded.

'For fuck's sake love, I'm trying to place a fucking bet. By the time you have finished with these questions, the fucking game will be over!'

I looked at Aria, panicking, but she gestured for me to continue. Keep going, she mouthed.

'I'm sorry about that Mr Adams, I just needed to get through security for you. Which bet would you like to place?'

'Finally. Fucking hell. I want £50 on the Chelsea game to end 2–1. To Chelsea. Obviously.'

'Okay, bear with me one minute. We've got that up at 5/2, do you wish to place your bet at those odds?'

He was not happy with that.

'5/2, it was fucking 4/1 on your website a minute ago!'

'I am sorry about that Mr Adams, the odds are live, and they do change,' I tried to explain.

'Well fuck your bet then! Fuck's sake.' He hung up.

I pulled my headphones off and sighed. Aria patted me on the back.

'You did really well there to hold your nerve. You don't need to take abuse from the callers though. You could have warned him about his language, and then if he carries on, our policy is that you can simply hang up on him. All calls are recorded anyway, so if it ever happens, we will be able to listen back.'

She smiled at me. She had been a brilliant mentor for the last few weeks. I never imagined myself working in a call centre for a betting company, but I needed the money. Jase was drinking us dry, hiding his wages, and leaving me and Oliver to struggle for nappies and milk. My nana had offered to babysit whilst I worked twenty hours per week, and I had been really enjoying it. My neighbour worked there too, and had kindly been giving me lifts to and from work, so I didn't have to spend my wages on the bus.

'So what are you doing later, then?' I asked her.

'Probably going out with my girls, getting smashed, then Ricky will pick me up. He's a good egg! That's why I'm marrying him!'

Her deep brown eyes beamed whenever she spoke about Ricky. They had been high school sweethearts, and were absolutely besotted with each other. They were both Italian, and he had asked her father for her hand in marriage before proposing to her at a beautiful restaurant in London. Ricky was a history teacher, and Aria was just about to start her teacher training, too. The job at the betting company was her stop-gap job between her degree and becoming a qualified primary school teacher.

'Doesn't he . . . mind?' I asked, lowering my voice.

'Mind what?'

'Picking you up when you have been on a night out with the girls?' I was so embarrassed to be asking her, but I couldn't help it. He just seemed so . . . nice.

'Why would he mind? He would rather pick me up than know I was getting in those dodgy fucking taxi companies in Stoke. If you turn up at your destination in one piece, and without being groped, or asked for a blowy, it's a fucking miracle!'

She was right. The taxi drivers where I lived regularly asked us if we wanted to pay in money or not. Only last week, and even with Oliver in the baby seat next to me, one had helped carry my shopping bags in for me, and then followed me into my kitchen and demanded sex.

You played Russian roulette when you got in a Stoke taxi.

'Doesn't your boyfriend pick you up when you go on nights out?' She watched me carefully, putting her dark hair up in a messy bun.

'He doesn't really like me going out with friends . . . to be honest . . .' I stared at my notepad, doodling.

She sat up straight.

'When was the last time you went out with your friends? Got proper hammered and had fun?'

'Never,' I mumbled.

We both knew what that meant. It was humiliating to admit. She sensed the tension, and changed the topic quickly.

'Isn't it funny how many English words there are for getting drunk?' she chuckled.

I suggested we try to list them. She looked over her shoulder. Our manager was busy.

'Go on then!' she whispered.

'You first!'

'Ummm drunk. Hammered. Smashed. Pissed. Fucked. Twatted. Battered . . .' Aria listed off with ease.

'Trollied. Paralytic. Steaming. Wasted. Plastered. Blotto. Lit. Sloshed . . .' I laughed as I added the ones I could think of.

'Haha! These are hilarious! Ummm . . . legless. Bladdered. Mullered. Tipsy. Trashed. Rat-arsed!' Aria thought of plenty more, and it felt like we could have gone on forever.

We fell about giggling as quietly as we could. This was definitely not part of my induction.

'It's like you can turn any word into meaning that you are drunk. Let's make a new one up!' I suggested.

'You are right. Hmm. What shall we go with? Varnished? No . . . no . . . Skated . . . Lemoned. Gonna go out tonight, get absolutely banana'd,' she giggled, her face on the table.

I thought about it. What word could we use?

'What about queenied. Queenied? Going out tonight, gonna get fucking queenied!'

We loved it.

'Oh my god, let's test it on someone. Let's just talk about getting queenied over lunch, and see if anyone notices! I'll say I'm going out with my girl mates tonight to get queenied, and then you say something like "the last time I got that queenied, I threw up next to B&M!"'

'Brill,' I giggled, wiping the tears from my eyes.

It was this close friendship I was building with Aria that meant she was the person who finally gave me the shove I needed to escape Jase. Weeks went by, and we talked more and more about our relationships. She was the first person I had ever told the truth to, and she couldn't hide her horror at my years of terrifying stories.

'You have to kick this bastard out. That, or I'm gonna ask my brothers to kill this motherfucker,' she had ranted to me one night, when she offered to drive me home. She stood in my living room, holding a chubby five-month-old Oliver in her arms, and kissing his slobbery face.

'I mean, where the fuck is he? You've just finished work, you've picked your baby up from your nana's for god's sake, and where is he? It's 10:30pm. He should be here looking after his fucking baby.'

I shrugged. I understood her anger, but I was used to his disappearing acts. I never really knew where he was, I only knew where he told me he was, and I knew those were two different things.

'Kick him out. Fuck him! He's ruined your fucking life for so long. I cannot believe no one around you has told you this before. He's a wanker. You are gorgeous, smart, funny, you're a brilliant mum, you have this beautiful little boy. Stop wasting your fucking life with this bastard and kick him out!'

She put her spare arm around me, and I put my tired head on her shoulder. She was right. I needed to escape this abuse. The violence had only been getting worse since Oliver was born, and I was terrified of Jase being able to influence my baby.

I don't know what on earth possessed me, but after she left, I text him.

I have thought about this a lot, and I have decided that this relationship needs to end. You treat me like shit. You have done since I met you when I was just a kid. I have no freedom, no life, and no friends. I don't want this any more. Please come and pick up your stuff, and go and stay with your dad for a while whilst we figure out what to do. Sorry.

I didn't even get chance to lie in bed, stressing about his response. My phone vibrated immediately.

Fine. I'm sick of u anyway. I'll go me dad's then! Don't expect me back tonight.

I starfished in my double bed. I had done it. It was going to end. I was going to get my life back. He hadn't even argued. Probably too wrapped up in some other girl's legs to care. Good. That suited me. I was so proud of myself. I fell fast asleep, and both me and my baby slept soundly all night.

But I should have known that was too easy.

Three weeks later, I was in the back of a police car. It was my second journey of the day. The first one was to the hospital to get treatment for my badly injured shoulder and neck. The second was to the interview suite. The two male coppers in the front were quiet, and were having their own private conversation under their breath. I didn't care that they weren't talking to me. My head was up my arse. I didn't want a conversation anyway.

Earlier that morning, Jase had turned up to my house after three weeks of living at his dad's, shagging anything that moved, drinking, doing drugs and having the time of his life.

'I want to see my son!' he had slurred at me as he wobbled on the step.

'Not in that state!' I had snapped back, and tried to shut the back door.

'Let me in to see my fucking son, you bitch!' He barged past me, swinging the old wooden door into me and sending me flying across the cold, peeling lino on the kitchen floor. I scrambled to my feet and ran into the living room to protect my baby.

'Hellooooo!' He was already stood over our son, stinking of fags and booze, cooing in that annoying baby voice, 'Your bitch mummy hasn't let me see you for weeks! I bet you miss me so much!'

'Isn't your mummy a fat bitch? Yes, she is! Oh, yes she is!'

I had never felt the urge to protect anything as much as I did in that moment. I wanted to choke slam him, throw him out of my house and keep him away from my baby. But I froze. Fuck. Not this again. Not now.

But something was different. Something overtook my deeply ingrained freeze response, and I broke out of it. I ran over to my baby and swooped him up before Jase could even process what had happened in his drunk and altered state.

'What the fuck are you doing?' he roared at me.

I stuttered. I held Oliver close to my chest.

'Please, calm down. You are too drunk to pick him up, Jase. You need to come back when you are sober . . .'

'I am fucking sober!' he exploded.

'Please don't yell, you are going to scare him. Please don't do this. Just go home, sleep it off, see him later. I will bring him round to see you and your dad . . .'

I was willing to say anything, do anything, to get him to calm down, and leave our baby alone.

'No! I want to take him to the duck pond. Put him in his fucking pram for me, and pack his baby bag. Now!'

I stood my ground. There was absolutely no chance that he was taking a five-month-old baby to a fucking duck pond in the state he was in.

'No, I won't do that. Go home, Jase. Leave us alone.'

I gripped my baby tighter, and tried to take a step back away from him.

'Give me my son!' He reached out, and tried to grab Oliver from my arms. I leant backwards, and his swipe missed by less than an inch. The rage consumed him, and I felt his hands on both of my shoulders. He looked at me and then tilted his head back.

Oh my god. I knew what was coming. As he went into to headbutt me in the face, every cell in my body screamed, 'protect your fucking baby!'

It was as if time had frozen. I could see it all in slow motion. His forehead hurtling towards my face. The back of Oliver's soft little head. His dirty hands on my shoulders. The smell of booze. The hatred and anger pouring from him.

I twisted my body as violently as I could to protect the tiny body of my baby. He gripped me tighter, and pulled me towards him as he tried to land the headbutt. He missed, but I felt my muscles tear open. I felt the shoulder dislocate from the socket. I felt the pain shoot through my chest and my ribcage. But I also knew I had protected Oliver from almost certain, instant death.

'You fucking slag!' he screamed in my face, as he grabbed me and shoved me as hard as he could.

Still holding my baby clamped to my chest, and with one shoulder dropped to the side, I held on with everything as I was launched off my feet, and my back slammed across the dining table. I slid right off the other side, landing on my neck. Oliver shrieked, but I didn't let go of him. He landed on my chest, and I sobbed in shock. I hushed my terrified baby, and told him everything was going to be okay.

The pain was indescribable. I didn't yet know what had happened to my neck and my back, but I knew I was seriously injured. One of my arms wasn't working properly, and my neck felt like I had been stabbed. Every movement hurt. Breathing hurt.

'Not so hard now, are you?'

Here he was. A twenty-one-year-old man stood over his teenage girlfriend and his five-month-old baby, heaving with rage, ready to kill one of them, or both of them. His fists were clenched. He was foaming at the mouth. I had one chance to get us out of this situation, or we were going to die.

I fumbled for my phone in my pocket, and for the first time in my life, I rang 999.

'Which service do you require?'

'Police!' I cried.

He grinned at me, a terrifying smile.

'What is the emergency?'

'Help me. My ex is attacking me and my baby. I am on the floor. I don't know what he is going to do to us next! Help us!'

He laughed, harder and harder. I could barely hear the woman on the end of the phone as he was laughing and taunting me.

'Is he still there?'

I stared up at him.

'Yeah, he's stood over me.'

'What address are you at?' she pressed.

'1 Duke Street, Biddulph.'

He laughed dramatically. 'You think I'm falling for that? You stupid fucking bitch!'

The woman could hear him.

'Ignore him, focus on me. Police are on the way. I've sent a car out to you. What is he wearing?' She was calm, but clear. I tried to focus on him. My head was throbbing.

'Uhhh stripy shirt. Grey tie. Black jeans . . .'

'Stripy shirt! Grey tie! Black jeans! You really are fucking pathetic!' He mocked me and laughed. Then he lunged at me, trying to grab Oliver again, and I screamed at him to back off.

I could hear the woman starting to panic.

'Stay with me, what is your name?' she yelled over the screaming.

'Jess,' I yelled back.

'Jess, how old is your baby?'

'Five months.'

'Is the baby hurt?'

'I don't know!' I cried down the phone.

'You will fucking pay for this!' Jase roared at me, spraying spit all over my face.

Jase had stopped laughing. At some point whilst I was answering the questions, he had realised I was not faking the 999 call. He panicked, and ran out of the house, smashing the mirror and throwing a chair as he left.

'Has he gone? the woman on the phone asked.

'Uhh. Yeah, I think so. He's ran off,' I sobbed.

'Do you know which direction he went?'

'No, I am on the floor. I can't move,' I said, remembering the pain.

'Police should be with you any . . .'

The sirens rang out through the estate. I heard car doors slam and footsteps run in all different directions around my house. Suddenly, I was surrounded by police officers, stood above me, looking at me and my screaming baby on the floor.

They took Oliver to Mum's whilst they accompanied me to the hospital to have my shoulder and neck examined.

As I sat in the hospital chair, a young female officer had come over to sit next to me.

'So has he done anything like this before?' she asked quietly.

'He's always like this,' I admitted, ashamed.

'He's attacked you before?'

'Oh yeah, loads of times.'

She sighed.

'Has he ever . . . raped you?' She lowered her voice, so the other patients didn't hear her.

'Oh god no. No . . .' I shook my head.

'So, he's never forced you to have sex with him?' she clarified.

'Oh that? Oh yeah, all the time. He's never raped me though,' I answered, absolutely certain there was a distinction.

She rubbed her head and sighed slightly.

'If he's forced you to have sex with him, he's raped you. That's rape,' she was gentle, and careful, but clear.

'Well, I mean . . . what?' I was lost.

'Has he ever physically held you down, or forced you to have sex with him? Or threatened you with a weapon? Or with being hurt?'

'Well . . . yes . . .' My mind played me a montage of hundreds of things I had just learned were rapes.

'How many times?' she continued.

'How long is a piece of string?' I shrugged. I didn't feel anything. No horror. No fright. No shock. Just the humdrum of sex I didn't want, that they were calling rape.

That answer seemed to earn me a second trip in the police car, to the interview suite. After two hours in the hospital, and then six hours in the interview suite, my brain was like a pile of useless mush by the time the police dropped me back off at Mum's house. They had found Jase hiding in a man's garden shed, and arrested him. He was charged with several counts of rape, sexual assault, ABH, threats to kill, and criminal damage.

Mum wasn't pleased to see me. I cuddled my baby in my arms and kissed his soft head over and over again. I was so glad he was safe, and I had protected him. My shoulder and neck were swelling up and bruising pretty bad, but it was worth it to have kept him safe in that moment. He cooed and giggled and tried to talk to me. He pulled my hair and nuzzled his face into my neck.

'Was that really necessary?' she snapped, hand on one hip.

'What?' I looked up, confused.

'Calling 999?'

'I don't get it.' I stared at her. I couldn't understand her reaction at all.

'You. Making a fucking mountain out of a molehill. As usual.'

My jaw dropped.

'Mum, he threw me across the dining table. He could have killed Oliver. My shoulder dislocated. I can barely move my neck!'

'It looks fine to me,' she quipped back heartlessly.

'What the fuck is that supposed to mean?'

'Well, I didn't need to be saddled with your baby all day whilst you went to the police!'

Just as I was questioning whether I had some sort of head injury, and was in fact dreaming this shit show of a conversation, my nana walked in from the kitchen and stood side by side with her daughter.

'Mum, they charged him with assault, criminal damage . . . and . . . well . . . rape,' I tried.

'Rape?' she gasped in horror.

'Uh . . . yeah.'

'You got him done for rape?' She spoke to me as if I was the worst human being alive.

I started to get nervous.

'You can't just go around accusing innocent young men of rape!' she shouted across the living room.

I understand that these are the moments that other teenage girls start to believe it was their fault – but I was incandescent. If anything, it was this conversation that cemented my belief that I was not to blame. I was shocked that my own mother would jump to defend a rapist instead of even asking how I was.

I lost it.

'He isn't fucking innocent!' I bellowed at her. 'He held a pair of scissors to my neck! He fucking ripped my episiotomy stitches out! I bled in a bath for hours! How can you fucking treat me like this?'

It didn't impact her. She had made up her mind.

'Oh, this is all convenient, all coming out now isn't it? How come we never knew anything about it?'

I knew what was coming.

'Because . . . I didn't tell you. I covered it up,' I mumbled. 'I was too frightened to say anything.'

'So you lied?' she snapped.

'Well . . . yes.'

'But we are supposed to believe you now, are we?'

She laughed. Nana laughed.

'Yes! He's just fucking attacked me and my baby! What more do you want?' I yelled at them both, and looked at my baby. I had just escaped one toxic relationship, and it felt as though the universe was instantly presenting me with another.

'You are going to send an innocent young man to prison!' she yelled at me, utterly appalled that I had reported him to the police.

'He isn't innocent! For fuck's sake!' I shrieked at her.

'Mud sticks, Jessica. You can never take that back if you brand him a rapist. He will carry that for the rest of his fucking life!'

'Good! Cos he fucking deserves to!'

Mum stormed out of the living room and back into the kitchen, and Nana quietly walked over to me. She got close to my face. She spoke in a lowered, seething voice.

'Do you know something, Jessie? You think you are something special, don't you?'

I stared at my nana.

'What?' I whispered back.

'You. You think you are the only woman in the world who has been beaten and raped? You think you are special? Like you deserve special attention? Special justice? Well, you don't!'

I took a step back from her in confusion.

'I don't think I am the only woman in the world that has ... you know ... I don't understand what you are saying ...'

She glared at me, turned on her heels, and went to find her equally annoyed daughter.

It was an exhausting walk with the pram back up the main hill of the council estate, back to my house with the smashed mirror, and the upside-down chairs. It was hard to walk into the room that echoed with my own screams. To look at the dining table and replay the moment I was thrown over it. To stand where I was lying on the carpet, frantically clinging to my baby whilst ringing 999.

One thing that is rarely talked about when you are a young mum in domestic abuse, is that no matter how terrifying your life becomes, you still have a job to do. My shoulder had completely stopped moving, and yet I still had to feed, change, rock, bath and cuddle my baby. I still had to do the laundry. I still had to wash his bottles. I still had to clean the house.

Motherhood doesn't stop when you are being abused. Life doesn't slow down for you. You still have to get up. You still have to work. You still have to be a good mum. Play with your baby. Smile with them. Sing to them. Read to them. Laugh with them. Teach them to talk. Hold their hand whilst they try to walk.

You live in heartbreaking turmoil, but they live in a fresh new world, filled with exciting and mind-bending possibilities. You have to be there for them, and give them every opportunity to grow, learn, explore and experience. If you weren't exhausted already, creating a safe space for your baby in a very unsafe environment will just about kill you off every day.

I was awarded an injunction, a restraining order to protect myself and baby Oliver, but Jase wasn't concerned. Most nights, I was on the phone to the police. He would sit in the garden, or at the end of the drive, sending me death threats, or describing what I was watching on TV.

One night, I woke up to him kicking the front door in. Another night, I woke up to 151 missed calls and forty-seven text messages, each one detailing the way he was going to murder me, and what he was going to do to my body.

Everything from burning me alive, to throwing me under a car. He terrified me. And it wasn't as if he hadn't done that to me before.

I shuddered as I remembered the night he grabbed hold of me, held me, and then deliberately threw me into oncoming traffic. A man performed a perfect emergency stop, and I could feel the heat of his engine as I lay on the road surface in the centre of Hanley, disoriented and terrified. As soon as the man got out of his car to try to help me, Jase had threatened him, and screamed at him to get back in his car – and the man had done as he was told.

The same thing had happened the day he was choking me in a stairwell because I wouldn't give him my debit card. He knew I had just been paid, and he wanted to go out drinking with his friends. He had no money left. As I was choking and gasping for air up against the cold wall in the shopping centre stairwell, a little old man on a walking stick hobbled up to us and started shouting at Jase to let me go.

He thought I was being mugged.

But Jase turned, and lunged at the old man.

'Fuck off now, before I do some real fucking damage!'

The old man had stared into my eyes, clearly feeling utterly helpless against the man towering over him. He stepped back, turned and walked away.

Even though I was supposed to have all these protections, and he was on bail, and I had a restraining order, he made my life hell for months. He told everyone his version of events, of course. A ridiculous story he made up and told everyone and anyone who would listen.

'Fucking slag!' a woman had yelled at me in Wetherspoons.

'Everyone in here knows what you've done!' the woman behind the bar said to me, slamming my drink down on the bar.

'And what am I supposed to have done?' I snapped back.

'That poor man. You've ruined his fucking life! He told us all. He came home from work and found you in bed with two other men, and your baby was right next to you in the Moses basket, screaming. He tried to drag the men out of the house, and you called 999! You should be ashamed of yourself. He's been in here, crying every night. Good job he's got some decent friends around him!'

'Is that what he's told you?' I burst out laughing at the stupidity of that story.

She stared at me.

'He's been charged with rape. And sexual assault. And sexual activity with a child: me. And criminal damage, for smashing my house up. And for ABH, for dislocating my shoulder. My story is a lot less dramatic, and there's no sordid threesome with a baby watching, but at least my story is the fucking truth!'

She shrugged and laughed at me whilst she dried some glasses and placed them on the wooden shelf.

'Predictable. He told me you would say that.'

'Maybe you should use your head, and have a good think about why that might be.'

Living in a small town where everyone knew everyone, and everyone knew him, was a nightmare. I was public enemy number one for daring to utter the 'R word', and it was being made clear to me. Loads of women and girls were being raped in that town, but you couldn't actually say it out loud. And you certainly couldn't tell the police.

My friends were nowhere to be seen. When I text Molly, she replied to say that she didn't want anything more to do with me, and that ever since I had started losing the baby weight, I thought I was god's gift. She said he had told her that's why I had cheated on him with two men from my new job.

When I text Hannah, she replied to tell me that she didn't believe me, and that if I had really been abused and beaten up, I would have left the first time he did it to me. She added another text message, to say that if she was ever being abused, she would leave the moment he put his hands on her. If it was true, and I had stayed, it was my own fault, she said.

When I called Bianca, she told me that she had decided to retract my invitation to her wedding, and she didn't want me as her bridesmaid any more. She said it was because she was disgusted by the 'lies' I had told the police. She told me that Jase had told her I had accused him of microwaving my arm.

'How do you tell such a stupid lie? A microwave won't even work if the door is still ajar! How would he have microwaved your arm?'

'I never said he did. He's lying to you. He's lying to everyone. To isolate me, and make me look stupid, probably.'

'Yeah, yeah. Apparently he's the one lying, right?'

I had known her for so long, and never ever heard her speak in this tone.

'Yes! Bianca, you have known me for five years, and I've never lied to you. Why would you suddenly believe such terrible shit?'

She sniggered.

'Well, let's put it this way Jess, I'm not the only one who doesn't believe you, am I?'

I was confused by her response.

'What is that supposed to mean?' I asked.

'Well, if your own mum can go drinking with him in the Red Lion, then maybe you're the fucking liar.'

I felt like I had been punched in the stomach. My mum? With Jase? Drinking?

'Yeah, thought as much. You got nothing to say to that, have ya?' she laughed, as if she had caught me out in my own lie.

She was right. I had absolutely nothing to say. My mouth couldn't even form the words to say. I felt like the ground was moving under my feet.

And it was in that moment that I realised I had no one.

13

Confessions of being from a council estate

Summer 2018

Ishook as I opened the huge white A4 envelope that had just landed on my doormat. I knew what it was. I saw the university logo on the front.

This was it. This was the day I was given copies of those anonymous emails. This was the day I was finally given access to what was really happening to me.

It was heavy. There must have been at least a hundred pages in there. The kids were at school, and so I climbed the stairs to my office and sat down. I took a deep breath.

'Whatever is in this envelope, you can deal with it,' I told myself, my voice echoing around my tiny little boxroom office.

In the request I made to the university, I deliberately made it as broad as I could.

'Please provide any data held in email inboxes, outboxes, sent boxes, deleted boxes and archived boxes which contain the names and phrases "Jess Taylor", "JT", "Jessica Taylor", "Taylor".'

I then included all of my social media handles, email addresses and my website. I knew that would capture what

I needed, and I named around five members of staff who I thought would have emailed each other about me. I made sure to include Melinda and Rosie, too.

There were many risks. First, they could simply lie and say they didn't hold any data. Secondly, they could redact things they didn't want me to see, or only give me the things they were comfortable with. Thirdly, they could realise what I was doing, and delete everything, and warn others to do the same.

I had no choice but to trust the process. I had to hope that the team doing the data access request would do it dispassionately, and honestly.

I pulled the lump of paper from the envelope and stared at it. I flicked through it all, reams and reams of redacted, black boxes and lines. Some text was left in places. Email addresses, and even the name of the senders had been blocked out.

My heart sank.

'For fuck's sake!' I slatted the paperwork across my little wooden desk. It scattered and slid. A few words caught my eye.

As you know, she has thoroughly annoyed my colleagues in the police force . . .

What? My mind raced. I jumped back up from my slump in my office chair, collecting the paperwork up, and stacking it in front of me. Were they a police officer? Or someone who worked with police? Was this someone I knew after all? How have I annoyed their colleagues?

I flicked overleaf.

I need you to keep my identity anonymous, because she has over 9000 followers on Twitter. Some of them can be very vocal, and I don't want to be on the receiving end of that, if people find out it is me.

Sneaky, cowardly fucker, I thought. I rolled my eyes. They want to be able to bully me, but not for anyone to find out. Lovely.

I kept reading.

As you know, she has started a campaign about the use of films with children who have been sexually abused. She even released a report about it a few days ago. The films have been made in conjunction with several police forces, and so I have alerted my colleagues in the police, so they can find a way to try to take action against her.

I sat at my desk in shock. The person was trying to encourage a police force to take action against me . . . because I didn't agree with them showing films? How could anyone have such a high stake in these films? Was the person a producer? Did they profit from the films?

As I read through page after page of emails, large black rectangles of redacted text sometimes gave way to a nugget of information. I ran my finger over the black redacted rectangles in dread. What was behind those?

I noticed another sentence in the middle of two blacked out rectangles.

My concern is that she will do serious damage to the discipline of psychology if she is ever allowed to qualify. I think we need to make sure that she is never allowed to become a chartered psychologist.

Hot tears filled my eyes. What damage could I possibly do? I was one young woman. Why were people so frightened of what I had to say? I stared at that final sentence, and couldn't believe that I was holding emails in my hand that were suggesting ways to ensure I never fulfilled my dream of becoming a psychologist. How could anyone be so cruel?

But the emails only got worse.

I think she is emotionally unstable. She has traits of personality disorder. One wonders if she could even manage being a psychologist at all, she carries a lot of baggage.

I stood up. I looked out of my little window, overlooking the park where my kids often played. I watched the wind blow through the huge pine tree outside. I watched a barge slowly make its way down the canal and under the bridge. Emotionally unstable? Traits of personality disorder? Baggage?

Who was this person? Why were they so intent on framing me as mentally ill?

And then I saw it.

I am concerned by her confessions of being from a council estate. She even started a hashtag (attached) #CouncilEstateProfessionals. It is frankly embarrassing. I am very concerned that she will bring you, and your university into disrepute by talking about being from a council estate.

The post was attached below, and I recognised the old tweet I had posted.

I remember growing up poor as fuck and hating living on the council estate. Now I love that I grew up there cos it gave me the connection to real poverty and real life I need to be a great psychologist and activist. Ain't enough of us in this field!

I stared at my post, and the little circle picture of myself next to it. How dare I expose my dirty, council estate roots in the perfect, beautiful upper echelons of academia? I laughed, but I was in shock. There it was. Right in front of me. This was about where I was from. This was about who I was.

I wasn't good enough to be a psychologist in their eyes. They had tried to claim I was unprofessional. They had tried to get the police to stop me from talking about my work. When those things hadn't worked, they had started to suggest I was mentally ill. But eventually, the mask slipped, and they were honest about their true dislike of me. It was 'frankly embarrassing' of me to 'confess' I was from a council estate.

I cried. I read my post again. I did hate living on that estate. I couldn't wait to escape it. I would never have defended it. I would never have defended myself, either. I did feel less than everyone else, and I did feel like I didn't belong. But something about reading those emails about myself motivated me to defend my estate.

Morning Laura, over the last few days, I have taken the liberty of collecting every social media post she has ever made where she has sworn, talked about her childhood, about her own abuse, and about her personal life. They are attached in this document.

I scowled at the email. I became angry at Laura. Surely, she could see this was personal. Who the hell admits that they have scrolled through thousands of posts, and collated hundreds of them into a document to discredit someone they didn't like. My blood ran cold. This person had been watching me for months. They had read thousands of my posts. They had sat down at a desk and made a document about me. It had taken them days.

I flicked through the pages, more and more of the same. And then a few from Melinda, that made me want to burn the university to the ground.

My mouth fell open. My eyes filled back up.

Thank you for circulating that interview she did about her rapes and abuse. Absolutely shocking. And disgusting. For someone who bangs on about trauma, she certainly seems to be getting off on talking about being sexually abused!

My skin prickled. My blood rushed in my body. I couldn't stop looking at the words 'certainly seems to be getting off'. It made me feel sick. I kept trying to look away, and focus on something outside, but I couldn't stop staring at those disgusting words. A clinical psychologist I had never met, had read one interview I had given about my life as a child, and had concluded that I was 'getting off on' talking about it?

I thought about the meeting, and the way Melinda spoke to me. No wonder she treated me so badly. She had already made her mind up about me before I had even set foot in the office.

But there was one more.

I think we talk to the Division of Forensic Psychology about finding a way to stop her PhD viva. There has to be something we can do. Obviously, we can't get her on her ability, and her work is of high quality, but there has to be another way.

I was incandescent. They wanted to talk to the national division of my regulatory body, to find a way to stop my PhD viva. Was that even legal? They clearly knew I was good enough to pass, but they wanted to find another way to fix it so I failed.

I sat back in my chair, and tried to take some deep breaths. I thought about all the years of studying I had committed to my work. Five years of a degree, and three years of a PhD – and all it would take to end my dreams is someone obsessive enough to influence as many people as they could that I was dangerous, unprofessional, mentally ill and . . . well . . . common.

But who was the sender? Their name and email address had been blanked out on over a hundred pages of evidence. I had learned very little about them.

The only thing I could say, from reading thousands of texts, case notes, journals, evidence, letters and statements over my years of practice, was that I was 100 per cent sure that the sender was a woman. The language, the tone, the approach, the way they typed and regarded Laura and other colleagues, it was obvious. There was no doubt in my mind. It was a woman.

I struck off three male names on the list in my notebook. I combed the pages for hours, only stopping to pick the kids up from school, feed them, and get them ready for bed. The moment they were asleep, I was back in my office. I wanted one more go at examining every page of the emails. There had to be a clue somewhere.

I was growing tired, and emotional. I could feel myself burning out when one of the emails caught my eye.

I know from behind the scenes, that she has reported a man for harassment. He has been investigated by the police. He was critical of her campaign, and she claims he had harassed her. I spoke with him.

I stopped. Dots started connecting in my head. I knew who they were referring to.

The sender was talking about a man who had used his work computer to harass and stalk me every day for nearly two years. Before reporting him to the police, I reported him to his employer. He seemed to know every move I made, everywhere I went, and every time I posted. He took obsessive screenshots of everything I said or did. One night, when I was up at 1am chatting to another professional, he was posting my comments and mocking them, one by one. He even started writing to people about me, and a few people had given me the heads up that he had become obsessed with me.

His employer took him through a disciplinary process and made him apologise to me in writing, but he had then left his job, and his behaviour had escalated. In the end, I went to the police, and asked them to take action. I had never reported anyone else to the police for harassment, so it had to be him.

So, the emails were not coming directly from him, but someone who knew him, or who had at least spoken to him. Could that hold the clue to who this was?

I sat at my desk, wracking my brain. Who was the sender of the emails?

It was almost midnight. I had the headache from hell, and I'd been having palpitations for hours. I was just about to give up and go to bed, when I got a private message on Twitter.

Do you know this woman? She seems obsessed with you.

I clicked the link, but I was already blocked. I didn't have any other way of looking, and unlike many academics, I didn't have any secret second accounts to use to circumvent a block.

I wearily typed back.

I can't see that link, I am sorry. Don't worry about it, lots of people troll me on social media, it's probably nothing. Goodnight!

I went to bed, and with the stress of the fact that several people in my faculty were trying to find a way to stop my PhD viva, I totally forgot about that message.

In the days that passed, I submitted a formal complaint to the university, including hundreds of pages of evidence. I relistened to the muffled, terrible quality recording of the meeting with Laura, Melinda and Rosie. I included several of the appalling comments they had made in my complaint, too.

As I pressed send on the complaint, I was filled with sadness. This wasn't how this was supposed to happen. I was in this top university, doing my dream PhD, to finally become a psychologist, to provide for my kids, to build a life, to escape poverty – and instead of studying and focusing on my research, I had just built a two-hundred-page evidence file for a formal complaint against a group of psychologists, one of which was my own professor. What an almighty mess.

I informed the university that I no longer wanted to work with Laura, and in light of my complaints, I asked for new PhD supervision. Whilst all of this had been going on, I had received virtually no supervision on my thesis, as every meeting had been consumed with those stupid fucking emails.

They didn't reply, but I didn't need a reply. I had been watching Laura for weeks as this had unfolded, and I had realised that she had no intention of defending me from the email sender. I had read her replies to the comments about my life, about my pregnancy, my council estate and my mental health – and she was pathetic.

The first investigation was a farce. They assigned David, a senior lecturer from within our department, to lead the process, and surprise, surprise, David and Laura had been firm friends for a decade. Not only was the investigation a complete cover up, but my meeting with David ended with him laughing at me.

'This is all a bit ... grand ... isn't it?' he chuckled, taking his glasses off to wipe them.

'What do you mean? You have seen the evidence, the emails about me are appalling!'

'Just your story, your belief that this is all deliberate. That some anonymous person is targeting you. It's all a bit ... conspiracy theory ...'

There were those words again. He had been talking to them about me.

It was being accused of being a 'conspiracy theorist' several times during that investigation which caused me to rethink my own understanding of it. I had always thought that a 'conspiracy theorist' was someone who was sharing wild, fantastical theories. But I had come to realise that being accused of 'conspiracy theories' was a quick way to shut down anyone who was raising concerns. If you could be framed as mentally unstable, or a conspiracy theorist, no one had to listen to you any more. You could be written off, ignored, mocked and discredited.

I didn't trust their systems, but I reported the investigation to the university, and asked for it to be escalated to a tribunal. I submitted a long letter explaining why I felt that the investigation was corrupt, and to my shock, the leadership team of the university agreed with me.

'We have made the decision to escalate this complaint to the Vice Chancellor tribunal process. If your complaints are upheld, you will be awarded compensation, and your PhD fees will be returned to . . .'

'What about my viva though? What can we put in place to ensure that it is safe? In one of the emails, the academics in my department even discussed deliberately appointing an external examiner who would fail me,' I cried to the man on the phone.

'We noted those emails too, and we are concerned about the viva process. For this reason, if your complaints are upheld, we will also be arranging an independent viva for you, and we will ensure that the examiner is not involved in this complaint at all.'

I started to worry. It all sounded very tentative.

'But I am supposed to be submitting my PhD in a few weeks. What do I do?'

'Just keep going, get your work submitted for examination, and we will schedule this hearing for as soon as we can,' he reassured me, gently.

He was the first person I had spoken to who made me feel like he believed me. Not just believed me. It felt like he had sided with me. He would have no power over the panel, but at least someone had read those emails and realised I was telling the truth.

I got off the phone to notification after notification after notification. Someone was sending me images of some kind. I didn't recognise the sender.

I watched as the notifications piled up on my screen.

Eleven, twelve, thirteen, fourteen notifications from Twitter.

What was happening? I stared at my phone.

I clicked into the app to find that the account with the grey avatar was messaging me again. I had totally forgotten about their warning about the troll, but they hadn't. They had taken screenshots of their tweets, comments, likes and posts – and were sending them to me one by one.

Wow! They were right. This woman was obsessed with me.

Something about her got my attention. An academic. A psychologist. A woman with long brown hair, thick glasses, and a mole on her top lip. She must have been in her forties. I had never seen her before. I had never even heard of her before.

Dr Macy Delaney? Who on earth was she? She sure hated me. Her account was a shrine to snide comments, subtle messages, comments aimed at me, sarcasm, and . . . what was that?

She had liked and shared several posts from the man who had been harassing me. Not only that, but she had publicly commented, asking to speak to him about me. She even liked several posts which claimed I should be kicked off my PhD course. And one saying I was clearly mentally ill.

My brain kicked in. This could be the sender. This could definitely be the sender.

This makes so much sense, I thought, I wonder what her connection is to the films, and to the work I do?

And that's when I spotted it. She worked with the police force I had criticised for showing the films to children. My stomach flipped. My heart pounded.

Could she have any connection to Laura?

I searched their names together in Google, and then in the academic library. Bingo. There they were. They even presented a paper together last month, a few days before my speech in London.

'Fucking got you! Macy fucking Delaney!'

I stood in my living room and laughed. The mystery was over. She had no power over me, unless she was anonymous. This was the end. I burst into tears.

Macy Delaney. I said her name over and over again. Finally. A name in my mouth.

I Googled her. An expert in deception, apparently. I laughed again. Not fucking expert enough though, Macy Delaney.

I rang the man back.

'I have just found out who the sender is. I am going to email you some more proof. I know you will be able to see the unredacted emails anyway, and you already know who it is, but I just want you all to know that I know who it is!' I couldn't keep my voice from shaking.

He paused, but I think he was smiling.

'Is that so? Can I ask you who you think it is?' he asked quietly.

'It's Macy Delaney,' I said confidently.

'Okay, thank you. I cannot confirm or deny that name, but . . . I'm glad you called back.' He was certainly smiling down the phone. I could hear it.

14

Sorry mate, wrong house

Summer 2009

*O*h, just go. What's the harm? I stared at the message.
Pleaaaaaaase don't make me go, I typed back.

That's the last time I drunkenly agree to a blind date.
The girl messaging me was the one, the only, Kaz. We had
bumped into each other in the pub, got queenied – ha! –
and then she had convinced me to go on a blind date to the
cinema with some dude she knew, called Ben.

I've told him you would now. The reply appeared.

I really don't have the energy for this. I'm not interested.

I was being short with her, but I was being honest. I was
in the thick of a police investigation. I had a nine-month-old
baby. I was working every hour I could to keep a roof over
our heads, and pay off the enormous debts Jase had racked
up in my name without telling me.

Come on. He's really nice. He's single. He's a lovely guy.
You'll have a great time.

I sighed. Since I had become single, I had men crawling
all over me. At first, it distracted me, but I had recently been
on a date with a guy I used to know, and it had ended in one
of the most peculiar ways imaginable.

After a great night out, dancing, laughing, shouting, and singing at the top of our lungs, we had gone back to his place, and I was expecting to be pushed into having drunk sex. We kissed, but I just wasn't feeling it at all. I was sat on top of him, and he stopped.

'Are you okay?'

'Ummm. I'm not really feeling it, I'll be honest.'

'Oh that's cool. Me neither, actually.'

Silence.

I got off him and sat next to him on the bed, cross legged.

'Wow, what a pair of wallies we are!' he laughed, and put his arm around me.

'Shall we get a drink?' I asked, and he nodded.

We lay on the large sofa in his apartment overlooking the city and talked about everything. Art, books we had read, cars we wanted to drive, music we loved. He pulled out his album collection, and we flicked through it together for hours.

'So, can I ask you something? Does that happen to you often?' he asked carefully.

'What?' I slurred back.

'Well, you just didn't seem to be into me. And I'm not offended or anything, cos I wasn't feeling it either . . .' he sipped at his drink.

I thought about it.

'Ummm well, I mean, I do feel like that a lot, but usually I don't stop, cos the guy doesn't want to stop. So I just have to carry on . . .'

He went quiet. He knew what I meant.

'But do you get off?' he asked directly.

'What do you mean?'

'Do you cum? Are you getting off on it or not?'

In the darkness, I blushed. But in the darkness, I told the truth.

'No. I've never had an orgasm during sex. Or any sexual contact with a guy. I just fake it so they stop.'

I couldn't believe that admission had just left my mouth. He raised his eyebrows.

'Wow. Have you ever had an orgasm when you do it yourself though?'

'Oh yeah, I know how to get there myself. Just . . . I dunno . . . I don't feel anything good when I have sex.'

He went quiet.

'Huh! Me too.' He shrugged and laughed.

'Really?' I sat up, I was intrigued.

'Yeah . . . fuck knows why. You're the first person I ever spoke to about any of this . . . Can I ask you something else? Do you actually like cock? Like the look of it?'

I nearly spat my drink out. This was the most direct, honest and graphic conversation I'd had in years. It was almost like being back at the sleepover with Emmy.

My answer didn't take much thinking about.

'Not really. They are pretty fucking gross, aren't they?'

'No comment!'

We both laughed.

'I've been wondering about going to the doctor for years. I think maybe there is something wrong with me. I dunno why I can't get off when I have sex,' I admitted to him.

He stroked my hand, looked into my eyes and smiled.

'I don't think there is anything wrong with you. And I don't think there is anything wrong with me. But I think we might be having sex with the wrong people.'

I wasn't sure what he meant, but we cuddled back up on the sofa, and listened to our favourite albums until the sun came up. I had thought about that conversation for weeks, and I had started to have a nagging feeling about what he was getting at. I pushed it away. Not now. This wasn't the time.

But what I was sure about, was that I did not want to go on that fucking blind date. I was in the taxi, on the way there, when I was still texting Kaz, trying to find a way out of it.

He's already on his way, you're already in the taxi. Just go, and if you don't hit it off, at least you had a nice night out with a new friend!

She was persistent, I will give her that.

I stood at the bar in the cinema and ordered myself a double vodka and orange juice to calm my nerves. I downed it, and ordered another.

'On a date, are you?' the barman laughed at me.

'How do you know that?'

'You are all dolled up, but you look like you're going to throw up.'

'Thanks mate,' I laughed. He was way too observant.

'So, is he hot?' the girl behind the bar chipped in. I had never met these two people in my life, but they were absolutely committed to the unfolding drama.

'I have no idea . . . it's a blind date,' I admitted, raising my eyebrows at my own stupidity.

'A blind date? No way! Do people even do that shit any more? You have no idea what this guy looks like then?' The girl behind the bar clapped her hand over her mouth.

'How will you recognise him when he gets here?' the barman asked, confused.

Shit. I hadn't thought of that.

'I don't know . . .' I admitted again. Fucking hell. Why have I done this?

It was 8:10pm. He was supposed to be here at 8pm. I tried to text Kaz, hoping he had backed out, or had forgotten, but there was no signal in the bar.

I watched as men turned up – some of them with their friends, some that turned up alone but walked over to people they knew, or met women who were waiting for them. The man and woman behind the bar were watching the door intently, desperate to catch a glimpse of the guy I was dating.

A man walked in. Tall, handsome, well-dressed, confident. It was 8:30pm. He was half an hour late. But at least he didn't look terrible. He had a friendly smile, a bit of stubble, light brown hair, and a slightly open shirt. He must have been in his late twenties, so quite a bit older than me. He looked around, and I tried to catch his eye.

He checked his phone, looked up, smiled, waved, and walked right past me.

It wasn't him. The only other possibility was the young kid who had just walked in behind him. Dread filled my body. No. He was walking towards me.

A strawberry blond lad made his way over to me. He was short. He was dressed like a twelve-year-old. His trainers looked like he had just trekked through mud to get there. He wore baggy jeans, and a white T-shirt with a stain down the front. What was that? Beans? Spaghetti hoops?

'Hey, you must be Jess?'

The barman burst out laughing and shouted his colleague over to laugh with him. I glared at them both as they hushed each other, and slapped each other on the back as they lost control of their giggles.

'Uhh. Yeah. Are you Ben?'

'I am!'

Oh fucking hell. Someone shoot me.

'Have you been here long?' he asked.

'I've been here since 8pm, which is when we were supposed to meet . . .' I said, pointing up at the clock on the wall next to the bar.

'Oh, sorry, I hadn't noticed the time.'

What kind of idiotic response was that? I frowned.

'Anyway, let me get us a drink each, what are you having?'

I looked at my two empty glasses. I guess another double wouldn't hurt.

'Double vodka and orange, please.'

The bartenders were just dying to come over and get in on the action, so they were astoundingly attentive when he gestured to them to serve us.

'Can I help you?' the barman asked Ben, glancing quickly at me.

'Yes, thank you. Could we have a double vodka and orange for her? And . . . I will have a blackcurrant,' he asked, totally oblivious to the fact that the bartenders were laughing at him. Or me. They were laughing at me.

'That will be £5.55 please,' the barman said, still glancing at me every now and then. He was desperate to laugh.

And then the worst thing imaginable happened. He reached into his pocket, and pulled out a neon Velcro folding wallet. If that wasn't bad enough, the Velcro wallet was attached to a long, springy, neon orange plastic key chain. I could have died.

The woman behind the bar walked off around the corner and burst into laughter. The man serving us cleared his throat, instead of laughing in my face, and looked at me with utter horror. I looked down, and saw that Ben was counting out loose change to pay for the drinks. I put my head in my hands and prayed to something, anything, to just knock me out.

'So, are you guys on a date then?' the bartender asked us, deliberately.

You fucking prick, I thought, glaring at him.

'Yeah, we are!' Ben beamed.

'Aww! That's so lovely! You make a wonderful couple, if you don't mind me saying.'

Oh fuck off. I gritted my teeth at the barman, but it just made him smirk more.

'Aw thank you so much! We do, don't we?' Ben smiled at me.

I smiled back and nodded. I was going to kill Kaz when I saw her next.

The bartender got through the interaction by the skin of his teeth, and then hid behind the bar whilst he giggled uncontrollably with his colleague on the floor.

I started hatching a plan to escape. I could say I had a family emergency. I could say my nan died. I didn't really care what I said, I just needed to get away from this date.

We went to see the film; some shoot 'em up action film that made me want to bash my own head in. I couldn't tell you a thing about that film. But I can tell you what happened when it ended. He stood up, and as I turned around to walk out, he belched in my face. It smelled like the extra large hotdog, the two litre Pepsi and the extra large popcorn he somehow managed to cram into him during the film.

'I just need to go to the bathroom,' I lied.

I stood in the sanctuary that is the ladies' toilets, staring at myself in the mirror, and asking myself what in the fuck I was going to do. I decided on a fake story about my babysitter calling me to say she had an emergency, and I walked out of the toilets. I hoped he had got lost, got distracted, or eaten himself into a coma, but he was stood right there waiting for me.

'Everything okay?' he asked.

'Oh, I am so sorry, I am going to have to go home. My babysitter has had an emergency and she just called me.

I am going to grab a taxi now,' I lied, looking at my phone, pretending I was finding a taxi company.

'No need! Let me give you a lift home! I only had a blackcurrant and a Pepsi!'

Hell fucking no. This idiot does not have a driving licence and a car, I thought, hoping my head wasn't shaking physically as much as it was mentally.

'No, it's okay, I will get a taxi. Honestly . . .'

'No, no, you must let me take you home!' he said, picking at some popcorn in his yellow teeth. He picked something out, flicked it on the floor, and pulled his car keys out of his jeans pocket.

I didn't know what to do. He linked my arm and pulled me along the carpark.

We got to his car, and I was genuinely stunned. You know how people apologise to you before you get in their car, and tell you it's like a mobile skip? And then you get in, and there are just a few bits, some tatty receipts, a crisp packet, maybe half a bottle of water? Well, when I tell you that every single window was filled with rubbish, I mean it. As he opened the passenger door to let me in, an avalanche of happy meal boxes poured out on to the tarmac. Weirdly, he didn't seem fazed.

Do you know those competitions on the TV where they filled a car full of ping pong balls, and you won ten grand if you could guess how many were in there? Well, it was like that, but with Happy Meal boxes.

He gestured for me to get in, as if he was welcoming me into a Bentley. I looked at the passenger seat, but there was still a pile of happy meal boxes in the footwell, and on the chair. Was I supposed to just sit on top of them all?

I was losing the will to live, and I just wanted to go home. I got in the car, and the boxes crushed down as I sat on them. I kicked some around my feet to make room for my legs, the way you would if you were kicking snow.

As we drove back to my house, he chatted away, talking absolute and utter bollocks. He told me that his dad was the inventor of the Boeing jet engine (which was invented in 1921). He also told me that for his eighteenth birthday, his dad had bought him a small island in the Bahamas.

I nodded along, thinking about how much I wanted to slap Kaz.

'So, what do you do for a living then?' I asked, hoping for even a shred of truth.

'I own a garage. I only sell sports cars. Bugatti. Lambos. Porsches. Range Rovers. I'm just about to open my second garage actually . . .'

I rolled my eyes, and looked around at the tiny, fifteen-year-old Ford Fiesta we were sat in. The total value of McDonald's that had been eaten in this car in the last six months was worth more than the car itself.

'Ah shit. Better stop for some fuel!' He pulled us into a late-night Shell garage, fuelled up and walked into the shop.

I was absolutely determined to find out more about this dude, and so I opened his glovebox, searching for clues. Of course, the first thing that happened was that even more McDonald's wrappers popped out, like they had been spring loaded in there for years. Like a McDonald's jack-in-the-box.

I sighed. Of course.

I picked up his ID card. He worked at McDonald's. At Alton Towers.

I shoved it back, and slammed the glovebox shut. It must have closed much easier than before, as all of the hidden contents were now all over my knees. I brushed them off me, into the footwell, and they blended in perfectly. There was no way he could ever notice.

317

As we pulled on to my estate, I realised that I did not want this idiot knowing where I lived. I panicked.

'Umm, I am just this house here, on the right . . .' I lied, pointing at a house around twenty doors up from mine.

'The one with the metal gates?'

'Uhh, yeah . . .'

He pulled up, and turned his car off.

'Well, I've had the best night with you. Do I get a kiss?'

'No,' I said. No is a complete sentence.

I got out of the car and walked towards the house I lied about living in. I had expected him to drive off, but instead, he stayed to watch me go in. I hesitated.

What do I do? I panicked.

He waved at me, and showed absolutely no signs of moving his car. I had to go in. I opened the gates, and walked in. I had absolutely no idea what I was walking into. I was on the council estate, walking into a stranger's house at 11:30 at night. I turned back, but he was still there.

Stop fucking waving at me, I begged him under my breath. Just fuck off!

I realised that I would have to walk into the house. What if someone in there battered me? What if I got savaged by a rottweiler? What if a wife thought I was her husband's secret mistress? What if it was someone I knew?

I took a deep breath, opened the door, and walked inside. I smelled the unfamiliar scent of someone else's house. Someone else's washing powder. Someone else's possessions.

I quietly looked through the blinds, and watched his car pull off and drive down the road. I breathed out. He was finally gone. Thank fuck for that.

'Can I help you?' a gruff, low voice shouted over to me.

I turned slowly, terrified of what I was about to see. There was a huge bald man with a beard, sat in his armchair, stroking his chunky Staffy, both of them just staring at me in the twilight.

'Umm. Wrong house!' I lied. 'I'm sorry. I'll go now.'

'Good lass,' he growled again. I opened his front door, walked out, and closed it behind me.

I walked back to my house, promising myself I would never go on a blind date ever again. Or any date. I just wanted to cuddle my baby and get in bed.

The nights were the hardest. I had no one left. My friends and family had abandoned me since I had reported Jase to the police. The only people in my inbox were men trying to fuck me. I text the radio to play my favourite song, and even the radio presenter stole my number and hit on me.

The stress, plus some pretty dangerous diet pills my doctor had given me, had left me skinny, tired and pale. Oliver was sleeping through the night, but I wasn't. I was waking up frequently to horrific nightmares of Jase breaking in and murdering me. When I wasn't dreaming that I was being stabbed to death, I was having raging revenge fantasies that scared me sick. I would wake up in cold sweats, breath heaving, heart pounding, because I had just dreamed that I had stalked Jase home from the pub, slit his throat, and watched as his life drained away. I even dreamed I invited him on a hot air balloon sunset experience, and then threw him out of the basket.

During the day, my mind wasn't any safer than it was at night. I had flashbacks and panic attacks all day long. Some of them were so bad that I passed out during them. I would be thrown back to moments I had repressed, smells that made me want to vomit, sensations I wished I could forget, and fear that took over my whole body. I was trying to look after a baby, whilst frequently picking myself up off the floor after passing out from the power of a panic attack.

The palpitations were out of control, and I couldn't get through a few hours without an attack of chest pain and heart palpitations. I would stand in the living room, holding on to a wall, whilst my heart felt like it was trying to escape through my throat. Sometimes, it felt like being strangled, which just triggered me even more.

Whilst I know all of this now, I had absolutely no idea what was happening to me at the time. I assumed I was dying of some freak heart condition. I hadn't put two and two together, and like many other teenage girls and young women who had been abused for years, I knew nothing about trauma, or trauma responses.

All I knew was that I wanted it to stop. I had been searching on the internet for months, and I was becoming more and more convinced that I had everything from heart failure to schizophrenia. I had been to my doctor so many times we were on a first name basis. Eventually, he referred me to a psychologist.

Oliver was asleep in the pram, and I was sat with the middle-aged woman in the small clinic in Stoke. I looked around nervously.

'So can you tell me what has brought you here today?' she started.

I talked non-stop for over an hour. I told her everything. Everything I could cram in. She listened to me intently, and took notes. She didn't say much, but I could tell she was listening. I told her about all the weird symptoms I was having, the way my mind raced, the nightmares, the chest pains, the fatigue, the fainting episodes, the palpitations, the shaking, the pins and needles. I told her that I thought I was mentally ill. I told her that I needed some pills. Something. Anything. I needed something to make me feel human again.

She put her pen down, and took off her thin varifocals.

'Jessica. Thank you for explaining all of that to me. I have listened to you. You have been through an enormous amount of . . . experiences,' she said.

'Do you know what's wrong with me? Is it bipolar? Mania? Schizophrenia? Can you prescribe something to make me normal again?'

She sighed.

'There is absolutely nothing wrong with you. You have been through a lot, and now you are very frightened, very angry, and very tired. You have a young baby. You are holding down a job. You have very little support, and you are waiting for a criminal trial.'

'What do you mean? Nothing wrong with me? It isn't normal to live like this! I never used to be like this!'

'I am saying that you are not mentally ill. You don't have any disorders.'

'But I want something to make it all stop,' I sobbed. 'Can't you just give me something?'

'There is nothing I can give you. Nothing I can give will solve how you are feeling. I think you might need some therapy, though. You have a lot to talk about, and a lot to understand.'

I was enraged by her. I stood up, and started to put my coat on.

'What a fucking waste of time! You haven't listened to me! You haven't believed me!'

She stood up next to me, and glanced over at the pram.

'I do believe you. I have listened to you. But you are not mentally ill. You don't have a mental health issue. You need some support, and you need someone to look after you, but you are completely normal. In fact, I think you are quite remarkable.'

'What the hell is that supposed to mean?'

'Just that you are eighteen years old, you have a baby, a job, a house. You have been through such a lot, but look at you, you are holding it all together. You have come here today for help. You are a very strong young woman.'

'I don't feel strong,' I sobbed into her shoulder. She put her arm around me.

15

I was just enjoying the drive

Spring 2019

The woman in the café had been watching me for over an hour. I probably did need to buy another cake, or a sandwich soon. But instead, I had been nervously watching the clock and checking my phone. The results of the tribunal were due, and I hadn't slept for two days.

Rachel text me, 'Any news yet?'

'No beaut. Nothing.'

I felt sick.

My PhD had been submitted, and it wasn't exactly the beautiful day I had imagined. It had been overshadowed by the stress and humiliation of the emails, and the way I had been treated. I was frantically trying to arrange my viva examination, but I had to wait for the outcome of the tribunal case to find out whether I could have an independent viva, to protect me from any interference.

My new professors had been wonderful. Mary and Harry had taken me under their wing, supported me, supervised me, challenged me and pushed me to my full potential. I had wasted months dealing with the complaints emails, but they had both helped me to catch up.

The research had been easy compared to the shit I had been up against. I had loved the process, the studies, the analysis, the interpretation and the discussions. I was immensely proud of what I had created, but my university experience had been truly ruined. This was supposed to be the exciting final weeks of my PhD, and here I was, sat in a small café, waiting to find out if the twelve counts of complaints I had submitted against the university were going to be upheld or not.

My phone buzzed again. This time it was Jaimi.

Are we still on for Thursday night? I would still like to come to your speech, if that would be okay?

I hadn't even thought about Thursday night.

Yeah that's fine. I dunno if I will still turn up to give it. I guess it all depends on the outcome of this tribunal, but I will let you know later on.

A text came straight back.

Thinking of you. You're stronger than you think.

I bloody well am not, I thought.

Jaimi was a fairly new friend, but we had become as close as Rachel and me very quickly. In fact, all three of us spent time together, went to conferences, went out for drinks, and went out for dinner whenever we could. It was wonderful having such supportive and smart friends around me, especially as I had been so lonely when I was younger.

We met in the summer at a protest against the Tories in the town centre. We had both been appalled by the recent actions of our local MP, and got talking about our placards. Mine said 'Time to resign, you misogynist swine!' Hers said, 'Boys will be boys' but she had struck out the words and changed it to 'Boys will be held accountable'. Jaimi was incredibly smart, funny, easy-going, and interesting. Just like Rachel and I, we hit it off right away, and we had been friends ever since.

I was giving a speech on International Women's Day at Cambridge, and she had asked if she could come along for the road trip. I was glad of the company, and so I had said yes.

It reminded me that yet again, I had not written my speech. I had been giving speeches for almost ten years by that point, and I had completely given up on planning. However, when giving a speech to over five hundred people in a lecture theatre, it is usually a good idea to have some slides, or some images, or something. I got my notebook out to sketch out some ideas, and my phone started ringing.

This was it.

I shook as I picked up the call.

'Hello . . .'

'Good afternoon. Is that Jessica?'

'Yes.'

'It's Gareth. I am calling with an update on your case. As you know, it was heard today at tribunal. I was present, but I couldn't influence the outcome,' he started.

The anticipation was caught in my throat. I could barely mumble two words to him. I made some weird noise, and he continued.

'Jessica, I am very pleased to tell you that every single complaint was upheld today. The university were appalled by the way you have been treated. They have awarded you the maximum compensation, they have decided to refund a year of PhD fees, and they have agreed to arrange your viva to ensure you can complete your PhD free of fear or intimidation from anyone.'

My body turned to jelly. If I had been standing, I would have fallen to my knees.

'What?' I cried. I had heard him just fine, but I couldn't believe what he was saying to me. I just wanted him to say it to me again, just to be sure I wasn't dreaming.

'I know this means a lot to you. You have been through a lot. All I can do is tell you how disgusted we were, and how sorry we are. On behalf of the university, we would all like to apologise for the way you were treated.'

I couldn't believe it. I had never felt justice before. Never felt validation before. Never been believed before. I had worked so hard to get to where I was, and I had expected to be treated with respect, surrounded by intelligent, compassionate, evolved academics and professionals. I could never have predicted such blatant classism and misogyny. I never saw it coming, and I couldn't have protected myself from it.

I made the mistake of believing that academia was a meritocracy. I thought that if I worked hard, demonstrated my ability, showed my talent and my knowledge, I would be respected and supported. I had never dreamt that my background would be used the way it was.

'I still can't believe it.' I shook my head a few days later, sat in my car, driving to Cambridge.

'You shouldn't have been put through it at all!' Jaimi replied. 'Do you think Laura will ever apologise to you?'

'Honestly? No. Mary told me that she emailed her the other day and asked for the dates and times I would be on campus, because she doesn't want to bump into me. She tried to convince Mary that it was because I was aggressive towards her, but Mary knew what she was playing at immediately. She emailed her back and told her that she wasn't entitled to that information.'

'Sounds like she is still trying to frame you as some wild, aggressive chav, then,' she chuckled, half amused, half appalled.

'Hmmm. Well, there you go. Can't imagine her apologising, can you?'

'No,' she sighed, lifting a handful of strawberry laces above her head and dropping them into her mouth.

'I had the last laugh though, I reckon,' I grinned devilishly at her.

'What did you do?' Her eyes lit up.

'I printed fifty posters. And stuck them all over the university. I made sure to put them on the backs of the doors in the women's toilets where I know the whole department go.'

She laughed. 'What did the posters say?'

I knew she was expecting something sharp, witty, offensive – but instead, I had made a heartfelt poster to remind young women from poor backgrounds that they deserved to be in our school.

'It is a poster of a young woman, walking through a library. Over the image, I wrote the words "No matter your upbringing, no matter your social class, you are smart, you are capable, and you deserve to be here. Don't you ever forget it."'

She watched the motorway speed past us. It went quiet.

'I love that. I'm so proud of you for that. You could have written something nasty, something petty, something shitty – and it all would have been justified. But instead, you wrote a poster encouraging other women like us . . .'

She smiled at me.

The journey was almost three hours long, and we talked about hundreds of things. Jaimi was in her early twenties, with a stretcher in one ear, two piercings in her nose, and bright green dip-dyed hair. She was studying politics at university, and was an active political campaigner in our local area. She was the women's officer, worked at the local soup kitchen, and did some work on the side as a private Maths and English tutor.

She was a tremendously talented musician, classically trained singer, and excellent guitarist. She was fascinating to be around, and talking to her made hours pass like a few moments.

She had been with her boyfriend for years, and I had been with mine for even longer. As the hours passed, and the honesty got more and more brutal, we both admitted to being pretty miserable with the men we were with.

'If I left him, I wouldn't get with another man for as long as I lived,' I laughed, driving along the long country roads to Cambridge.

'Me neither.' She looked across at me. 'Would you just stay single for everthen?'

I blushed.

'Ummm . . . probably not.'

She smiled. 'You're bisexual then?'

'Ummm . . . maybe. I mean. Yes. Well, I am attracted to women, if that's what you are asking . . .'

Oh my god. Did that just come out of my mouth? I hadn't even admitted that to Rachel. I stared at the road ahead of me, panicking.

'Oh, yeah . . . me too,' she mumbled.

I glanced at her. Suddenly, I was in uncharted territory. There had been girls when I was younger, but we had never admitted what it was before.

I felt uneasy.

'I've never told anyone that before. That I'm attracted to women,' I admitted to her.

'Does your partner know?' she responded.

I let out a wry laugh.

'Yes. Well. He is in denial about it. He accuses me of being gay all the time. He told me once that his sexual fantasy was to have sex with two women at once. I told him that it sounded great,' I laughed.

She snorted, laughing at me.

'He kept pushing me, asking me what I would do with a woman. He was like, would you fuck a woman then? I was like, yeah dude. He was like, would you eat her out then? I was like . . . yeah absolutely . . . And then he didn't speak to me for two fucking days!'

We both giggled at his fragility.

'Oh, so he can tell you that he wants to fuck other women, but you can't say the same thing? About right!' She laughed, eating three strawberry laces she had carefully plaited whilst we talked.

When we got to Cambridge, I met the hosts of my speech, and asked for somewhere to get changed. They took me to a small room, and I took off my oversized hoodie, and my baggy T-shirt, to replace it with a blouse. I was stood in my skinny jeans and a black lace bra, checking my shirt for any marks or wrinkles.

'Oh, excuse me. I didn't realise you were . . . undressed,' I heard Jaimi's voice behind me and spun around.

I went to apologise, but she didn't move. I didn't move. We just looked at each other. I could feel her gaze. I smiled. She smiled back.

'I'd better get ready . . .' I said softly.

'Uhh. Yeah. Sure. Sorry.'

As I started my speech, she mouthed 'good luck' at me from the front row, and I was 'on'. I hosted an evening of discussions and interactive Q & A about my PhD research, and then about my campaigns and resources. The room was packed. The questions were lively.

The room was buzzing by the end of the night, and I was rewarded with an applause that lasted way too long. A long line of people wanting to talk to me formed, and Jaimi nipped over to me to bring me a cold drink and a snack.

'You were amazing,' she whispered, handing me the drink.

'I won't be long, I will just answer these questions and then we can get you back. It will be a long drive!'

'Oh don't worry about that. Do what you gotta do, I'll just wait here and chat to people.'

The roads back home were dark, quiet, and starry. We were still an hour from home at midnight, and we hadn't shut up from the moment we had left the venue. The three-hour drive had disappeared behind us, and I realised that I was sad that it was nearly over.

I was conscious that her boyfriend would be waiting up for her, and so I noticed that my satnav offered us a quicker route home. I clicked to accept it.

'Oh, are you taking us on a detour?' She noticed everything.

'This route is about fifteen minutes quicker, because there is a road closure. The satnav says . . .'

She looked sad. Annoyed, even. I stopped talking.

'Is everything okay?' I asked eventually. I could feel her energy change.

'I was just enjoying the drive. I don't really . . . want to go home,' she said, looking at her feet.

'Nor me . . .' I agreed.

What was happening here? Was there something between us?

Absolutely not, my mind shouted. She is way too beautiful for you. Don't be ridiculous!

I agreed with the voice in my head. She was the most beautiful woman I had ever met. There was no way she would be interested in me. She must have meant as a friend.

'Well, this is my house,' she sighed as we pulled up, looking at the dark windows of her home.

'Is he in?' I asked, looking at the stillness of the house.

'Oh, probably.' She dismissed my question. 'Anyway. Thank you so much for inviting me tonight, well, I invited myself, but thank you for the road trip. The university was beautiful. You did a brilliant job . . .'

She held me in her gaze.

'That's okay, thank you so much for coming. It was great to . . . spend time with you . . .'

I could feel the tension rising. She must have been able to feel it too. My temperature was soaring, and I was thankful she couldn't see me blushing.

We sat in the dark of the car. She looked at me the way I was looking at her. I felt her little finger brush against mine, and I looked down at our hands. She followed my line of sight, and then looked back up into my eyes.

And then we were kissing. Soft, gentle, perfect kisses. One, then another, then another. We pulled away from each other and couldn't keep the smiles from our faces.

'What does this mean?' I asked her.

'I don't know . . . but I don't want it to end . . .' she played with my fingers and wrapped them around her own.

The morning of my viva, a few weeks later, I was a complete wreck. Whilst the kiss had been beautiful, and perfect, and wondrous, it had turned my life upside down. As much as I had tried to repress it, my body had punished me for it. I became ill. My hair fell out. I stopped eating. I couldn't focus. I couldn't remember anything. I felt sick. I couldn't sleep.

I was having to finally face reality: I was lesbian.

And any unfortunate woman who has been through the realisation that she is gay, and been through the torture of the PhD viva, will tell you that you can do one or the other, but you cannot do both. No human can survive both. They will combust.

Of course, my brain was doing both at once.

That meant I had been seeing Jaimi as much as I could, revising as much as I could, and spending the rest of my time in existential crisis. I desperately wanted to pass my viva and become Dr Jessica Taylor, but my mind was filled with dilemmas.

Instead of revising my thesis, I was daydreaming about running away. Instead of studying my theories and models, I was having to process the reality of why I had been miserable with men, having terrible sex, and been attracted to girls and women since I was a teenager. Instead of considering my tactics and approaches to passing the viva examination, I was sat in my office, worrying about what would happen if I came out as lesbian.

As I went to do my hair and makeup, a card arrived through the front door. It was huge. I took it back upstairs to my bedroom and opened it.

INCREDIBLE! DR JESSICA TAYLOR PLANS WORLD DOMINATION!

I laughed at the front. It was a collage of photos of me, made to look like the front cover of a newspaper. I opened it to find a warm, supportive message, filled with love and pride. And her name at the bottom.

All my love, Jaimi x

I walked into the viva, and I was absolutely certain I was going to throw up.

On top of processing that I was a lesbian for the past few weeks, I had been having crushing catastrophic thoughts. I had become convinced I was going to die on the morning of my viva. That I would die on the train on the way to the viva. That I would die of some mystery illness before I got a chance to finish my PhD. That I would trip, fall down the steps on campus, crack my head open, bleed out and die on my way into my viva meeting.

My phone vibrated. It was Jaimi.

> *You are going to smash it, Jess. See you on the other side! X*

Another from Rachel.

> *So proud of you! Can't wait for you to be Dr in a few hours! xxx*

The room was tiny. Just like everything else in academia, it was grossly underwhelming. For three years, I had pictured my viva to be this prestigious, traditional, beautiful ceremony. Instead, we were back in Harry Potter's under-the-stairs closet, near the office filled with the oily tangle of bikes. I had been in nicer rooms for detention. In fact, I had been in nicer rooms in the fucking prison.

It was a dusty little side room with one table in the centre. There were two women I didn't recognise, and a woman I vaguely recognised from the university leadership team. She was there as part of the agreement to keep my viva safe.

We talked through my research, they asked me questions, I answered them, they challenged some of my findings, but I found it easy to defend. They asked me questions about analysis and methodology. It was fun. Before I knew it, it was over. I thought we were still having a warm-up chat.

Was that it? I wondered. Maybe that was just part one?

They asked me to wait outside whilst they made their decision. I was supposed to stay still, but I ran to the bathroom to be sick. As I washed my face, I stared at myself in the mirror that resembled the ones in my old school toilets, and looked deep into my own green eyes. There I was, staring back into myself. I zoned out.

I looked tired. I looked pale. I looked stressed. To be honest, I looked like a woman trying to pass her PhD viva to become a doctor after months of being bullied, whilst also going through a life-changing crisis of her sexuality.

I walked back to the room, and they were already outside looking for me.

'Oh, there you are!' the chair of my viva gasped. 'We were looking for you!'

'I am so sorry, I have been feeling really unwell,' I muttered.

'Ah, just nerves, I am sure. We have all been there!' she reassured me, patting me on the back. I nodded, knowing this was not the time or the place to say, 'Well, actually, I just recently realised I was gay after repressing it for fourteen years . . .'

I walked into the tiny room and it had suddenly become more crowded. My supervisors were in there, too. As I made my way in, they handed me a huge bouquet of flowers, and they all cheered.

'Congratulations, Dr Jessica Taylor!'

'You did it!' Mary cried, wrapping her arms around me. 'You fucking did it!' she added, a whisper in my ear.

I did it. I am finally a psychologist. I did it.

16

The sky is the limit

Autumn 2009

I scoured the internet for houses. I didn't really care where I went, but I couldn't stay in Stoke any more. I couldn't stay on that fucking estate. My life was a living nightmare. Jase had been on bail for almost six months, and he had breached it more times than I had changed nappies. The police were treating me like I was their annoying mother-in-law, and either ignored my calls completely, or talked to me like a piece of shit.

Manchester. I could live in Manchester, I thought. My whole family are from there, so it's not like I would be alone . . .

I clicked on one of the houses. A terraced two-bedroom house. It was lovely. The garden was pretty. It was right near a primary school. Maybe I could live there?

£700 a month? Fucking hell. Maybe not.

Birmingham. I could go there, I guess. I had never been there, but it seemed to have some cheaper areas.

Derby. What about Derby? That was much cheaper than Manchester.

I realised that I hadn't been to many places at all. In fact, I had rarely left Stoke. These cities all looked much posher than Stoke, and I couldn't even work out where their council estates were. Most of them didn't seem to exist any more, and had been bought up by housing associations and private landlords. I guess it wouldn't be long until this estate was all bought up.

Already, in the years I had been there, more and more houses were being bought, and then rented back to us. When you were in crisis, you used to be able to turn up at the town hall and ask for somewhere to live, and they would give you a tour of a few suitable properties. Then you could pick your favourite. My mum turned down four houses they offered her, once. Bathroom was too small. Rooms were too dark. Needed new carpets. You couldn't afford to be that choosy any more. If you turned down a council house, you were doomed.

Life was certainly going to be very different, but the more I thought about it, the more certain I was.

Especially since Jase had grabbed me the day before.

He held me by the throat, and whispered in my ear.

'You told the fucking police I raped you?'

I couldn't move. I didn't answer.

'I denied it. Obviously. But you . . . You fucking loved it. I enjoyed doing it to you,' he snarled, and ran his other hand over my body.

I shook with terror.

'If I ever get the chance to do it again, I will fucking kill you.'

I sobbed, and gasped for air.

'And I will tell you another thing. I am going to wait for that baby to grow up, and then I am going to come back for him. I will tell him what a fucking slag his mum is, and make sure he hates your fucking guts. I will make sure he never speaks to you again. So at least you have that to look forward to!'

He let me go, and I collapsed into a coughing fit on the dusty driveway, next to the pram. I tried to summon some physical and emotional strength from somewhere. I rose to my feet, dragging myself up using the handles of the pram. I turned my back on him, walked away, and didn't look back. I knew he was watching me as I left, and I knew he was waiting for me to look at him. The tears rolled down my face, but I did not turn to him.

The death threats hadn't stopped. Nor had the late-night silent phone calls. The attempts to break in. The stones thrown at my bedroom window. The watching me and texting me to tell me what I was wearing. I was absolutely certain that he was going to murder me, but no one seemed to care.

One night, I was walking home from town with the pram when I noticed Jase's dad walking towards me. This cannot be good, I panicked. I tried to cross the road, but he followed me, and crossed over to meet me.

'Look, Jess. I need to talk to you.'

He was a frightening man. He had been in prison many times when he was younger, and I had seen him lose his temper enough times to know where Jase got it from. I stood still, afraid of what he would do if I tried to walk away.

'I didn't believe you. I thought you were lying about him. But I overheard him threaten you on the driveway. And I'll be honest with you, every time he demands that you bring that baby over, he goes out and gets drunk, and leaves the baby with me. He's never once looked after his own baby.'

I was speechless. A tear fell from my eye.

337

'You have been so good to him. All these years. He has treated you like shit. I have seen it all. Heard it all. He's cheated on you so many times. He lies to you every day. He has ended up a violent, evil bastard. I'll be honest, I'm ashamed of him. He could have had a family and a life, but instead, he's on bail for . . . rape . . .'

The word cut through him.

I ignored the fact that I knew he himself had done the exact same thing to his ex-wife. But now wasn't the time. And at least he was being honest. At least I wasn't being threatened, or beaten up.

'Well. Thank you. I'm sorry it's been horrible, and that I had to go to the police. I just couldn't live like that any more . . .'

'You don't need to apologise for him. He deserves everything he gets.'

I hesitated. And then I blurted it out.

'I am leaving. I can't stay here. He's too dangerous.'

He went quiet.

'So I won't see the baby grow up?' His voice cracked.

I shook my head. I had no choice. He knew that. I knew that.

'That fucking bastard . . . anyway . . . I should go. I don't want him giving you aggro if someone sees us talking . . .'

And with that, he turned and walked back towards the big roundabout at the bottom of the estate, and into the darkness.

I chose a house around 30 miles away, in a town I had never even heard of. The house looked nice enough. It was cheap. There seemed to be lots of factories near the house, and I figured I could get some temporary work to keep me and Oliver afloat for a while.

I had been saving up my wages, and refusing to pay my rent because the landlord wouldn't fix my front door (which Jase had kicked in months earlier). I had just enough to put a deposit down on the new house, and hire a van.

I spent four days packing up my house in secret. I couldn't let anyone on the estate know that I was leaving. If they found out, I would never be able to leave. Someone would tell Jase immediately, and I would be trapped there forever. Or worse.

I asked for the van to be hidden round the corner until around midnight, when my stepdad drove it around for me, and parked it on my driveway. He had offered to drive my things up to the new house, and I was so grateful to him. I packed the van at a speed I wasn't aware I was capable of. I wanted to pack the entire house and leave before sunrise. It was the only safe way out.

The sweat poured off me whilst I dragged, shoved, threw, ran, pulled, pushed and stacked everything I owned into the back of the small moving van. Every now and then, I stopped to check on my baby, cuddle him back up in his travel cot, and sniff his nappy. He was almost one, and had been up on his feet for two months. If you took your eye off him for a few seconds, he would be climbing on the sofa, running into the kitchen, or even trying to climb the stairs. He was turning into a lovely little toddler, and he was smarter than I had anticipated. He had a head full of floppy blond hair, huge blue eyes, and a set of perfectly pearly teeth.

I looked down at him, cuddled up with his favourite blanket, sleeping on his front, on his knees, with his bum in the air. I couldn't let him grow up here. No matter what was coming next in my life, he would not be growing up on this estate. Fuck the consequences. I would take them all.

The only option was to run away.

We pulled away from the house as the sky turned pink. We drove out of the estate, and I watched the streets pass by. Up Church Road, where Mr Tompkins would soon be awake, to start rolling his golf balls down the hill. Past the park, where Reece had pelted golf balls at anything and everything whilst the residents screamed and hid.

Past the fields where that lad had stabbed his girlfriend. Past the pub, where the microphone had dropped to the floor as my dad ducked out with the blonde woman. Past my childhood house, which probably still had UV-pen graffiti on the skirting board in the box room.

Past Kalen's house, past my old house next to his. Past the bus stop where Kenny had been run over by the 6A bus. Past the garage roof where I used to sit on and smoke weed. Past the gully where I had been choked. Past the house where I had been raped on a dirty mattress. Past the moors where Jase had abandoned me in the middle of the night. Past my high school, where I spent months of my time in an isolation booth.

Past Dad's house, where he had cooked his leg. Past the junction where I found Mr Edwards. Past the Chinese restaurants I had defrauded with my old cheque book. Past the house with the rat infestation. Past the carpark that Birchy had knocked me out on. Past Jodie's house. Past the graveyard where I told her I was pregnant. Past the retail park where I learned to race cars.

I was eighteen years old, and I already felt like I had lived ten lives. I looked down at my sleeping baby. I didn't know what was coming next, but I had to try to give him a better life than I had. I had to try.

Whilst other people my age were just starting their lives, I was running away from mine. In the dead of night, I had packed up my life, put my baby in a van, and driven away from everything and everyone I knew.

'Are you sure about this?' Mark asked me, after miles of silence.

'No,' I murmured, 'but I know I can't stay here. We will have no chance if we stay here.'

We slept upright in our seats, in a carpark near the new house, and waited for the estate agent to open so I could pick up the keys.

When I walked into the little terraced house for the first time, it felt eerily familiar. Something about it felt like my first house. It had the same layout. It had the same smell. I sighed.

A bathroom downstairs, at the end of the house past the kitchen, was not going to be easy to adjust to. Especially with a baby. I walked into the kitchen to find that there wasn't one. Just an empty, cold room. No worktops. No cupboards. No sink. The backdoor was smashed, and had been boarded back up.

Upstairs were two large bedrooms. In the first bedroom, the sash window was smashed. There was glass all over the carpet. The cold breeze blew through the house. I shut the door, and decided to check out the other bedroom. It was huge, and airy. I liked it. But I could feel another breeze. I looked around, and saw more glass. One of the windows was smashed.

I rang the estate agent, and they said they would send a maintenance team over immediately. 'Immediately' meant at least a week in landlord-speak, and so I set about boarding up the windows and securing the house myself.

It took days to unpack, and the house wasn't perfect, but there was something wonderful about being totally anonymous. I had moved to an area where I didn't know a soul. I could walk down the street, and no one knew a thing about me. I explored the town, and no one looked at me.

I wasn't the girl who reported her ex to the police, here. I was nobody. I was invisible. I didn't exist.

It was liberating. I could stand in the supermarket, babbling to my baby, choosing some baby food, and not one person would stop me and ask me a question. I wouldn't bump into six people from school. I didn't have to worry that Jase would walk in and start threatening me.

It could have felt like loneliness, but it just didn't. For the first time in years, it felt like safety.

It was a cold, windy winter morning when I was sat on the sofa and watching TV. I had been searching for jobs for hours, and had a list of them I was going to call and email to register my interest. One was in a cosmetics factory. One was in a ready meals factory. The other was at a betting shop. I would take anything. I just needed solid income, and a way to look after us both.

There were so many other jobs available, but I had no qualifications. I left high school, and spent years trying to survive. I had nothing to offer employers, other than a bit of experience as a waitress, and a few months in the call centre.

I had no idea how I was going to provide for us. I had to figure something out, and quick. No one was coming to save us. The only hope we had was me. I looked up as the TV played another advert.

'Do you want a career? A way to study around your family and your job? Flexible, affordable payment options? A chance to follow your dreams, no matter your background?'

You have my attention, I thought.

'Why not explore the options at The Open University? You can study all of these fantastic topics, including mathematics, computer science, geography, politics, and psychology . . .'

University? From home? I was baffled. I had never heard of anything of the sort. I stared at the screen, wondering if it was a scam, or a joke.

I ran around the room, looking for a pen and something that would pass as paper. I wanted the phone number. I scribbled it down, barely legible, and stared at it. Could I go to university? Could I be a psychologist?

I went to check on Oliver, who was having his afternoon nap, and came back down to sit on the sofa. I fidgeted. I procrastinated. I looked at the phone number on the back of the envelope. I picked it up. I put it back.

Just call them, the voice in my head prodded.

Just do it . . .

Just call the number, and tell them that you want to be a psychologist. Ask them how it works. Tell them you want to study.

My hands trembled as I typed the number into my phone. Was I even good enough to study at a university? Would I even get in?

I deleted the number. I would never get in anyway. Who would accept someone like me? An eighteen-year-old mum, with a one-year-old baby? No one is going to let me into their university. And who would ever let me be a psychologist?

But I paced the living room. I couldn't let it go. I couldn't stop thinking about it. It was burning a hole in my brain. I had never been so indecisive. So frightened. So ashamed of myself. So scared of rejection.

'Jessica. You are going to pick the fucking phone up, and call the number!' I said out loud, into the cold air of the living room. I stared into the mirror above the fireplace, willing myself to get a grip.

I pressed the call button on my phone, and listened to it ring. Ring. Ring. Ring.

For god's sake, pick the fucking phone up, before I put the phone down . . .

'Welcome to The Open University, you are speaking to Andy. How can I help you today?'

I froze. Oh no. No. Not now.

'Hello?' he asked again. I panicked. I needed to make a noise. Ideally, I needed to talk.

'Uhh . . .' I managed.

'That's okay, take your time . . .' the kind voice came again.

'Uhh . . . I saw your advert on . . . the TV . . .'

'Okay, great. Are you interested in learning more about studying with us?'

'Yeah . . . I think so . . .'

I had absolutely no idea what I was doing. What was I thinking? How would I juggle a baby, and study for a degree? This was ridiculous.

'What would you like to study with us? Do you have a preferred topic, or a job you are working towards?'

Why was I so embarrassed? I felt stupid. Did I dare admit my dreams to this stranger on the phone? What if he laughed at me? I cleared my throat, and closed my eyes.

'I . . . I want to be a psychologist . . . maybe one day . . .'

'Okay, great . . . well, we have a psychology degree. Would you like to learn more about that?'

I recoiled. I couldn't do this. I was just some stupid kid from Stoke. How would I ever afford a degree? I can't go to university. Where would Oliver go?

'Well. I'm not sure I will be able to get on it anyway. Just to be honest with you. I am eighteen. I have a baby. I work as much as I can. I don't have a lot of money. I got my GCSEs, but I didn't get any As. I didn't go sixth form. I probably can't get a student loan thing like everyone else . . . so I dunno why I even rang, actually . . .'

I went to put the phone down as the tears of embarrassment welled up in my eyes.

'No, no. Wait. This is what OU is for . . .'

I heard him try to keep me on the phone as I went to put it down, and I stopped for a moment. I put the phone back to my ear, and tried to hide my wobbling voice.

'So you're saying I could be a psychologist one day?' I whispered into the phone, feeling a lump form in my throat.

'Oh, definitely!' The guy encouraged me. 'The sky is the limit. You can be whatever you want to be!'

I could be whatever I wanted to be?

I looked around me at the simple house in the town I didn't even know. I thought of Oliver napping upstairs. I remembered the years of violence and abuse. The hours spent frantically calling the police for help. I could be whatever I wanted to be, the man said.

'Oh . . . well . . . how do I sign up?'

In the end, the case against Jase was dropped over a year later, due to the failings of the police to follow correct procedures. This case was referred to professional standards and IOPC. Five years later, I was offered the opportunity to reopen my case, and have it re-investigated in 2014 when police forces were encouraged to reopen failed sexual offences cases nationwide. At this point, I had just found out that I had been accepted on to my PhD, and after much reflection, I decided not to reopen my case, knowing full well that would have been my last chance at justice. I knew that I had to let go, and I was worried that I didn't have the strength to unearth years of violence, abuse and fear at a point in my life where I felt that I was finally getting somewhere. Jase was later charged with, and convicted of, other offences of domestic violence against several other women and one teenage girl. I took my case to the Criminal Injuries Compensation Authority and was awarded compensation for the abuse that I suffered at his hands, both sexual abuse and domestic violence. I am one of many thousands of women who never got justice for anything done to her, and had to find ways to move on with her life.

17

The watcher of your own flame

September 2023

This book was two stories of two small parts of my life. The similarities between them. The way they dance, intertwine, move and grow as one. I've found that many themes in our lives repeat themselves. Some say they repeat themselves when we have lessons to learn from them, but others believe that there is no purpose or reason to these experiences.

I met a spiritual man recently who said to me, 'History doesn't repeat itself, but it does rhyme'.

Maybe some of us are prone to be subjected to thousands of harms in our lives, whereas others seem to glide through life seemingly unscathed. Who really knows? I had never noticed how much I had already lived through until I started telling parts of my story.

I get three main responses to talking about my life. The first is horror. The second is disbelief. The third is awe. I resonate with none of them.

The horror tends to come from people who have never lived lives like mine, where the mere mention of child abuse, rape, drugs, poverty and exploitation causes them to recoil.

Devastated. Horrified. Appalled. Disgusted. Saddened. The way they look at you like you should be dead or in prison, wondering how on earth you got out alive. The way their mind whirrs at the realisation that the human being stood in front of them was savagely beaten, raped and violated – and yet somehow, just looks like any other run of the mill person they walk past in the street every day.

I can't relate to that level of horror, because I was surrounded by kids like me. I wasn't anything out of the ordinary by any stretch. Several of my friends are already dead. Several more are in prison. Many of us are parenting teenagers now, because we all had children when we were children ourselves. To feel a sense of horror would mean I would have to be shocked, and I would have to be much less desensitised than I am now.

Instead, I move through the world knowing that millions of people have lived lives like mine, and much worse. I know when I walk down a busy street, or wander around a shop, I am surrounded by humans who have been subjected to some of the darkest and most terrifying experiences we can imagine. They might have lived with those burdens for decades. Some will die, having never processed or discussed them.

There is truth in the cringey internet meme cliché of 'everyone is fighting a battle you know nothing about'. In my other books, I have written about the broad experiences of human trauma, and the way we repress and minimise it on a daily basis, smiling the short lies of 'I'm good, how are you?' to each other in an endless circle of empty bullshit.

Or maybe it's just years on the estate, and then even more years working in forensic settings, prisons, rape centres, courtrooms and police stations that has left me severely desensitised and weirdly accepting of the level of human trauma and abuse around us all. But horror is not something I feel any more.

The second response is disbelief, and that can range from momentary disbelief whilst someone is listening to my story, right the way through to outright denial of everything I have ever said. The kind of psychological defence response of, 'This is too far-fetched, how could anyone possibly have lived through so much? She must be lying!'

I had never really come across that response until I left the estate and ended up surrounded by middle-class professionals, activists and academics. When I talk about my life to those who grew up in Stoke and other similarly deprived areas, they nod, they laugh, they acknowledge, and then they often respond with an experience equally as gruesome from their own journey. It has been a strange experience to be surrounded by people who would sooner believe that nothing I say is true, and my life story must be a load of old bollocks because as one woman said about me, 'no one could possibly have experienced so much stuff by her age'.

But again, the reality is more common than we like to admit. I know of many women who have lived through decades of endless battles, trauma and chaos. Abuse, house moves, miscarriages, divorce, loss, debt, fear, violence, poverty, relationship breakdowns, unemployment, injuries, accidents, assaults, drugs, drink, harassment, bereavement, loneliness and confusion.

More recently, Jaimi and I have started teaching about trauma in a different way. We present our students and professionals with a long list of possible traumas and distress, and let them process how many of them they have already lived through. I tend to start at the position that most humans have lived through more traumas than they have ever realised.

And so, disbelief is not something I can relate to, either. And as Taylor Swift quite rightly said, 'Life is emotionally abusive.'

The final response then, is awe. Sometimes when I talk about my life, people respond with a feeling of total astonishment and admiration. They ask me how on earth I made it out, so they can learn how to make it out, too. They write to me and tell me that they don't understand how I can put one foot in front of the other each day. They want to know why I don't blame myself for any of it. Why I don't wake screaming in the night from the memories and the sensations. They ask me how I can love myself, trust my decisions, and believe in my abilities. They question how I have 'bounced back', and why they don't seem to be able to do it.

And so, I wanted to finish this book by showing you how this is possible. I could never write one book that encompassed my whole life, and so this book is only a snapshot. But even in this snapshot, there is enough shit to last any of us a lifetime.

I truly believe that one of the things that has carried me through, and enabled me to process everything that was done to me, is respecting and loving myself. My current self, but most importantly, my child self. I don't blame her. I don't chastise her. I don't criticise her. I don't spend my nights questioning why she didn't see it coming, or why she didn't figure it all out sooner. I don't wish she had got away faster, or fought off the rapists more. I don't think she was stupid. I don't think any of it was her fault.

Quite the opposite in fact, I think that younger version of me was truly remarkable. Much more awesome and inspiring than I could ever be now. I honour her, and I love her – even if no one else did. Especially because no one else did.

Sure, I could spend my life tearing her to bits, wishing she had done something different – but then I would be no different to anyone else who sank their teeth in. I regard earlier versions of myself with respect and love. Every step I have taken has led me to where I am now. There is something poisonous about self-hatred, and self-doubt – and I didn't need that shit coursing through my veins.

Instead, I want to use this final space to write to my younger self, in full view of the world, to demonstrate my love and loyalty to the version of myself that pulled me through the darkest and most dangerous moments of my life. Lots of psychologists like me understand the value of writing honestly and lovingly to our younger selves, and even imagining ourselves writing back. I can't think of a better way to end this memoir, even if kid version of me would tell adult version of me to fuck off and mind her own damn business.

Hey Kiddo,

I know, I know. You're not a kid.

You know it all, yada yada. Shut up for a moment and listen. You will wanna hear what I have to say, I promise.

As I'm writing this to you today, I'm thirty-two years old, and you will never believe where I am. Nope. Not in a nursing home, you cheeky little fucker. We don't die after twenty-five, you know. Jeez.

Anyway, you won't guess it. Never in a million years!

I'm in Australia. Yeah. You read that right. I'm on a book tour. You heard.

You know how I got here? On a business class flight. With a bed and a pillow. I ate a steak at 40,000 feet with a glass of port. With my beautiful wife right next to me. On the way to deliver sold out lectures all around New Zealand and Australia.

I can imagine your face. I swear to you, I am not lying. Take it in, kid.

Oh yeah, shit changes. Shit changes a LOT for you. For me. For us. Forever.

You don't know it yet, but everything you've ever seen, heard, learned, lived, felt, thought, said, written and drawn has led you to the other side of the fucking world. You did all of this. You are the constant. You are my instincts. You are the strength inside me, the core of me that no one can touch.

I know you don't feel like it right now, but you are the strongest, most tenacious, most determined, most surprising person I've ever known.

I can't fathom how you did it, but you did.

And I just wanna say to you that you're right about everything by the way, none of the shit that was done to you was your fault. It was never you. I am so proud of you for never blaming yourself. That took serious resolve. You were treated appallingly by so many people for so long. You were so right to run away. From everyone. From everything.

Everyone tells you that you were wrong, but you were SO right to protect Oliver from the estate. I cannot thank you enough for having the insight and strength to escape when you did. Your tiny baby grows up to be a brilliant teenager who decides he wants to study psychology like his mum. You've been teaching him to cook from scratch since he was five, and now he's better than you and wants to open his own restaurant one day.

So many of your decisions were the right ones, babe. I wish I had even half of your certainty. If people think I am self-assured, they should have met you!

And despite all this, the first time someone will tell you that they are proud of you is when you are twenty-seven years old. And it will hurt. It won't feel like a compliment at all, it will feel like being stabbed in the throat. It will feel like being given a gift at the same time as being punched in the stomach. You will drive home in tears, at the realisation that no one has ever said that to you before. That you've never had someone you love look you in the eye and tell you how proud they are that you didn't just survive, you smashed it.

If I could go back and be the person you needed when you were younger, I would tell you that I was proud of you every goddamn day. How you had the strength to get up out of bed and start a new day over and over again is beyond me. How you juggled two babies, a full-time job and a degree is nothing short of miraculous. How you escaped abuse and worked through thousands of traumas – I still don't know how you did that shit. You didn't get nearly enough credit for what you did, so I am writing this to you to give you all the love, grace, respect and thanks that you deserve.

***You** are the reason I am here today.*

But let me tell you some shit. There are so many qualities people are going to attempt to beat out of you kid, but those are the ones that kept you pushing forward. It turns out that people do not like unwavering confidence. They don't like self-love. They don't like ambition. They don't like it that you are not interested in popularity or cliques. They don't like that you walk away from situations and people who harm you, and never look back. But no matter what happens, never lose the essence of who you are. Hell, I know you won't. You never did.

There are times when you will be made to feel ashamed of your roots. You'll wish you could hide them, or be someone else. You'll pick up on attitudes and body language that you can't quite place. You'll get the feeling you're not welcome. People will make jokes about your background and your childhood. People will try to claim that you are not good enough. Some people will find out that you had a baby as a kid, and use it to position you as some Vicky Pollard tribute act that accidentally found herself on a PhD programme.

You'll try to fit in, only to realise you don't want to.

You're going to need to learn how to respect and thank your council estate for making you who you are, whilst also accepting that it nearly killed you. You're going to need to learn that academia is a vile, elitist, oppressive place, whilst also accepting that you need your PhD to achieve everything else you go on to do. Annoying. Uncomfortable. Conflicting. But real.

Thank you for never allowing yourself to be moulded into someone else's ideals of you. Thank you for your stubbornness. Thank you for your rawness, for your sharp edges and blunt walls. Thank you for your ambition. Thank you for your undying love of books and art.

Thank you for your curiosity about the world, the universe, the human mind, and spirituality. Thank you for your fucking dogged determination that your kids wouldn't live the way you did. Thank you for cutting people out that needed to be far, far away from you. Thank you for being brave and speaking your mind no matter who tried to shut you up.

Thank you for being the young woman who stood firm, took the shit, the side eye, the insults, the slurs, the abuse, the lies – and was still able to look at yourself in the mirror and know that no one can blow out that spark you can see in your eye. I know you smile at yourself every morning in the bathroom mirror, and remind yourself how strong you are. It pays off, by the way.

Thank you for being the watcher of your own flame.

You were the young sage who realised that your energy is best spent building something new, and developing your future, than fighting with your past.

Thank you for letting other people's words wash over you. You knew you were never to blame. You knew you weren't crazy. You knew you weren't lying. You knew you could survive. You knew you would come good one day. You knew the truth and it kept you warm when you were alone with it.

You always trusted yourself, your mind, and your body to do what they needed to do for you, even when they are being a total prick. Thank you for never being frightened of the inside of your own beautiful, complicated mind, even though that is also, very often, a total prick.

Thank you for being the spirit who could get up off the floor for the thousandth time, brush herself off, smooth down her hair, wipe the blood off, and start all over again.

You've always been the underdog, the underclass, the underestimated, but to me, you were always gonna win. There was no other outcome for you, was there?

'Success is my only motherfucking option, failure's not.'

I know you know what I'm talking about, kid.

Keep working hard. Keep sinking into your music. Keep writing your diaries, your stories and your poems. Keep focused on your future. Self-development is a gift to yourself. Don't be scared to be different from everyone around you. You are not in competition with anyone else, you are on your own path.

Girl, you're gonna make it through. I'm not saying it doesn't hurt like fuck to make it through, cos there are gonna be days when you wonder if death would be easier, but you do get to the place you dream of. Promise.

I mean, you don't become a stripper with Isabelle, and you don't end up having baths in Lambrini like you are planning right now, but with the benefit of hindsight, you're going to have to trust me when I say that you enjoy your Breakfast Martini at the bar on the aeroplane much more. And that baths in Lambrini would probably give you thrush. Don't ever do that.

You somehow became almost everything you instructed us to become in your letter. Admittedly, you are not Prime Minister, though. Yet. There's still time though.

And when you get to where you want to be, you're gonna need to draw from the deepest parts of yourself to stay healthy. The bottom might be ugly, but the top ain't pretty either, our kid. I know you know the Lennon lyrics, 'There is room at the top, they are telling you still. But first you must learn how to smile as you kill, if you want to live like the folks on the hill.'

Well, let's just say, you are not like the folks on the hill, and you need to keep that in mind. Not everyone who bares their teeth at you is smiling. And you'll figure that out slowly. Very slowly.

Oh, and before I forget, I just wanna tell you that Emmy was right. Lots of girls are 'just experimenting', but some of those experiments confirm the hypothesis, if ya get me.

Love you Tayla,
Jess x